CBT *for* Beginners

WITHDRAWN oke Park
GUILDFORD COLLEGE

Praise for the Book

This book delivers what it promises. Simmons and Griffiths provide a well thought out introduction to the subject area of standard CBT. Their illustrated case material balances the theoretical and empirical information and brings the book alive. This text should be on the shelves of trainee cognitive behavioural psychotherapists for a considerable time to come.

Dr Alec Grant, Lecturer and Course Leader, MSc in Cognitive Psychotherapy at INAM (Institute of Nursing and Medicine), University of Brighton

Students will find the text easy to read and incredibly helpful, both as a textbook to read alongside completing a basic course in CBT and as a reference text that will continue to be helpful while delivering CBT ... the strong practical focus of this book is its main strength, helping to equip the therapist with skills needed to deliver CBT and giving advice/guidance on ways to use these skills.

Hannah Bailey, Assistant Psychologist, NHS

This book clearly is for 'beginners', as the title suggests; a splendid strength in many ways ... the contents are very comprehensive, and, as a guide for beginners' CBT, it really does include the main competences that are required.

Andrew Stevens, Director of Cognitive Behaviour Therapy Programme, University of Birmingham

CBT *for* Beginners

Jane Simmons and Rachel Griffiths

Los Angeles • London • New Delhi • Singapore • Washington DC

616.89142 SIM
186599

© Jane Simmons and Rachel Griffiths 2009

First published 2009

Apart from any fair dealing for the purposes of research or private
study, or criticism or review, as permitted under the Copyright,
Designs and Patents Act, 1988, this publication may be reproduced,
stored or transmitted in any form, or by any means, only with the
prior permission in writing of the publishers, or in the case of
reprographic reproduction, in accordance with the terms of licences
issued by the Copyright Licensing Agency. Enquiries concerning
reproduction outside those terms should be sent to the publishers.

SAGE Publications Ltd
1 Oliver's Yard
55 City Road
London EC1Y 1SP

SAGE Publications Inc.
2455 Teller Road
Thousand Oaks, California 91320

SAGE Publications India Pvt Ltd
B 1/I 1 Mohan Cooperative Industrial Area
Mathura Road
New Delhi 110 044

SAGE Publications Asia-Pacific Pte Ltd
33 Pekin Street #02–01
Far East Square
Singapore 048763

Library of Congress Control Number: 2008927210

British Library Cataloguing in Publication data

A catalogue record for this book is available from
the British Library

ISBN 978-1-4129-4806-7
ISBN 978-1-4129-4813-5 (pbk)

Typeset by C&M Digitals (P) Ltd., Chennai, India
Printed and bound in Great Britain by TJ International Ltd, Padstow, Cornwall
Printed on paper from sustainable resources

Mixed Sources
Product group from well-managed
forests and other controlled sources
www.fsc.org Cert no. SGS-COC-2482
© 1996 Forest Stewardship Council
FSC

Contents

List of Figures

Introduction

As clinical psychologists working in a community mental heath team, we are regularly asked to provide CBT training, consultation and supervision. Colleagues have often asked us to recommend a basic easy-to-read text to complement our training, so we decided to write one.

We hope that this will be both a useful text in conjunction with your clinical training and development and also a reference guide to recap and refresh the principles of CBT when required. The CBT methods we have highlighted have been chosen from our own experiences for their simplicity and usefulness in clinical practise. There are many different ways of delivering CBT and we recommend further reading (see reference lists at the end of each chapter), particularly if you are actually planning to practise CBT, to broaden your perspective and enhance your clinical skills. If you do not actually wish to practise CBT, but have an interest, you will also find that this book will help to guide your thinking in terms of referrals and case discussions.

We have included many examples throughout the book but we focus on three main case examples covering anxiety/panic attacks, obsessive compulsive problems and depression. These are common problems that can usually be helped greatly through the use of CBT techniques. These three case examples are fictional but we believe they encompass many of the characteristics of the types of people and problems that might be seen by CBT therapists. Any resemblance to real clients is coincidental. There are role-play scripts of assessments and interventions and we also explore where things might get 'stuck'. We strongly advise that anyone planning to use the techniques in this book seek the guidance of a supervisor who is experienced in CBT, and access basic-level CBT training.

We have chosen to focus on the aspects of CBT that are common to all problems, rather than the specifics of how to use CBT with a particular diagnostic group. One of the strengths of this book is that we focus on case formulation. We believe this to be one of the most important aspects of CBT and we describe it in great detail in the book. However, in brief, formulation is about building up a 'picture' of each individual client and using their case history to inform interventions. It is individual case formulation that we see as essential to planning treatment rather than using the diagnostic category as the sole guide. We do discuss strategies that are particular to categories such as anxiety, depression and obsessional problems, but we rarely see people who do not have

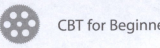

some form of dual diagnosis, and we therefore feel that the case formulation approach is the most useful one.

In writing this book, we are assuming that the readership will have generic therapeutic competencies such as those outlined by Roth and Pilling (2007) in their Department of Health paper covering the core competencies required to deliver effective CBT for people with anxiety and depression. This book makes use of their guidelines throughout in order to ensure that all the core competencies for CBT are covered, and these are referred to throughout the book. Roth and Pilling's generic therapeutic competencies assume that clinicians will have a knowledge and understanding of mental health problems and the ability to function within professional and ethical guidelines. Also assumed is that clinicians will have knowledge of a model of therapy and the ability to assess and engage clients as well as the ability to nurture and sustain a good therapeutic relationship. The capacity to handle the emotional content of sessions and manage endings is important, as is making use of supervision.

The worksheets from the appendices will be available to download from www.sagepub.co.uk/simmons

PART ONE
CBT – WHAT IS IT?

1

What is CBT?

What is CBT? It is currently a much 'bandied about' term, especially as it is used liberally in the NICE (National Institute for Clinical Excellence) guidelines (http://guidance.nice.org.uk/CG22/guidance/pdf/English) and recommended for use with most common mental health problems. It is often described as a guide to thinking positively, which is somewhat misleading. Curwin, Palmer and Ruddell (2000) provide a comprehensive list of characteristics of CBT as follows:

1 therapeutic style
2 psychological formulation of the problem
3 collaborative relationship
4 structure to sessions and to therapy
5 goal-directed therapy
6 examines and questions unhelpful thinking
7 uses a range of aids and techniques
8 teaching the client to become their own therapist
9 use of homework or assignments
10 time-limited
11 audio-recording sessions

1 Therapeutic style

The style is different from some other forms of therapy. It assumes that clinicians bring with them a range of skills and ideas about intervening. It is more than just active listening. The clinician is active and works with the client to elicit information relevant to the client's difficulties.

2 Psychological formulation of the problem

Briefly, a psychological formulation is a 'picture' of why someone is experiencing the problems they are. It differs from diagnosis in that it provides an explanation rather than a label. Psychological formulation is covered in detail in Chapter 8.

3 Collaborative relationship

The client and therapist work together to build up the formulation, with the therapist using a questioning process to develop a picture of the difficulties with the client. CBT is very transparent and each stage of formulation building is shared with the client. It is as though the client and therapist are going on a voyage of discovery, with the therapist asking curious questions and building hypotheses, and the client regarding the difficulties being experienced.

4 Structure to sessions and to therapy

CBT therapists tend to make an agenda at the beginning of each session – this is negotiated with the client and helps to make use of limited time and to give the sessions a 'problem-solving' atmosphere. Sessions tend to be offered in a series of blocks followed by a review, which gives the client the opportunity to give feedback formally or opt out of therapy. It is always assumed that therapy will come to an end at some point, which can aid clients with dependency issues. Structure of therapy and sessions is discussed in detail in Chapter 5.

5 Goal-directed therapy

The client and therapist work collaboratively to develop goals – these may change over time and at reviews. The goals are most useful if they are quite specific. For example, a client may say 'I want to go out more', but this does not give them anything concrete to work on, and so goals need to be more defined. 'I want to go out more' becomes ', I want to go to the local shop.' Goal setting is discussed further in Chapter 9.

6 Examines and questions unhelpful thinking

This is the main foundation of CBT and it is what everyone tends to think of when CBT is mentioned. The CBT approach uses a series of questions to enable clients to examine their thought processes and assess whether their approach is most helpful to them.

Several chapters in this book cover this topic as it is laced through CBT from assessment to formulation to intervention.

7 Uses a range of aids and techniques

The course of therapy is directed by the formulation, which can be developed over time. This includes the use of a range of techniques which are described in the intervention chapters. Questionnaires may also be used to evaluate the changes clients make during the course of therapy and this is discussed further in Chapter 7 on assessment.

8 Teaching the client to become their own therapist

Hopefully, the client will be able to see their own part in overcoming their difficulties throughout the therapy process. Some clients find this easier than others. Tasks between sessions can help the client to feel that they are working on their difficulties themselves. It can be important to remind the client regularly that they are in control of the changes they make, and also that the time spent in sessions with the therapist usually accounts for either an hour a week or an hour fortnightly. Not very much! Relapse prevention and 'end of therapy letter' are discussed further in Chapter 19 on endings. These are both very useful tools towards the end of therapy.

9 Use of 'homework' or assignments

'Homework' essentially refers to tasks that the client conducts between sessions. It is important for the client to be able to do work between sessions, especially as time within therapy sessions is limited to an hour every one or two weeks. It helps with the continuity of making change and gives clients the feeling it is they who are making changes, rather than a therapist with a magic wand. An example of a piece of 'homework' is to complete a thought record (see Chapter 13) or to walk to the end of the garden once a day. There can be difficulties with the term homework as it can conjure up images of school – not always the happiest time for many people; other terms can be 'assignment' or 'between-session tasks'.

10 Time-limited

CBT is time-limited which means that the therapy always has an ending in sight. The goal of the therapy is to teach clients to become their own therapist rather than becoming dependent on therapy. Regular reviews help to keep this goal in mind.

11 Audio-recording sessions

Audio-recording of sessions is often used in CBT, especially during training of therapists. It can also be helpful for clients to listen back over sessions. However, this method is not used by all therapists.

Empirical basis of CBT

As well as having the above characteristics, CBT is a therapy that has developed through rigorous research and outcome studies. Behavioural therapy was the first to emerge, based on principles of animal learning and the work of Pavlov in the 1890s and 1900s (Pavlov 1927), as well as research on human anxiety by Watson and Rayner in 1920. Behavioural approaches subsequently became popular for work on problems such as anxiety, and research was being conducted routinely (e.g. Shapiro 1961 a, b). However, it was not until the 1970s that behavioural therapy really came to the fore. It was now being routinely used to work on problems such as anxiety, although some noted that it did not work for every person or problem. Foa and Emmelkamp (1983) wrote a book on treatment failures, which served to highlight some of the gaps in a solely behavioural approach.

Behavioural researchers started to get interested in a cognitive approach, and 'self-instructional training' (Meichenbaum 1975) became popular at this time. Briefly, 'self-instructional training' worked on the premise that behaviour change could be brought about by changing the instructions that patients gave themselves, away from unhelpful, upsetting thoughts and towards more helpful self-talk. Traditional cognitive therapy as described by Beck (1970, 1976) gradually began to be adopted on a wide scale and has been extremely influential in the development of CBT, an integration of cognitive and behavioural approaches.

As CBT has become more widespread, it has been subjected to rigorous outcome research and has been shown to be a valuable approach with a considerable range of psychological problems (Roth and Fonagy 1996). However, Dudley and Kuyken (2006) note that one of the key aspects of CBT, the concept of formulation (see Chapter 8) has yet to be fully researched, although pertinent research is beginning to materialise (see Kuyken 2005).

Summary

- CBT is currently a much discussed therapy.
- CBT is recommended by NICE for many common mental health problems.
- It has a number of characteristics and has developed through rigorous research and outcome studies.

Further reading

Beck, A. (1970) *Depression: Causes and Treatment*. Philadelphia: University of Pennsylvania Press.

Beck, A. (1976) *Cognitive Therapy and the Emotional Disorders*. New York: New American Library.

Curwen, B., Palmer, S. & Ruddell, P. (2000) *Brief Cognitive Behaviour Therapy*. London: SAGE.

Dudley, R. & Kuyken, W. (2006) 'Formulation in Cognitive-behavioural therapy', in L. Johnstone & R. Dallos (eds), *Formulation in Psychology and Psychotherapy: Making Sense of People's Problems*. Hove: Routledge.

Foa, E.B. & Emmelkamp, P. (eds) (1983) 'Failures in behaviour therapy'. New York: John Wiley.

Kuyken, W. (2005) 'Research and evidence base in case formulation', in N. Tarrier (ed.), *Case Formulation in Cognitive Behaviour Therapy: The Treatment of Challenging and Complex Clinical Cases*. Hove, UK: Brunner-Routledge.

Meichenbaum, D.H. (1975) 'A self-instructional approach to stress management: a proposal for stress inoculation training', in C.D. Spielberger & I. Sarason (eds), *Stress and Anxiety* (vol. 2, pp. 237–64). New York: Wiley.

Pavlov, I.P. (1927) *Conditioned Reflexes: An Investigation of the Physiological Activity of the Cerebral Cortex*. Trans. and ed. G. V. Anrep. London: Oxford University Press.

Roth, A. & Fonagy, P. (1996) *What Works for Whom? A Critical Review of Psychotherapy Research*. New York: Guilford Press.

Shapiro, M.B. (1961a) 'A method of measuring psychological changes specific to the individual psychiatric patient', *British Journal of Medical Psychology*, 34: 151–5.

Shapiro, M.B. (1961b) 'The single case in fundamental clinical psychological research', *British Journal of Medical Psychology*, 34: 255–62.

Watson, J.B. & Raynor, R. (1920) 'Conditioned emotional responses', *Journal of Experimental Psychology*, 3: 1–14.

2

Who Benefits from CBT?

As mentioned above, CBT is now a very popular form of treatment for a whole range of different psychological problems. The NICE guidelines put forward CBT as the psychological treatment of choice for most mental health disorders. It is therefore tempting to think that CBT should be used with every person to solve every problem. Referrers and clients can get quite hopeful about the power of CBT to resolve all difficulties. It is therefore useful to think about certain issues during a CBT assessment and, even better, at the point of making a referral for a CBT assessment.

Safran and Segal (1990a; 1990b) have devised a 'Suitability for Short-term Cognitive Therapy Interview' and a corresponding rating scale to help identify the clients who are likely to benefit most from CBT. Although these tools are designed to identify clients who will benefit from short-term therapy, they have also been useful in our clinical practice with clients who require longer-term therapy. There are ten items the authors consider to be important when assessing clients:

1　accessibility of automatic thoughts
2　awareness and differentiation of emotions
3　acceptance of personal responsibility for change
4　compatibility with cognitive rationale
5　alliance potential: in-session evidence
6　alliance potential: out-of-session evidence, including previous therapy
7　chronicity of problems
8　security operations
9　focality
10　general optimism regarding therapy

The above items are each discussed very briefly below, and then we have expanded on the ones we feel are most important later in this chapter.

1 Accessibility of automatic thoughts

Clients need to be able to access their thoughts about situations and events. This can be very difficult for some clients and may take some prompting and education.

2 Awareness and differentiation of emotions

Clients need to be able to recognise emotions and the differences between them.

3 Acceptance of personal responsibility for change

The degree to which a person identifies their own part in creating their emotional difficulties will often predict how much work they are prepared to put in towards making changes in their lives in order to address their difficulties.

4 Compatibility with cognitive rationale

The cognitive model/rationale is described in detail in Chapter 3. However, in brief, the client needs to be able to accept the rationale that our thoughts affect the way we feel and, in turn, the way we behave.

5 Alliance potential: in-session evidence

This is the ability of the client to form a reasonable therapeutic relationship with the therapist.

6 Alliance potential: out-of-session evidence, including previous therapy

This item is about the client's ability to form positive relationships with other people in general. Clients who have relationship problems with other people are likely to need longer-term therapy.

7 Chronicity of problems

The longer the person has been experiencing difficulties, the more sessions they are likely to need in therapy.

8 Security operations

This refers to the extent to which the person relies on 'props' such as alcohol which may make them feel safer in the short term but may cause more problems over time.

9 *Focality*

Clients who are able to remain focused in sessions are likely to benefit more.

10 *General optimism regarding therapy*

Greater optimism about the potential of therapy to bring about change has been shown to affect therapy outcome in a positive way.

During our work in community mental health team settings, we have used the above criteria and, over time, adapted them to suit our needs. This allows us to provide referrers with as much information as possible in order to allow them to make decisions about which clients to refer, without feeling overwhelmed with jargon. The information below can be given, in handout form (see Appendix I), to potential referrers.

Referral criteria for cognitive behaviour therapy

The list below gives some pointers to look for during a general assessment to see if referral for a CBT assessment might be relevant. The person doesn't have to fulfil *all* the criteria but it does help if they fulfil most of them. On page 13 are some sample questions to ask clients before making a referral for CBT assessment.

Accessibility of automatic thoughts

- The person needs to be able (even if it takes some prompting) to access negative automatic thoughts, e.g., 'I messed that up'; 'People will think I'm odd.'
- It is okay to suggest examples of thoughts that other people sometimes have in these situations, especially if the person is finding it hard to access their own thoughts.
- However, part of CBT is about teaching the client to access thoughts and not all clients may be able to do this to start with.

Awareness and differentiation of emotions

- The client needs to be able to gain access to emotions and differentiate between emotions, such as guilt, anxiety, sadness, anger, etc. The therapist needs to be aware of differences in language: 'depressed' may just mean low in mood to some people. Be aware of cultural differences.

- This is not quite as important as the ability to access negative thoughts and some people may not be able to do this at first. For these people, there may need to be some preliminary work on accessing emotions before they start CBT (see Chapter 17).

The client's ability to make use of therapeutic input – very important!

- An important aspect of therapy is how prepared clients are to make changes in their lives so that they can work on the problems they have. A negative indication might be the question: 'Have you got a tablet that will make it all go away?'
- How motivated is the client? Are they able to collaborate? Or have they been told, by social services or their partner, to come? If the client needs to be persuaded to start CBT, it's most likely an indication that it is not for them at this time. They can always be referred in the future.
- Clients' ability to remain focused on the problem in hand. This may be something that clients have to work towards.

Barriers to therapy

- If someone is 'floridly psychotic'. However, a level of psychotic symptoms can be fine, and CBT for psychosis could be considered.
- If someone is in a current manic phase.
- If clients are cognitively impaired, this may make therapy more difficult but not impossible.
- If there are practical issues, or other referrals are being made, the person will need a care co-ordinator as well.
- If the setting is the NHS, the client will also need to be accepted into the relevant team before therapy assessment can commence.

Questions to consider asking to see if therapy would be helpful

It is most useful to ask the client to describe situations in which they feel anxious/low/scared, etc. The following questions can then be put.

Accessibility of automatic thoughts

When that situation occurred:

- What were you thinking?
- What went through your mind?

- Sometimes people worry that, for example, if they have a panic attack they might faint, or sometimes people might worry that, for example, if they go out, others will stare at them, etc. Do you ever get similar concerns?

Awareness and differentiation of emotions

When the situation occurred:

- How did you feel?
- What was happening in your body at the time?
- Ask about different situations and how the person felt at that time.

The client's ability to make use of therapeutic input

- What changes would you like to make? (Specific goals are best.)
- What are the advantages and disadvantages of making changes:
  - to the client?
  - to the client's family?
  - to any other significant others?
- What might get in the way of making change, attending sessions on a regular basis, etc.?
- Be aware how focused the client is able to remain on the issue being discussed.

Referral letters

Most clients enter mental health services (both primary and secondary care) via a referral letter, often from their General Practitioner (GP). Some clients enter the services through different routes such as Accident and Emergency departments or a Mental Health Act assessment. In some parts of the country, mental health services allow for self-referral. However, referral letters from the GP are probably the most common route.

The quality of referral letters can vary and, for this reason, we felt it would be helpful to write about referral letters – which ones might be suitable and which ones might require you to ask the referrer for more information. The more a clinician knows about mental health and therapy, the more helpful the referral letter is likely to be. Below are some examples of referral letters and each is followed by a discussion of what might be the next appropriate action. Do please note that when teams go through the referral letters each week, there is often much debate about each letter, and therefore the discussions we present here could be hotly debated by other professionals and are only meant as a general guide.

Referral letter 1: Andy

Dear Mental Health Team,
Re: Andy, DOB: 26.08.82

I am writing to refer the above-named young man, whom I saw in my surgery today. He attended surgery as he was concerned about chest pains and palpitations, and was wondering whether there might be something wrong with his heart. I conducted a physical examination and could find no abnormalities. He appeared very tense and anxious, and reported that he is not coping at all well. I was quite concerned about him as he normally appears quite confident and together.

Andy works at the local bank as a bank clerk; however he has recently gone on a period of extended sick leave, and is unsure whether he will be able to go back. He lives on his own in a flat in the city centre, and currently spends most of his time actually in the flat. He told me that today was the first day he had left the flat since he had to go out to buy food a few days ago. He appeared embarrassed about his difficulties and was reluctant to go into detail. However, he did finally agree that I could make a referral to yourselves. I would value your assessment and advice.

Yours sincerely,

Dr X

Discussion of Andy's referral letter:

It is important that Andy has had an examination by his doctor as this helps to exclude possible physical causes for his symptoms of chest pain and palpitations. If this had not been clear in the referral letter, it would be a good idea to speak with the GP. This does look like a suitable referral for an assessment. There are some issues to consider, which may influence the plan for assessment. The referral letter states that Andy 'finally' agrees to a referral being made, which may indicate that he has some reservations about a psychological approach to his problems. It may therefore be important to include questions about his beliefs around his difficulties and whether he has an explanation for what is happening. It may also be helpful, as part of the assessment, to ask some questions about the client's motivation. The referral letter suggests that Andy finds his problems embarrassing and it would be important to be sensitive to this during assessment (this will be elaborated on later).

Referral letter 2: Anne

Dear Mental Health Team,
Re: Anne, DOB 14.03.53

I am writing with reference to Anne … whom I have been seeing on a regular basis in my surgery over a period of approximately six months. She frequently attends surgery complaining of poor sleep, lack of appetite and a lack of pleasure in things that she used to enjoy. It is difficult to know what has set this off and she has been unable to identify specific triggers. She is frequently tearful and has stated that she sometimes feels as though there is no point in going on. I note that her two children have now left home and, indeed, her daughter has moved to Australia.

I do hope that you can help as she does feel rather desperate.

Yours sincerely

Dr Y

Discussion of Anne's referral letter

This does look like a suitable referral for assessment. It is interesting that she is finding it difficult to identify specific triggers and this may need some careful questioning. The GP has identified some possible triggers in terms of her children leaving home and it would be useful to gently question her about this. Given that she may be depressed, it would be important to enquire about any suicidal thoughts (this will be elaborated on later).

Referral letter 3: Anne-Marie

Dear Mental Health Team,
Re: Anne-Marie, DOB 02.10.65

Thank you for seeing this lady who has had some courses of CBT in the past. She reports that she misses her weekly contact with her last therapist who retired six months ago, and whom she had been seeing for a number of years. I note that she had psychological input including CBT prior to her most recent therapy. She has been attending surgery more regularly since her therapy ended and she does appear to need to talk to someone.

Yours sincerely,

Dr X

Discussion of Anne-Marie's referral letter

This is less likely to be a suitable referral for CBT. More information is required, especially regarding symptomatology and whether previous therapy actually helped Anne-Marie to make changes in her life. After this information is obtained from the GP, decisions can be made regarding the suitability of assessment for CBT. It may be that other forms of help are indicated rather than CBT. Possibilities include befriending, supportive counselling, etc.

Referral letter 4: Marcus

> Dear Mental Health Team,
> Re: Marcus, DOB 14.07.88
>
> Thank you for seeing this young man for CBT as his mother is worried about him.
>
> Yours sincerely,
>
> Dr X

Discussion of Marcus's referral letter

In this case it would be advisable to contact the GP for information it on his symptoms, and how long he has had them. In addition it would be important to know whether the referral had been discussed with Marcus.

Referral letter 5: Megan

> Dear Mental Health Team,
> Re: Megan, DOB 29.11.84
>
> I am writing with regard to Megan who I am very worried about. She came to see me today and reported that she has been having some very distressing thoughts regarding her baby daughter, Molly, who is now four months old. She was extremely tearful and said she was very worried about telling me about her thoughts as she thought I might arrange to have Molly taken into care. She eventually said that she is having recurrent thoughts that she might harm the baby in some way, which she is finding extremely distressing especially as she is a very caring mother. I have no concerns about her risk to Molly and the health visitor is in agreement.

Megan also reported that she is very concerned about the cleanliness of her hands and I noted that they were very red and chapped. I would appreciate it if you could see her as soon as possible as I am concerned that the problem is getting worse.

Yours sincerely,

Dr Z

Discussion of Megan's referral letter

This does seem like a suitable referral. It would be important to get more information on the content of the thoughts and to ask questions about things that she might be avoiding, and checking rituals that she carries out in response to her anxiety. It would also be relevant to ask how she copes with being a mum. It appears that there are no risks to the child, but it would be a good idea to cover this issue again in assessment. Psycho-education is very important for people presenting with these types of thoughts as it can help them to make sense of their problems and feel less guilty. If appropriate, this could be touched on during assessment (this will be illustrated later).

What constitutes a good CBT referral?

It is all well and good discussing the above referrals, but it is also helpful to think about the basics of a good CBT referral. For this purpose, we have included in Appendix I a handout to give to potential referrers. Educating referrers tends to be a process that occurs over time and it is important to keep an open dialogue with referrers so they can ask questions and learn more about CBT.

Summary

- CBT encompasses a number of characteristics which sets it apart from other therapies.
- Not everyone benefits from CBT and there are a number of factors to be aware of during assessment and also when looking through referral letters.
- There are certain barriers which mean that people might not be able to take part in therapy at the current time but this does not mean that they could not benefit in the future.
- It is important to get certain information from referrers before deciding to assess for therapy – this can sometimes save a lot of time and disappointment.

Further reading

Curwen, B., Palmer, S. & Ruddell, P. (2000) *Brief Cognitive Behaviour Therapy*. London: SAGE.

NICE (National Institute for Clinical Excellence) (2004, 2005) *NICE Guidelines* http://guidance.nice.org.uk/CG22/guidance/pdf/English

Safran, J.D. & Segal, Z.M. (1990a) *Interpersonal Process in Cognitive Therapy*. New York: Basic Books, Appendix II.

Safran, J.D. & Segal, Z.M. (1990b) *Interpersonal Process in Cognitive Therapy*. New York: Basic Books, Appendix I.

3

The CBT Model

The cognitive model was first put forward by Beck (1976). Beck's model illustrated how emotional problems could be driven by patterns of negative thinking, and proposed that problems could be alleviated by changing thinking processes. Since the 1970s, the cognitive model has been developed, refined and extended. The roles of physiology, behaviour, environment, motivation and process in therapy have all now been considered. The cognitive-behavioural model incorporated the role of a person's behaviour in the development and maintenance of their problems. The terms 'cognitive' and 'cognitive-behavioural' are however sometimes used interchangeably in the literature. There is now a vast literature of CBT theory and models of varying complexity relating to different client groups, professionals and disorders. We will use a basic CBT model in this book which focuses on the four key elements of psychological distress – thoughts, feelings, physical sensations and behaviour – and the relationships between them. This basic CBT model is illustrated in Figure 3.1.

The CBT model hypothesises that situations in themselves do not cause psychological distress, but rather what is important is the way that people interpret, make sense of and react to situations. People will experience distress if they construe a situation negatively, or react to it in a negative way. Interventions based on the CBT model therefore aim to correct negative biases in thinking processes and behavioural reactions. The CBT model can be used diagrammatically throughout the course of therapy in the form of a 'maintenance cycle'.

We will now define each element of the CBT model in more detail.

Thoughts and beliefs

The term negative automatic thought (NAT) is often used to describe the cognitive element of distress. The thoughts are automatic as they are not usually under conscious control of the person. NATs are thought to result from maladaptive core beliefs and assumptions (for a fuller explanation of cognitions see Chapter 4). Core beliefs and assumptions are

Figure 3.1   The cognitive-behavioural model

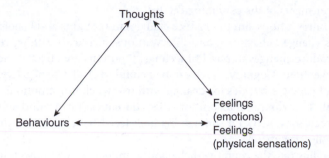

developed through our experiences as we grow up. If a person had difficult or traumatic life experiences in their childhood they are more likely to develop negative core beliefs and assumptions, which result in everyday NATs. These NATs are often experienced as a 'running commentary' on a person's experiences and expectations. As circumstances change as a person grows up, the negative core beliefs, assumptions and NATs may no longer be necessary or appropriate, yet if they have been left unchallenged they may remain.

Feelings – emotions

Emotions such as anger, sadness, guilt and fear are an important element of psychological distress, and are often the reason for seeking help.

Feelings – physical sensations

Psychological distress is often manifested physically. Anxiety usually produces marked physiological changes, such as increased heart rate or shortness of breath. Sadness is often accompanied by a lack of appetite.

Behaviours

Another element of psychological distress is behaviour, that is, what a person actually does. This can include changes in activity levels and avoidance, as well as coping strategies such as drug and alcohol use and self-harm.

The cognitive-behavioural model suggests that all these elements of distress are related, so that a change in one element can produce a change in any one of the others. In this way, a negative change in one element can start a 'negative spiral', or 'vicious cycle', through the impact that it has on the other elements of psychological distress. Cognitive-behavioural interventions break vicious cycles by creating positive changes in one or more elements of the psychological distress.

Cognitive interventions aim to produce changes in thoughts and beliefs, behavioural interventions change behaviours, and interventions such as breathing retraining and relaxation produce changes in physical feelings. Emotions are affected indirectly by all of these interventions. Cognitive work can be helpful to challenge negative beliefs about emotions, and coping strategies for dealing with overwhelming emotions can be developed through behavioural interventions. Psycho-education around emotions is an important precursor to CBT for some individuals (see Chapter 17, 'Working with Emotions', for a fuller discussion).

In order to illustrate the cognitive-behavioural model, we will now describe some of our own personal experiences. The example we will use is the first experience we had of teaching cognitive-behavioural therapy to mental health professionals. Three of us were involved in this training; two of us had very similar thoughts and one had very different thoughts, resulting in different feelings and behaviours, and these are shown in Figure 3.2 and Figure 3.3.

Figure 3.2   Thoughts about teaching CBT for Person 1

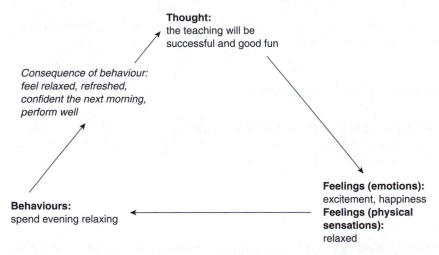

Person 1

Thought:
the teaching will be successful and good fun

Consequence of behaviour: feel relaxed, refreshed, confident the next morning, perform well

Feelings (emotions):
excitement, happiness
Feelings (physical sensations):
relaxed

Behaviours:
spend evening relaxing

As you can see, a positive cycle is set as a result of the positive thoughts of Person 1. Persons 2, and 3 however, experience a negative cycle as a result of negative thoughts about teaching. All of us experience a mixture of positive thoughts and negative thoughts in our day-to-day lives, but the more negative thoughts we have, the more likely we are to get trapped in negative patterns of thinking, feeling and behaving. These negative patterns are called maintenance cycles, but are also sometimes referred to as 'vicious cycles' or 'negative spirals'. The cognitive-behavioural model suggests that intervening to change any of the different elements of psychological distress, can produce changes in the other elements of psychological distress. Figure 3.4 shows potential CBT interventions that could break the maintenance cycle of Persons 2 and 3.

Therapist and client will decide together where first to intervene in this maintenance cycle. This will depend on the nature and severity of the client's problems and will be explored in more detail in Chapter 5, looking at the structure of therapy and sessions.

Figure 3.3   Thoughts about teaching CBT for Persons 2 and 3

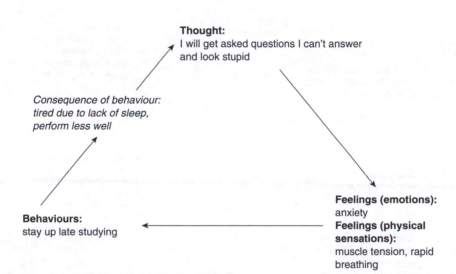

Persons 2 and 3

Thought:
I will get asked questions I can't answer and look stupid

Consequence of behaviour:
tired due to lack of sleep,
perform less well

Feelings (emotions):
anxiety
Feelings (physical sensations):
muscle tension, rapid breathing

Behaviours:
stay up late studying

Explaining the CBT model to clients

In order for therapist and client to work together collaboratively, it is important that the client has a good understanding of the CBT model and treatment rationale. We find that this is best explained making use of lots of everyday examples such as the ones illustrated in Figures 3.2 and 3.3. The best examples are ones that are relevant to the client's own experiences, life and culture. The important point is that different thoughts can arise from the same situation, resulting in different maintenance cycles. We find it helpful to first illustrate positive 'maintenance cycles', that is, how positive thoughts set up positive patterns of feeling and behaving which reinforce the original positive thought. Having worked through some examples like this, we discuss the point that it is not a situation in itself which causes distress, but the interpretations and meanings that we make in a situation. Some situations or life events will of course result in very negative thoughts for almost everybody who experiences them, such as losing a job or suffering a bereavement. This is to be expected and entirely natural. People with anxiety or

Figure 3.4 Where CBT interventions break the maintenance cycle

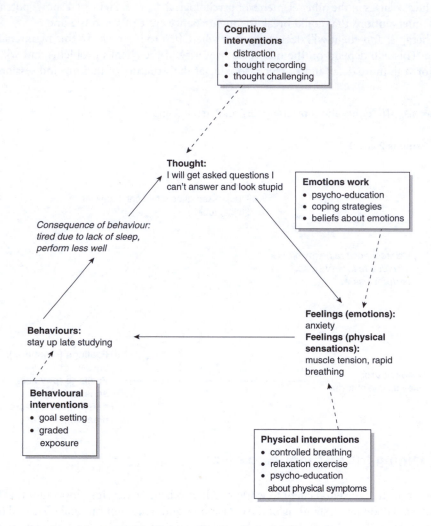

mood-related problems tend to have a bias in their thinking, so are prone to making negative interpretations. It is this bias in thinking that CBT aims to address.

Recognising the difference between thoughts, feelings, behaviours and physical sensations

In order for cognitive-behavioural interventions to be successful, it is important that clients are able to distinguish between the different elements of the CBT model – namely thoughts, feelings, physical sensations and behaviours. These are often mislabelled at the start of therapy; here is an example from our case study, Andy:

Therapist: What thought did you have when the phone rang?
Andy: I felt really anxious.

In this example, the client has labelled the emotion rather than the thought. It is the therapist's job to prompt the client into accessing the relevant thoughts associated with the emotion, for example:

Therapist: So when the phone rang you felt really anxious. Looking back can you remember what went through your mind at the time the phone started ringing?
Andy: Yes, I think I was thinking about work.
Therapist: Okay, so the phone rang and you remember thinking about work. What was it about work that you were thinking about?
Andy: Well I thought it would be my boss.
Therapist: And what did you think your boss was phoning for?
Andy: To ask me to do a presentation.
Therapist: And the thought of doing the presentation made you feel anxious?
Andy: Yes, because I would make a fool of myself.

The therapist finally elicits the NAT in this example, which is 'I will make a fool of myself.'

Practical Exercise

When teaching CBT to other professionals we use an exercise to identify thoughts, feelings, physical sensations and behaviours. It is also a useful exercise to complete with clients early on in therapy when confusion around the elements of the maintenance cycle is common. The client needs to be able to correctly identify these different elements of distress before moving on to interventions to break the maintenance cycle. The identification of NATs will be covered in more detail in Chapter 13.

The thoughts, feelings, physical sensations and behaviours listed in Appendix II can be photocopied and cut up into the individual statements. The exercise is to sort the statement into groups of 'thoughts', 'feelings', 'behaviours' and 'physical sensations'. This exercise is not as easy as it first seems. It does not matter if you do not get this 100 per cent right – there are usually discrepancies between people regarding what constitutes a thought and what constitutes a feeling.

Summary

- The CBT model suggests that the way people interpret and react to situations can cause psychological distress.
- Interventions based on the CBT model aim to correct negative biases in thinking and behaviour.
- The model proposes that the elements of psychological distress – thoughts, emotions, physical sensations, and behaviours – are related. A change in one can produce changes in the others.

4

Levels of Cognitions (Thoughts, Beliefs and Assumptions)

Most theorists in CBT acknowledge that there are three different levels of cognitions. These are usually referred to as 'core beliefs', 'dysfunctional assumptions' and 'automatic thoughts'. Our minds are filled with a constant array of changing thoughts and ideas. Usually, we are not even aware of these many thousands of thoughts. Sometimes these thoughts are positive, but they can also be negative and therefore have a negative impact on our moods and feelings.

This chapter is an introduction to the different levels of cognitions.

Automatic thoughts

Automatic thoughts tend to be more available to the conscious mind than assumptions and core beliefs, and can be verbal or appear as images. They are labelled 'automatic' because they tend to pop into the mind without prompting. Even though automatic thoughts tend to be more accessible to the conscious mind, we often tend not to notice that they are having an effect on our moods in either a positive or a negative way. One of the tasks of CBT is to help clients to start noticing these automatic thoughts, particularly the negative ones, and how they have an effect on mood and feelings. Obviously it is not possible to get clients to identify *all* their thoughts, as we are constantly thinking. The task is to learn how to identify thoughts that lead to powerful feelings.

Clients can start to identify their negative thoughts by becoming aware of what goes through their minds when they feel a strong emotion of any kind. We will be discussing this in far more detail in Chapter 12.

Assumptions or 'rules for living'

Assumptions, sometimes known as 'rules for living', tend to be less easy to identify than automatic thoughts. They are most easily noticed when put into words, and are usually defined by 'if … then … ' phrases (e.g., '*If* I make a mistake, *then* I will be a complete failure') or 'should' statements (e.g., 'I *should* always be able to cope well'). 'Rules for living' are developed as a way of 'protecting' people from their negative core beliefs. For example, a person with a core belief about failure may strive to make sure they don't fail and they may have the following 'rule for living': 'I must not make any mistakes or I will be a complete failure.' In this way, people are constantly striving to make sure they don't trigger negative core beliefs.

Core beliefs

Core beliefs are the deepest level of cognition and they are global and absolute beliefs, rather than being conditional on certain terms. Examples include statements such as: 'I am worthless', or 'The world is against me.' Core beliefs differ from automatic thoughts in being global rather than specific – for example 'Everyone hates me' rather than 'Ian hates me' – and they differ from assumptions in being absolute rather than conditional – for example, 'I am a bad person' rather than 'If I don't get on with everyone, I am a bad person.' Core beliefs may be latent and some people may have many negative beliefs but if their lives are going very well, these negative beliefs are rarely triggered and their positive beliefs have the opportunity to become more prominent and have more of an impact on their thoughts, feelings and behaviour. This helps to explain why certain events tend to trigger episodes of mental health problems: certain events may trigger the person's negative beliefs and they may then start filtering in information according to these negative beliefs.

Greenberger and Padesky (1995) provide a helpful analogy for describing to clients these cognitions and how they fit together. They use the analogy of a garden to describe the different levels of cognitions. Automatic thoughts are thus described as being like the parts of flowers and weeds that are above ground level. The automatic thoughts are thus rooted beneath the surface in assumptions and core beliefs (see Figure 4.1). Explaining CBT to clients, along with the ability to demonstrate the rationale for CBT, are core therapist competencies (Roth & Pilling 2007).

Figure 4.1   Analogy from Greenberger & Padesky (1995)

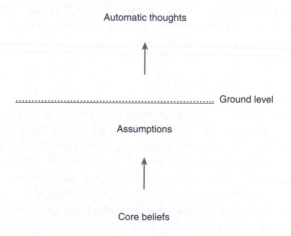

Automatic thoughts

··· Ground level

Assumptions

Core beliefs

Thus, for many people, negative automatic thoughts (or weeds) can be kept in check by using thought records, behavioural interventions and problem solving. However, for other people these tools are not enough to remove the weeds and they just keep on coming back – very much like a garden. For these people, the roots may need more work. Interventions for this level of cognition are discussed in Chapter 15.

Clients often ask where these cognitions come from and why they might develop certain beliefs over others. Sometimes clients ask why they still feel bad about themselves even when people compliment them or they are told they are doing well at work. The following explanation can be useful.

How we filter information into our brains and develop core beliefs

A useful example that we have heard CBT therapists use to explain how we filter information into our brains is to think about the child's shape-sorter toy where you have to slot shapes into various differently shaped holes.

Let's imagine someone has had a very difficult early life. They may grow up with lots of unhelpful and negative beliefs about themselves, the world and other people. People who have had a good start in life will tend to grow up with many more positive beliefs. So if someone has had a difficult time of things they may tend to take in mainly negative information (let's call it square-shaped information) because it fits with their view of themselves and the world. People who have had a good life and have positive beliefs will tend to take in positive information (let's call it star-shaped information) because it fits in with their view of themselves and the world.

So people who have had had a difficult early life tend to take in square-shaped information, and as they take in more and more their negative view of themselves is strengthened and the square-shaped filter becomes increasingly rigid. Star-shaped information (e.g. compliments from others) may try and get in but, as it doesn't fit with the person's view of themselves, it hangs around on the surface and is eventually lost. Or, it may be that the person does hear the star-shaped information but they 'yes but' it out – e.g. 'Yes but she only said that because she's my therapist.' The job of CBT is therefore to help people to become aware of this process and gradually help the shapes (filters) to become more flexible so they take in more information.

The prejudice model (Padesky 1991)

Padesky (1991) states that one of her favourite metaphors for explaining the development of core beliefs and filtering of information is to discuss them with the concept of 'prejudice' in mind. Socratic questioning can be used to enable the client to start thinking about the concept of 'prejudice'. It is important to get the client to think about someone they know who holds a prejudice with which they disagree. Suppose the client thinks of a friend called Chris who holds a prejudice against the drivers of red cars. The therapist then asks the client a series of Socratic questions about red car drivers:

- Chris sees a red car driving really badly. What does he say?
  (The client may say things like: 'Chris says, there you are, yet another red car driver being selfish.')
- A red car cuts in front of Chris. What does he say?
  ('Well that's just typical, another red car driver driving like all the rest of them.')

Next, the therapist asks a series of questions where it is clear that the red car is actually driving well:

- A red car lets Chris pull in front of it. What does Chris say?
  (As Chris has prejudice about red cars, he may say 'The car only let me in because I pushed myself forward in front of it') *or*
  ('The red car is an exception; most red cars drive badly') *or*
  ('That red car is actually more of a maroon colour.')

The second set of questions/answers illustrates how the prejudice acts to discount positive information. The client can be asked why the therapist might be asking these questions after describing the cognitive model and the development of core beliefs. Many clients will get the link at this point, although some might need more direction. At this point, the metaphor can just be used to explore how core beliefs might be like prejudices in a general way. However, this metaphor can be utilised later in therapy, when core beliefs are being examined and challenged in more detail, to explore whether individual core beliefs are acting like prejudices.

Summary

- There are three levels of cognitions: automatic thoughts, dysfunctional assumptions/ rules and core beliefs.
- Clients can have lots of conflicting cognitions all at the same time and one of therapist's jobs is to help the client pick out the cognitions that are leading to the negative emotions.
- Metaphors can be a helpful way of explaining CBT to clients.

Further reading

Beck, A.T. (1976) *Cognitive Therapy and the Emotional Disorders.* New York: International Universities Press.

Beck, J.S. (1995) *Cognitive Therapy: Basics and Beyond.* New York: Guilford Press.

Greenberger, D. & Padesky, C. (1995) *Clinician's Guide to Mind over Mood.* New York and London: Guilford Press.

Padesky, C.A. (1991) 'Schema as a self prejudice', *International Cognitive Therapy Newsletter,* 6: 6–7.

Sanders, D. & Wills, F. (2005) *Cognitive Therapy: An Introduction* (pp. 3–24) London: SAGE.

5

Structure of Therapy and Sessions

The ability to structure CBT sessions and the therapy as a whole are core therapist competencies as outlined by Roth and Pilling (2007). Without sound structure therapy sessions and the therapy as a whole can lose focus and direction. This usually results in the therapy becoming less effective and efficient than it might otherwise have been. The therapy structure, along with the CBT formulation of the client's problems, provides a solid foundation on which therapy is built. This chapter will cover how to structure individual CBT sessions and plan the length and course of therapy. We would argue that there is no 'standard' course of CBT, as each client has a different set of circumstances, problems and symptoms. We have, however, outlined an example of what a course of CBT might look like. Throughout the chapter we will look at some of the variables to consider when planning a course of CBT in order to individualise it to the specific needs of your client. We will also address some common problems that you may encounter when trying to maintain therapy structure.

Length of therapy

A 'typical' course of CBT lasts 12–20 sessions, depending on the nature, severity and complexity of the client's problems. Howard et al. (1986) conclude that most of the 'impact' of therapy occurs in the first 10–20 sessions, suggesting that there may be little benefit in lengthening therapy. CBT is a time-limited, 'skills'-based therapy which requires active participation by the client. Therapist and client work together to enhance the client's understanding, insight, and use of cognitive-behavioural strategies so that the client will continue to use CBT techniques long after the end of therapy.

Frequency of sessions

The optimal frequency of sessions is usually weekly or fortnightly. This allows enough time for practice, experimentation and reflection between sessions without running the risk of losing momentum, which can happen if longer gaps are left between sessions. Frequency of sessions can be adjusted as therapy progresses. At the start of therapy it can be beneficial to have sessions closer together to work on the early therapy goals of building a trusting therapeutic relationship, developing a formulation and giving the client a good understanding of the CBT model. Later in therapy the main goals are practice and review of the cognitive and behavioural interventions. At this stage bigger gaps between sessions can be beneficial as they allow for more experimentation by the client. Length of time between sessions can be reviewed and negotiated between therapist and client as the therapy progresses.

Session length

Optimal session length for both therapist and client is usually between 45 and 60 minutes, which allows enough time for all the agenda items to be covered, without 'burnout' of either the client or therapist. If the client has difficulty in concentrating for long periods of time, for example as a symptom of depression, the session length can be adjusted accordingly.

The following may suggest that a shorter session length is needed:

- The client starts to appear restless or fidgety.
- The client is unable to reflect back an understanding of what has been discussed. This may indicate a difficulty in concentrating.
- If the client is very socially anxious and finds it difficult to sit in a room with a therapist. In this case, sessions can be gradually lengthened as the therapy progresses and the client becomes more comfortable.

Structure of therapy

Although there is no 'fixed' session-by-session structure that must be adhered to, there are some useful principles to consider when planning a course of CBT. Early sessions should focus on engagement and assessment, leading on to education around the cognitive-behavioural model and then to the development of a CBT formulation (an understanding of the client's problems from a cognitive-behavioural perspective). The main goal of the middle stage of therapy is the practice and review of cognitive and behavioural techniques and reformulation. The later stage of therapy focuses on relapse-management work, coping with setbacks and a review and summary of formulation and the skills and techniques learned. Figure 5.1 illustrates the timing of the key tasks of a course of CBT. The therapist might adjust the timing of later tasks, based on what is learned through the assessment and formulation stages.

Figure 5.1 The structure of therapy

Task	Session															
	1	2	3	4	5	6	7	8	9	10	11	12	13	14	15	16
Engagement	*	*	*	*	*											
Assessment	*	*	*	*												
Education around CBT model			*	*	*											
Developing shared formulation			*	*	*	*	*	*	*	*	*	*	*	*	*	*
Behavioural interventions				*	*	*	*	*	*	*	*	*	*			
Cognitive interventions						*	*	*	*	*	*	*	*	*		
Relapse-management/ending											*	*	*	*	*	*

Regular reviews

It is helpful to review the therapy regularly. We would suggest reviewing the therapy every six sessions, but the frequency can be agreed between the therapist and client. Review sessions provide an opportunity for the therapist and client to reflect on the therapy together. They can help to keep the therapy focused and problems and issues that have arisen can be discussed. The goals of therapy should be reviewed and the therapist and client should check that they are on target to meet these goals by the agreed number of sessions. Therapy length can then be adjusted in light of the things that therapist and client have learnt about the problem. Keeping the end of therapy in mind is another important function of having regular reviews, and is discussed in more detail in Chapter 19 on therapeutic endings. Techniques for assessing symptoms are discussed in Chapter 7, and include self-monitoring and self-report questionnaires, which may be used again in the review sessions in order to monitor change through the therapy.

Sometimes clients can find it difficult to engage in therapy. This can happen for a number of reasons: some clients may be expecting a different kind of therapeutic approach; they may wish that the therapist has a magic wand; they are finding it difficult to make the commitment to change; change means their family will offer less support; they don't get on with the therapist; or they don't fully understand or like the model. Regular reviews can help to identify situations where the client is having difficulties engaging in the therapy. Some clients may be able to identify the difficulties in engaging while other clients may not see the lack of change as a problem, as they are valuing the supportive element of the therapy.

As discussed above, it can be helpful to review the client's goals with them in some detail during the review process and explore if there are any difficulties tackling any of the goals. If clients are finding it difficult to comment on the goals, therapists can be open and transparent and say: 'I note that you have been having difficulty tackling … Do you know why you are having difficulties with those goals? … What might be stopping you moving forwards?' Some clients may need to look at the pros and cons of making changes in certain areas of their lives, as change can be challenging. We have included a chapter on motivation for change interviewing (Chapter 18), which specifically deals with exploring the pros and cons of making change. This process can aid the therapist and client in making decisions about future therapy. In some cases, the therapist and client may choose to have a break from therapy, or to end the therapy. This might be because of a lack of progress, changes in life circumstances or a worsening of symptoms. If you are unsure about whether it is appropriate to continue along the same therapeutic path, it would be important to seek supervision.

The structure of therapy illustrated in Figure 5.1 is not fixed and should be adjusted for each individual client. But there are some general considerations when deciding on the length and course of therapy. If your client has long-standing or very severe depression it is likely that his or her thoughts and beliefs will be very negative and fixed, resulting in a limited capacity to see things from alternative perspectives. Cognitive work involves consideration of alternative explanations and perspectives, which may be difficult at this stage. It is therefore usually better to start with small behavioural goals for clients with very severe depression. Success at these can then be used as 'evidence against' negative beliefs when you come on to the cognitive work.

Somebody with severe anxiety or agoraphobia may find it impossible to attempt a behavioural goal until some of their catastrophic thoughts about what might happen have been addressed using cognitive strategies. Figure 5.2 lists some potential issues that may affect the structure of therapy.

Structure of the CBT session

A typical structure of a CBT session is outlined below. The structure of the session will vary according to the stage of therapy. Early therapy sessions will follow a different format, as they will focus on assessment and formulation, and later sessions will have a focus on maintaining progress and ending. The structure of these early and late therapy sessions will be discussed in more detail in the chapters on assessment and endings. The example below is for a mid-therapy CBT session when CBT strategies are being actively practised.

Figure 5.2 Factors to consider when planning therapy structure

Clinical Issue	Therapy Structure Considerations
Client finds it difficult to express feelings or communicate problems.	Client may be embarrassed about problems, or find it difficult to build trust. Spend time on engagement. Non problem-focused talk may be helpful. Assessment may take place over a number of sessions.
Client seems confused or has a lack of insight around problems.	A lengthened formulation period is indicated. The formulation should be revisited frequently.
Client is uncertain about whether problems can be addressed psychologically.	Spend time on formulation and education around CBT model. This may need to be revisited during therapy.
The client has very fixed negative thoughts, or capacity to view things from alternative viewpoints is limited.	Start with behavioural work. Introduce cognitive work once client has had some success in behavioural tasks.
Client is very anxious about completing behavioural goals.	Spend time planning behavioural goals. Plan very small goals if necessary; this can be adjusted as confidence builds. Consider using cognitive work to challenge negative beliefs about completing the goals.
Client finds it difficult to identify thoughts, feelings and behaviours.	Spend lots of time on education around the cognitive model, and the difference between thoughts, feelings and behaviours. Allow lots of session time for cognitive work.

1 Setting the agenda (5 minutes)

Setting an agenda helps to keep the session focused so that all the relevant issues are addressed within the time constraints of the session. Therapist and client should set the agenda together and agree on the goals of the session. The therapist first asks the client what he or she would like to include in the session and then adds any additional issues to the agenda. Once therapist and client have generated a list of items, time can be allocated to each one. If there are too many items on the agenda for each item to have adequate time, therapist and client can discuss which should take priority and which can be postponed until the following session.

Agenda setting is important from a practical point of view but it is also important for the client/therapist relationship. The client's active involvement in agenda setting helps a collaborative relationship to develop between the therapist and client. Setting the agenda together with your client underlies the general philosophy of CBT, that of active collaboration between therapist and client. Some clients do, however, find being asked to contribute to the therapy process in this way intimidating to start with. Be aware that your client may not know what would be relevant or appropriate to add to a session agenda when they first start CBT, and consequently might need more guidance and suggestion from the therapist in early sessions.

2 Update (5 minutes)

This can contain a review of the previous session, including how the client felt after the session. A brief general review of life and events can provide a useful introduction to the session and help establish rapport. A risk of asking 'general' questions about events in the client's life is that the session can lose its focus and become more of a 'chat'. This can be avoided if the therapist uses the cognitive-behavioural model to help understand experiences that the client brings to the session. In this way, general 'catch-up' conversation can be linked in to the therapy and the direction and focus of the session can be maintained.

3 Homework review (5–10 minutes)

It is important that homework tasks are not just set, but reviewed in the following session. Reviewing homework tasks in session makes it more likely that they are completed by the client and this is associated with better therapy outcome. Homework review is therefore a very worthwhile agenda item although it can be overlooked by therapists. The CBT model should be used to understand the client's experience of completing the homework tasks and the consequences for his or her thoughts, feelings, physical sensations and behaviour (i.e. the effect of the homework on the CBT maintenance cycle). If the client was unable to complete the task, the reasons for this should be explored.

4 Specific CBT strategies (20–25 minutes)

These will depend on the stage of therapy and the nature of the client's problems. These will be discussed in detail in later chapters on cognitive and behavioural interventions. The specific problems that the strategies aim to address will of course also be discussed.

5 Agenda items that do not fall under 2 or 3 (time varies)

Setting homework tasks/experiments (5 minutes)

These should be discussed between therapist and client and made clear and explicit. The rationale for the homework assignment should be discussed; if the client has a clear understanding of the purpose of the task then compliance will be more likely. It is also important to identify any potential problems in completing the homework task. This gives the client and therapist the opportunity to overcome potential difficulties, and increases the chances of the client completing the task successfully. It is important that the client gains a sense of success, especially at the start of therapy, as this can increase hopefulness and self-esteem. It is important to give adequate time to planning homework tasks as the completion of homework tasks is a factor that is related to the success of therapy as discussed above. The nature of the homework task will depend on the client's particular problems as well as the stage of therapy; they will be covered in more detail in Chapters 11–15 on CBT interventions. Compliance with homework tasks has been shown to be related to better outcome in CBT (Persons et al. 1988; Niemeyer & Feixas 1990) and Roth and Pilling (2007) identify planning and reviewing homework as core competencies for therapists.

6 Reflections on session (5 minutes)

This is a time to summarise and get feedback on the session. Therapist and client can both take a turn in saying how the session has gone. The therapist's reflections will hopefully make the client feel listened to and understood. It is important that the therapist reflects on the positive aspects of the session as well as what was more difficult. Client reflections are very valuable to the therapist as they provide an insight into the client's emotional state, their hopefulness and their understanding of the session.

Common problems in maintaining therapy and session structure

It is not uncommon for CBT therapists to find it difficult to stick to the structure of therapy and agreed agenda of each session. We will outline below the main issues that we have come across in our practice as CBT therapists.

Setting the agenda

As discussed above it is important the agenda is set collaboratively with the client. A typical problem with collaborative agenda setting is that the client does not contribute to the items on the agenda. Reasons for this can include lack of confidence, low mood and uncertainty about what to suggest. Taking an active part in treatment is often a new experience for our clients, who may have been used to a more 'expert-and-patient' approach to health problems, resulting in a belief that the therapist is there to 'cure' them.

From the therapist angle, one of the blocks to collaborative agenda setting is the therapist having a preconceived idea about the session and how therapy should progress in general. The therapist has a dilemma – on the one hand a robust structure and focus to therapy is needed, but on the other hand collaboration with the client (who might have different ideas) is vital. We can recall countless sessions ourselves, when we have devised a session plan before meeting with the client, only to find later in the session (or therapy) that the client had completely different priorities. If the client senses that the session has been pre-planned by the therapist (for example by seeing a list of goals) then he or she is less likely to feel able to contribute to the agenda process. On a practical level, consider starting the session with a blank piece of paper. This gives a different message from starting with a visible 'list' of items that has been drawn up prior to the session. There is nothing wrong with having a list, but consider referring to this after you have had an opportunity to raise the issue of agenda setting with the client. You can suggest that the client also jots down some potential agenda items to bring along to the session. If possible, try and place the agenda between you and the client as you are setting it, or at least make sure that you can both see it. This might seem trivial, but if you can both see it, you can both 'own' it.

If there is a lack of collaboration in agenda setting this should be explored in session with the client and reflected upon in supervision. Once the therapist has an understanding of the reasons behind the lack of collaboration it can be addressed. Recapping on the CBT model and the rationale for a collaborative approach, addressing negative thoughts about treatment, and reflecting on your own anxieties and concerns about the therapy in supervision are strategies that can all help overcome this problem.

Therapists often complain that they feel uncomfortable with agenda setting in therapy. It is our guess that this is because it can sometimes feel too 'businesslike' or 'formal'. Some therapists also feel that it makes the therapy feel less personal or warm. For these reasons, it is essential that the client is actively involved in the agenda setting, and the rationale behind an agenda is explained, for example in the following way:

> I think it is important that we make sure that we cover all the important issues each week. How about we make a list of these at the start of each session, and decide 'roughly' how long we should spend on each? That way we can be sure that we don't overlook anything important. How would you feel about that?

Sometimes the process of thinking about important issues and making a list results in the agenda setting developing into a full description and discussion of the topic. This can feel awkward for the therapist, as it can feel insensitive to interrupt. It is important that the therapist does interject to ensure that the agenda is set, and the session maintains a focus, as in, 'That sounds really important/difficult/good. Let's make sure we allow plenty of time to discuss it later on … Is there anything else you feel we should discuss today?'

Problems with the update

Sometimes clients give too lengthy, detailed or unfocused accounts of events since the last session. In early sessions this might be because the client does not know what is required of them. It can feel awkward to interrupt the client as they are describing how things have been to them, but not intervening can be at the expense of the other agenda items. When an interruption is needed, we have found that following sequence is useful:

- Interrupt with a brief reflection of what the person has said.
- Reinforce how important it is that the therapist hears about significant things that have happened.
- Remind the client that to start with, it would be helpful to have a brief overview of how things have been, before discussing specific examples.

If this problem continues, consider asking the client to prepare a brief (a few sentences) written summary of how things have been.

Here is an example of an interruption for a client who goes straight into details about specific events:

> *Therapist*:   Can I just interrupt for a moment? It sounds like a lot has happened since we last met up, and I want to make sure that we can to talk about everything we need to. Can you just summarise how things have been for you overall, before we go on to talk about some of these specific examples. That way we can be sure that I will see the whole picture.

Some clients may understand what is required of a brief update, but still provide lengthy and unfocused summaries. It may be a symptom of anxiety, or apprehension about what the rest of the session will hold. The CBT session may be the only time that the client stops and thinks about how they are feeling, and the problems that they are experiencing. Having problems and emotions focused on can be difficult, and sometimes a lengthy introduction can be a way of avoiding this. If you suspect that this may be the case, ask the client how they were feeling before the therapy session. What thoughts went through their mind about it? What emotions did they notice? It can then be helpful to normalise anxious feelings about therapy sessions and discuss anything that might make them feel easier. The therapist should remind the client that they do not need to talk about anything that they do not feel ready to discuss, and that they can feel free to say this to the therapist. If you do identify high levels of anxiety around talking about problems or emotions, then frequent 'check-ins' on how the client is feeling through the therapy session can be helpful. For clients who are very averse to discussing emotions, some preparatory work on emotions (see Chapter 17) may be helpful.

Homework review

As discussed earlier, the homework review is an important part of the CBT session, but is often overlooked by the therapist. It is important that the therapist keeps an accurate

Figure 5.3   Common reasons for non-completion of homework tasks

- lack of understanding of the task
- lack of confidence in ability to complete task
- the task is too difficult or complicated
- a lack of belief that the task will help
- not seeing the relevance of the task to treatment
- fear of change
- avoidance of thinking about problems between sessions
- lack of motivation to change (see Chapter 18)
- problems in the wider system (e.g. family, work)
- fear of unmanageable emotions (see Chapter 17)
- time constraints
- embarrassment should others see
- unpleasant association with 'school' homework
- wanting to be 'cured' by therapist rather than taking an active part in treatment
- feeling better, so do not feel that the task is necessary
- previous negative experiences of therapy and homework
- practical constraints (e.g. transport problems, financial constraints)
- forgetting what the task was

record of the homework task and remembers to ask about it. If the therapist does not enquire about the homework task it can make the client less motivated to complete it. The therapist should enquire about the homework task and help the client to understand their experience from a CBT perspective. In order to do this, specific questions should be asked about thoughts, feelings, behaviours and physical sensations. Noncompliance with homework tasks is a common issue and the reasons for it should be explored. Common reasons that we have encountered for non-compliance with homework are shown in Figure 5.3.

It is important that the client feels able to discuss the real reasons why they have not been able to complete the task. We often find that the client will initially say that they did not have time to complete the task, but after further discussion other reasons come to light. If you suspect that there might be reasons other than the one given, ask the client about their thoughts and feelings about the homework task.

Specific CBT strategies

One of the biggest problems that can occur in this part of the session is that the discussion is too general and not focused on CBT interventions. The conversation can be brought back to a CBT focus by asking for specific examples of thoughts, feelings and behaviours. Listening to the client's problems is an important part of the therapy, but usually a specific intervention is also needed for change to occur. It is therefore important that specific CBT strategies are discussed (see Chapters 11–15). Timing and pacing are often problematic – if the therapist underestimates the time it will take to discuss agenda items, then time can run out for important issues. This problem can be avoided if issues are prioritised during the agenda setting.

Setting homework tasks

Lack of collaboration can be a problem in setting homework tasks and can be addressed in the same ways as lack of collaboration in agenda setting. It is important that the client understands the homework task and the rationale for doing it. This is more likely if the client has played an active part in designing the task, rather than just having it 'prescribed' by the therapist. Homework tasks should be pertinent to the session and phase of therapy, but if the session has had a lack of focus or has not covered specific CBT strategies then it is difficult to base homework on what has been covered in the session. Make sure that setting homework is not just a rushed afterthought at the end of the session, by allowing adequate time to discuss it with the client.

Reflections on the session

A common problem here is that the client is unable to say how they have really found the session. Common responses are 'fine' or 'a bit tired'. Reasons for this can include not wanting to offend the therapist or seeking the therapist's approval. The therapist can increase the likelihood of an honest and open response by encouraging it, and also assuming that there will be both positive and more difficult aspects of the session. For example:

Therapist: So before we finish for today it would be good to discuss how you feel the session has gone and how you are feeling now.

Megan: Fine, it's gone OK.

Therapist: Well I guess that you may have found some parts of the session more helpful and maybe other bits less helpful. It would be really useful for me to hear about what you feel went well and what went not so well.

Megan: I thought it was really helpful when you drew out what happened in the supermarket on the diagram.

Therapist: Yes, when you felt panicky doing the shopping how did drawing that out help?

Megan: Well, it helped me understand what was going on, and made the problem seem a bit smaller somehow – like I might be able to do something about it.

Therapist: OK, so it sounds like that was helpful. Perhaps we could do that again with the examples you bring next time?

Megan: Yes, I think that would be a good idea.

Therapist: So were there any bits of the session that you didn't find so helpful?

Megan: Well, you didn't ask me much about my sister's birthday. I found it really difficult but I didn't think you were interested in talking about it.

Therapist: Yes, we didn't discuss that in much detail did we? It sounds as though you felt I was dismissing that experience, and I am sorry that it came across like that as it was obviously a very difficult experience. Would it be helpful if we prioritise that discussion next time and leave 10 minutes at the end of the next session to make sure that we have given everything enough time?

Megan: Yes, that might be good.

Therapist: So how are you feeling now, at the end of our session?

Megan: I feel a bit worried about the homework task but I think I can do it. I am really hoping that this is going to make a difference, but don't want to be disappointed.

Summary

- Length of the therapy, frequency of sessions and session length are important considerations when planning CBT.
- The focus of sessions changes through the course of therapy.
- Regular reviews can help to maintain therapy structure.

Further reading

Beck, J.S. (1995) *Cognitive Therapy: Basics and Beyond* (pp. 25–75). New York: Guilford Press.

Howard, K.I., Kopta, S.M., Krause, M.S. & Orlinsky, D.E. (1986) 'The dose effect relationship in psychotherapy', *American Psychologist*, 41: 159–64.

Niemeyer, R.A. & Feixas, G. (1990) 'The role of homework and skill acquisition in the outcome of group cognitive therapy of depression', *Behaviour therapy*, 21 (3): 281–92.

Persons, J.B. Burns, D.D. & Perloff, J.M. (1988) 'Predictors of dropout and outcome in cognitive therapy for depression in a private practice setting', *Cognitive Therapy and Research*, 12: 557–75.

6

The Therapeutic Relationship

The therapeutic relationship has always been of importance in the practice of CBT, but has not always been regarded as such. However, in recent years, CBT has undergone a transformation and the quality of the therapeutic relationship has become much more central. Sanders and Wills (2005: 53) argue that 'relationship issues can also be helpfully used to form a more vibrant and emotionally engaged practice model for all cognitive therapy'. This part of this book briefly discusses some of the issues regarding the therapeutic relationship. However, when relevant, the therapeutic relationship is discussed through the book in some of the individual chapters. As this is a basic CBT book, we do not discuss the therapeutic relationship in as much depth as more advanced texts and we point the reader towards the Further Reading section for more in-depth discussions.

Despite the therapeutic relationship previously not being given central importance in CBT, there has always been a recognition that certain conditions need to be present for therapeutic work to be successful. These are generally acknowledged to be 'empathy, understanding, genuineness, respect, congruence and unconditional, non-possessive positive regard' (Sanders and Wills 2005: 55). One of the core competencies of CBT is the building of a trusting relationship, as outlined by Roth and Pilling (2007). Hardy et al. (2007) state that the building of a therapeutic relationship involves three core elements (based on Bordin's 1979 definition): bonds, tasks and goals. Essentially 'bonds' refers to the development of the therapeutic relationship, and the way this relationship develops has an effect on the types of tasks and goals that are selected. The relationship history of both therapist and client also has an effect on the therapeutic relationship.

Therapy can be extremely painful and challenging at times, and it is at these times that the therapeutic relationship is especially important. The key concept at the heart of CBT is collaboration, a concept that can be foreign to many clients and is quite different from the medical model, in which the doctor is seen as the expert who heals the patient. In CBT, the client is seen as an expert in their own difficulties, and works alongside the therapist to make life-changes. We have often noted that clients can find it difficult to know how they 'should be' in therapy: 'What is a client supposed to be like?'; 'What is it okay to say?'. CBT has, in more recent times, used the concept of self-disclosure to build relationships with clients (Beck 2007). We have found that a small amount of self-disclosure can be useful if the content is relevant and likely to be helpful to the client.

Using the therapy relationship to inform the formulation

The above indicates how an empathic and genuine therapeutic relationship can form the basis for an effective therapeutic intervention. Persons (1989), in her case-formulation approach, illustrates how the therapeutic relationship, the client's inter-actions with the therapist and also the therapist's feelings towards the client, can inform the formulation/case understanding. CBT formulation is covered in depth in Chapter 8, but for the purpose of this chapter, formulation is described as an under-standing of a client's difficulties incorporating past history, the factors that seemed to set the problem off and the factors that are keeping the problem going. The client's behaviour with the therapist can give an indication about their behaviour with others and may help to highlight their underlying beliefs about themselves, others and the world. In turn, the therapist's feelings and responses to the client's behaviour can help the therapist gain an understanding about how others might feel when the client behaves in certain ways.

For example, if the therapist, usually punctual, is late for a session and the client becomes incredibly angry, it may suggest that the client has high expectations of oth-ers and may find it difficult to tolerate mistakes, or could feel that the therapist does not like or respect them. Careful questioning can be used to get more information about what thoughts/beliefs triggered the anger. The therapist should also pay atten-tion to their own feelings to give clues as to how others around the client may feel and react. It is important that therapists are able to remain calm and in the position of an observer while questioning the client and gaining an understanding. The inability to do this could lead to the therapist becoming entangled in the client's beliefs in an unhelpful way.

Sanders and Wills (2005) discuss the concept of personal therapy for therapists to help them come to terms with their own issues and gain an understanding of what may be triggered for them in certain interactions with clients. However, for those therapists not undertaking personal therapy, Persons (1989) has written an excellent chapter enti-tled 'Cognitive therapy for the cognitive therapist' which summarises some of the issues involved in being a therapist and also suggests some ways of recognising and dealing with these issues. There is not scope to elaborate on this further within this book, but we highly recommend the above chapter.

Summary

- CBT has undergone a transformation and the quality of the therapeutic relationship is now much more central.
- One of the core competencies of CBT is the building of a trusting relationship.
- The key concept at the heart of CBT is collaboration.
- The clients behaviour with the therapist can give an indication about their behaviour with others and may help to highlight their underlying beliefs.

Further reading

Beck, J.S. (2007) 'Self-disclosure in cognitive therapy', *Cognitive Therapy Today*, Beck Institute's blog http://cttoday.org/?p=146

Bordin, E.S. (1979) 'The generalisability of the psychoanalytic concept of the working alliance', *Psychotherapy: Theory, Research & Practice*, 16: 252–60.

Hardy, G., Cahill, J. & Barkham, M. (2007) 'Active ingredients of the therapeutic relationship that promote client change', in P. Gilbert & R.L. Leahy, *The Therapeutic Relationship in the Cognitive Behavioural Psychotherapies*. London: Routledge.

Persons, J.B. (1989) *Cognitive Therapy in Practice*. New York, London: Norton.

Sanders, D. & Wills, F. (2005) *Cognitive Therapy: An Introduction*. London: SAGE.

PART TWO
CBT- HOW DO YOU DO IT?

7

CBT Assessment

In this chapter, we will describe the CBT interview first, then other modes of assessment. After that we will present role plays of our three case studies to give you an idea of how assessments can be run and also the sort of specific questions that might be relevant to each of the three disorders we have chosen to focus on: anxiety/panic, depression and obsessive compulsive problems.

The first few sessions of CBT are used to gather information in order to start developing a hypothesis/idea (also known as a psychological formulation) and treatment plan. Briefly, a psychological formulation is a picture of why someone is experiencing their particular problems. It differs from 'diagnosis' in that it tends to be an explanation rather than a label. A formulation can be in the form of a diagram or it may be written down in some other format. It essentially contains the following information:

> **Predisposing factors:** Information about a person's past history (usually childhood and teenage years) helps to explain 'why me?' This is usually the time that a person's core beliefs about the world, themselves and others are formed.
> **Precipitants:** Information about what was happening just before the person developed their symptoms, that is, events or circumstances that may have contributed to the person developing their current symptoms.
> **Protective factors:** These are factors which might have helped the person cope thus far or helped them to survive a very difficult situation. Examples might be having had a good relationship at some point or a supportive friend, or possessing determination or intelligence, etc.
> **Triggers:** These are any issues at all that set off the symptoms on a regular basis. For someone who is anxious about going out, an example of a trigger might be stepping out of the front door.
> **Symptoms:** These are any symptoms the person is experiencing. They fall under four main categories: physical (e.g. heart racing, hyperventilating); thoughts (e.g. 'everyone is staring at me'); feelings (e.g. sad, anxious); behaviour (e.g. avoiding going out).
> **Maintenance cycles:** this is how all the above information fits together – look back at Chapter 3 for an explanation of the cognitive behavioural model.

So, during the assessment, we need to ask questions in order to get the above information. Sometimes we don't get all these answers in the first instance so it's a case of filling in the formulation as therapy progresses. With clients with very complex histories, we may just be trying to get an idea of the current symptoms (physical symptoms, thoughts, feelings and behaviours) and studying the maintenance cycles and how we may start to break them, rather than going into histories in a great deal of depth in the first instance. The history may be explored in more depth further into the therapy. For the basic level of CBT we would be working at the 'current symptom' level but we would get some background history so we can help the client to make sense of *why* their difficulties developed. We will be discussing this in more depth in the next chapter. CBT makes use of a questioning technique called Socratic questioning, which is described in detail below.

Socratic questioning: guiding discovery

An important aspect of CBT is Socratic questioning. It is a form of questioning named after the famous philosopher Socrates who used systematic questioning to arrive at 'the truth'. It is also one of the core competencies of CBT as outlined by Roth and Pilling (2007).

This form of questioning is used throughout each stage of CBT, from assessment through to intervention, to gain information about the client's view of their lives and to explore alternatives together. Padesky (1993) argues that the real purpose of Socratic questioning is to guide discovery, rather than trying to change the client's mind about a particular issue. Therefore, the therapist may be asking a series of questions without having a goal in mind and without knowing where the conversation may end up. The idea is to find out more about the client's view rather than trying to change the view. This gives the client the opportunity to be more active in the therapeutic process. During the assessment phase, the questions may be based on finding out more about the presenting difficulties and later the questions may move towards how the client would like things to be different and what the client could do to create this change.

The use of Socratic questioning does not preclude the psycho-educational aspect of CBT. It is a tool that can be used alongside other methods to gain more information, as well as insights into the client's difficulties. Padesky (1993: 4) offers the following definition of Socratic questioning:

> Socratic questioning involves asking the client questions which: 1. the client has the knowledge to answer, 2. draw the client's attention to information which is relevant to the issue being discussed but which may be outside the client's focus, 3. generally move from the concrete to the more abstract so that, 4. the client can, in the end, apply the new information to either re-evaluate a previous conclusion or construct a new idea.

Padesky (1993) also suggests that there are four main stages to the Socratic questioning approach:

1   *Asking informational questions:*
    This essentially means asking questions to which the client has the answers, but which he/she may not be aware of prior to the question being asked. An example of this might be questions about the meaning of the intrusive thoughts or images the client experiences: 'When you have thoughts about harming your child, what are you worried it might mean about you?'

2   *Listening:*
    Here the therapist actively listens to the answers the client gives and builds up information over time. This information can be drawn upon at later points and may lead to discovery of new information. As well as listening, the therapist is watching for emotional reactions and questioning what else is going through the client's mind at these times.

3   *Summarising:*
    Padesky (1993) suggests that a summary should occur every few minutes during the Socratic questioning process. The purpose of summarising is to give the client and therapist the opportunity to check that they are thinking along the same lines, and for the therapist to reflect back to the client the information that has been gained during the questioning process. Additionally, the use of summarising techniques can be helpful in structuring the sessions as described by Roth and Pilling (2007).

4   *Synthesising or analytical questions:*
    This aspect of the questioning process requires the therapist to use the new information gained and apply it to the client's original concern or belief. It helps to tie the new ideas together in a meaningful way: 'Megan, how does the information we've been discussing fit in with the idea that you're not a good mum?'

These types of questions are used throughout the process of therapy. They can be used to gather information at the beginning during the assessment phase and to help bring about insight and change in later stages (although this can also happen at the assessment stage for some people).

The assessment interview therefore includes questions to gain information about predisposing factors, precipitants, protective factors, triggers and symptoms/behaviours which make up the maintenance cycles. Socratic questions can be used at this point in the process as well as in later stages of therapy. Below is an outline of the sort of information and questions to be included in the CBT interview.

The CBT interview

The following is an outline of 'the ideal interview'. Hint: it never (ever) runs this smoothly!

You may find (particularly with clients with complex difficulties) that you get a lot of information on the current problem and initially work with the 'here and now' rather than getting a lot of detail on history. That part of the assessment may come much later … or it may happen the other way round. Some clients may have a need to tell you their stories before they can give any other information.

Initial stage

- Explain that the purpose of the assessment is to get an overview of the client's difficulties and to see if therapy might be helpful. Explain that the first meeting will take about an hour. Confidentiality needs to be discussed: 'Everything is confidential except in cases where we feel concerned about risk, either risk to yourself or to another person. In some cases we might need to pass this information on, but we would discuss this with you fully first' – this should be standard practice anyway. However, we would advise that you check the policy and procedures of the organisation you are working for, as this may change depending on the context in which you are working.
- Rapport building: you can let the client know that you have some information from the referrer but would like to hear from them how things are and what issues are causing difficulties.
- Get a brief description of the problem to start with – this can be expanded upon later.
- Typical questions:
  'Can you describe the last time you felt upset and what was happening?'
  'How long ago was that?'
  'What has changed in your life since you developed these difficulties?'
- Explain to the client that there is no need to get lots of detail at this point – it's just to start things off.
- It is helpful to give a summary at the end of this section.

Initial problem list, onset and course

- The person can be asked what they would describe as being the main issues/problems for them at the moment.
- Information should be gathered about how the problems have developed over time – whether they have steadily got worse or if there have been times when they have been better.
- Why has the client presented now? That is, has the situation changed? Or has the problem got worse? It is very useful to establish this.
- Examples of helpful questions are: 'What did you find difficult about what happened?' Or 'How did you manage to cope in that situation?'

Triggers

- These are situations or thoughts or feelings (or pretty much anything, actually) that set the symptoms off on a daily or regular basis.
- What seems to set the problem off on a daily or regular basis?
- Sometimes people can't identify any triggers. This may be because the triggers are internal. For example a trigger can be a thought such as, 'If I go outside, I'll faint'. Thoughts can sometimes set off feelings, such as anxiety, very powerfully indeed and may then lead the person to avoid a certain situation.

Symptoms (maintaining factors)

See Chapter 3, 'The CBT model' – for an explanation of how the symptoms often fit together in maintenance cycles.

- It can be very helpful at this stage to get the person to come up with examples about how they're thinking and feeling, e.g., 'How did you feel about coming along here today?' 'What were you thinking?'
- Thoughts: 'What runs through your mind when you get into these situations?' It is also useful to try and identify the person's worst fears about the situation: 'What are you most worried will happen?' One helpful way of eliciting thoughts is to give an example of other people's thoughts: e.g., 'Sometimes in those kinds of situations people have thoughts like … "I'm not very popular"' This can also help people to feel they're not alone. Some people have real problems identifying their thoughts and it can take time for them to get used to doing it.
- Feelings: 'When you have thoughts like that, how do you feel?' For some clients, identifying feelings/emotions can be very difficult. We have included a chapter to help with this difficulty (see Chapter 17).
- Physiological: 'What does your body feel like when you experience this problem?'
- Behaviour: 'What do you do to cope in these situations?' 'Do you find yourself checking, washing a lot?' 'Do you ask other people for reassurance?'
- Avoidances (a sub-section of behaviour): A very powerful maintaining factor. Ask questions such as: 'What things have you stopped doing since you've experienced these difficulties?' 'What have you been doing to cope with this problem?' 'How would life be different if this problem went away?' Clients sometimes use subtle avoidance, for example going to parties but not eating soup in case their hands shake, or going out but only with the use of tranquillizers. These may also be known as 'safety behaviours' (covered in some detail in Chapter 10 on coping strategies) and it is important to be aware of them as they can also keep the avoidance, and therefore the problem, going.

Ways of coping

- How has the client been coping with the problem? As discussed before, some coping strategies can be helpful in the short term but not the long term.
- Questions can be asked about how the client copes both with the current problem and with past problems.
- 'What sorts of things make the problem feel better or easier to manage?' 'What sorts of things have been helpful?' 'Which situations/thoughts/feelings, etc., seem to set the problem off?'
- 'When are the difficulties easier to cope with?'
- 'Can you think back to another time in your life when you had to get through a difficult situation – how did you come out the other side?' It can be quite useful to bring in solution-focused strategies here – such as noticing and commenting on a person's strengths.
- Sometimes a person may find ways of making the problem feel easier in the short term – however, this may lead to difficulties in the long term because the person starts avoiding things or engaging in 'safety behaviours' (see pp. 93–4 for a full explanation of 'safety behaviours').

Precipitating factors – (why now?)

- There does not have to be lots of detail about this at this stage.
- You may only need to collect information relevant to the problem in question.
- It's about finding out what was happening at around the time the person developed the problem – sometimes people find this difficult to identify.
- It may also help to describe some common life events to the client if they are finding it difficult to name any themselves.

Predisposing factors – sometimes known as vulnerability factors (why me?)

- Information is sought about anything in the client's background which would make it more likely that they would develop the target problem. Clients can sometimes find it strange or off-putting that you are asking them about their childhood. Some clients can see the relevance, while other clients may wonder why you are asking them questions about how they were as a child. It can be helpful to add a sentence like: 'It might sound strange but it would be helpful just to find out a bit more about you and how things were when you were growing up, as that can help put things into perspective a bit and give some background information to the difficulties you are experiencing now.'
- It's sometimes helpful to ask more specific questions, depending on what the person is coming up with.
- See the assessment dialogue (later in this chapter) for each case study to get some ideas about specific questions, depending on what the problem is.
- In some cases it is not necessary to go into detail about the history in the first assessment interviews, and this may be left until later.

Protective factors

- Questions are asked to gain information about the person's strengths and the factors that have enabled them to survive.
- Examples might be a good relationship at some point, the presence of friends, motivation, determination, and so on.

The above forms the main basis of the CBT interview. Clinicians will have their own style of working and there is no exact way of doing it. Often these interviews are led by the client and you may find yourself spending much longer on a particular area than you expected. Sometimes you may have to spend several sessions getting the information and, occasionally, while the information is very sparse to start with it starts to change as the client gains trust in their therapist.

As well as the CBT interview, other tools can be used to aid the assessment process and give further information.

Other assessment tools

Self-monitoring

This generally occurs in the form of diary sheets. These can be developed to measure behaviour (e.g. number of times someone with obsessive problems checks that the oven is switched off per day), thoughts and also intensity of feelings/emotions. Diary sheets are more commonly used once interventions have begun, so diary sheets are discussed in detail in the later chapters on interventions.

Self-report questionnaires

These are standardised questionnaires, often with 'norms' and can be used to measure change over time. The use of self-report questionnaires is described by Roth and Pilling (2007) as a core competency for CBT. It can be helpful to use one or two of these at the start of therapy and then at subsequent reviews. Examples of these are the Beck Depression Inventory II (Beck et al. 1996) and the Beck Anxiety Inventory (Beck et al. 1988). A couple of questionnaires that are now being used routinely in primary care mental health are the GAD-7 (Spitzer et al., 2006) to measure anxiety, and the PHQ-9 (Spitzer et al., 1999) to measure depression. Sometimes clients have difficulty noticing the changes they have made, so these questionnaires can help to give them evidence of change.

Below are excerpts from the assessment sessions for the three case studies we use throughout the book – Andy, Anne and Megan. There are also pointers to specific questions that might be asked, depending on the presenting issue. There is not enough room to give dialogue for full assessment sessions, but the following excerpts should give a flavour of what a CBT assessment might be like.

Assessment Session Andy

Therapist:	As you know, this is an assessment for cognitive behaviour therapy, or CBT for short. We will be talking through what's been happening for you and possible ways we can help. This particular assessment is to see if CBT would be helpful. Very briefly, CBT is designed to explore how your thoughts and ideas about the world affect how you feel and how you behave. But we will give you lots more information on that and examples of how it works after we've finished the assessment. So, what would be helpful is if you could start by letting me know what has been happening for you recently.
Andy:	I have been worried about my health, haven't wanted to go outside…
Therapist:	Can you say a bit more about that. What is it about being outside that feels difficult?
Andy:	I don't know, I just don't want to go out, I don't really know what else to say. I went to the doctor because my chest was hurting and I thought there might

be something wrong with me, but he thought I was okay and sent me here …
I don't know what else to say, I'm not sure I should be here.

Therapist: You mentioned being uncertain about being here and what you need to say, just to let you know that lots of people do feel a bit worried about coming here and talking about their difficulties. From the letter your doctor sent and from what you have said so far, we do see a lot of people with similar difficulties. Can I just ask you a bit more about when this seemed to start?

Andy: [*Nods*]

Therapist: When did you first notice that it was feeling difficult to go out?

Andy: I'm not sure really. I think looking back I haven't been feeling quite right for about six months now; for the last couple of months it has been a lot more difficult.

Therapist: So thinking back to six months ago, that would have been July. What was happening around that time?

Andy: Not much really… work was okay, although, actually, I think that was around the time that my old boss left, and my new one started.

Therapist: And what was that change like?

Andy: Well my old boss was really good and I felt like I was doing well at work, but my new boss has changed things. He made me do presentations which I hate doing, and he pointed out that I didn't speak much in meetings. My old boss used to just let me get on with things, as long as I got my work done. I started to dread going into work… but anyway the main thing is that I have noticed my heart beating really fast, and I have had really bad pain in my chest. I was sure that there must be something wrong with my heart. One time I thought I must be having a heart attack it was so bad. My breathing also seems to go all over the place – I feel like I just can't control it.

Therapist: When did you first notice your heart beating fast and the chest pain?

Andy: Don't know really, that was probably about six months ago, maybe not quite that long.

Therapist: So what did you think when your GP said that your heart was okay?

Andy: Well, I thought he must have missed something … but then he said it might be stress … panic attacks … but the thing is, I just can't see how stress can affect my body as much as it is … I just can't see how that works.

Therapist: Anxiety can have a huge effect on the body and it can really feel quite frightening, but the good news is that there are lots of things that you can do to change these symptoms. It's also much more common than most people think. I won't go into detail about this today but we can spend some time exploring how anxiety and stress affect the body if you wish to meet again after today.

Andy: I suppose it might be worth a try …

Therapist: So, I'm wondering – as well as worrying that you might be having a heart attack, are there any other thoughts that go through your head as you're having these … shall we call them 'anxiety attacks'?

Andy: Ummm, don't know … what do you mean?

Therapist: Well, sometimes people have thoughts such as 'I'm going to collapse', or 'Everyone's looking at me, they can see I'm nervous.'

Andy: Yes, yes … those are my exact worries. I get really worried when I'm out and also what if I can't get back home and who's going to rescue me if I don't know anyone when I'm out and having an attack … I also think everyone will see me sweating, especially if I have to stand in front of people at work.

Therapist: It sounds really distressing for you … I'm wondering how your mood is?

Andy: Eh? Do you mean am I moody with people?

Therapist: Well, I just wondered how you feel in yourself. Do you find you feel 'down in the dumps'?

Andy: Oh right, yes, I get really down sometimes, I just want all this to go away …

Therapist: I'm just wondering how you're managing to cope with these situations and feelings … it does sound really difficult.

Andy: I really don't know … How do I cope? Hmm … actually I have felt quite a bit better since I've been off work, and it's been helping to not go out as much … actually it's been much better since I've not been out as much … Not sure what else has been helpful.

Therapist: So being away from the situation is helpful … but do you think it also makes you worry about going back into the situation again?

Andy: Yeah, I suppose … 'cos I really feel worried about going into town now and places where it's very crowded.

Therapist: Okay … and sometimes people cope by drinking alcohol or taking drugs, as it helps to shut out the worries.

Andy: I never take drugs … no, no … but yes I do drink alcohol, it seems to calm my nerves a bit.

Therapist: It's a way of coping isn't it? … Okay, so I'd like to change tack a bit. It might sound strange but it would be helpful to just find out a bit more about you and how things were when you were growing up as that can help put things into perspective a bit and give some background information to your current difficulties.

Andy: Well, everything's been normal till now, so I'm not sure it's worth saying anything … it's all been fairly normal, childhood was fine, happy …

Therapist: Do you mind if I just ask a bit more … we don't have to go into loads of detail.

Andy: Okay.

Therapist: Did you grow up round here?

Andy: No, I went to university round here, grew up near Oxford which is where my parents live now.

Therapist: And who did you live with when you were growing up?

Andy: Mum, Dad and Brother … all got on okay … brother was a bit of a pain but I suppose that's normal.

Therapist: It certainly is … is he older or younger?

Andy: Older, used to bully me a bit but he's fine now.

Therapist: And how about your parents, what was your mum like when you were growing up?

Andy: Fine, very loving … actually I think she used to suffer with nerves a bit, I seem to remember … but I don't think it was really spoken about. She always wanted me to do well at school and stuff … very supportive, but it was expected that I worked hard … actually they were both like that …

During the assessment, it can be helpful to have specific questions in mind, depending on the type of difficulties the client is presenting with.

Specific questions about anxiety and how it developed

- What sensations do you experience in your body when you get anxious?
- Do you experience anxiety before going into situations? (Also known as anticipatory anxiety.)
- Do you worry about what others will think if they notice you are anxious?
- What are you afraid might happen?
- Do you remember being an anxious child?
- Did you worry about going into school when you were a child?
- Do you remember others in your family being anxious or 'worriers'?

NOTE: People who suffer with intense anxiety may have developed beliefs about the world not being safe or ideas that other people might judge them if they appear vulnerable. It can be helpful to explore these ideas with the client. Obviously, anxiety and fear are the most common emotions experienced.

Assessment Session Anne

Therapist: As you know this is an assessment for cognitive behaviour therapy or CBT for short … [as before – see Andy's assessment]

So, what would be helpful is if you could start by letting me know what has been happening for you recently.

Anne: Oh … [*sighs*], I just feel so tired and like I can't be bothered with anything. I don't want to be bothered with seeing people or doing anything. All I feel like doing is crying … and that's not me (*tearfully*), that's just not me.

Therapist: How long have you been feeling like this?

Anne: You know, I'm really not that sure … it seems to have gradually got worse over time. Really the last couple of years, I've just not been myself but it's hard to see what's caused it. I've not got many things to be depressed about really – I think about other people and how much they have to deal with and then I look at me and think what have I got to feel down about? I really should be coping better than this.

Therapist: It sounds as though it's difficult to identify why you're feeling like this.

Anne: Mmm … yeah.

Therapist: Sometimes that can make people feel worse because it just feels as though the low mood has come out of the blue and they then feel they have no control over how they're feeling. Have you had any difficult or unusual events happen over the last year?

Anne: The menopause is pretty difficult … I just feel so hot and irritable a lot of the time … and it reminds me I'm getting old … The children leaving home also makes me feel old and I miss them … especially Jess, who's moved to Australia, because she used to pop round quite a lot and although we talk on the phone, it just doesn't feel the same … there is something else but I feel really ashamed about it … I may as well tell you. I had an affair with someone I work with … it's not still going on but it was for a year and I just feel really guilty.

Therapist: So you've been feeling low about that … What prompted the affair, do you think?

Anne: Me and Jack were going through a rough patch and he just wasn't listening to me and the guy at work did, but I know it wasn't the right thing to do. Jack and I are getting on much better now but I've just got this guilty feeling hanging on and I just don't feel I can talk to anyone about it – you're the first person I've told …

Therapist: It sounds as though that has been quite an important event for you and left you with a lot of guilty feelings. It must have been so difficult to cope with this on your own.

Anne: It has been … actually it feels like a real relief to tell someone. … I've been so ashamed of myself.

Therapist: So it may be something we come back to and spend some time talking about during sessions. … Do you think that would be helpful?

Anne: Yes, I think that would be really helpful, definitely.

Therapist: Okay, I'll make a note of that. So, I just want to change tack a bit now and ask you a few specifics regarding your sleep, appetite, mood and so on … How are you sleeping at the moment?

Anne: My sleep's not good at all … It takes me ages to get off to sleep and then when I do, I sleep for a while but often wake up and toss and turn, thinking over things … I do get off to sleep again but often wake up several times and I never sleep past 6 o'clock.

Therapist: So what are you thinking about when you're tossing and turning?

Anne: Oh … all sorts of things. Often I'm thinking about what a waste of time I am and that I've never got anything to say when I see friends … and I feel like they're all ignoring me anyway. I just don't know why I'm feeling like this and that worries me so much … Things just go round and round in my head.

Therapist: Makes it so much harder when it's dark as well for most people …

Anne: Yes it's like that for me … I do feel better in the day and that's when I can sleep, so my sleep pattern is all messed up – I suppose you're going to tell me off like my doctor.

Therapist: No, I don't like to tell people off, but it does sound as though it would be good to work on getting your sleep pattern sorted out a bit, as that will help.

Anne: Well, that would be really great.

Therapist: How about your appetite?

Anne: I just don't feel hungry. I've lost loads of weight and that's not like me …

Therapist: How much are you eating in a day?

Anne: Not breakfast but I try and have a bit of lunch and tea. It's really hard to get the food in but I am trying.

Therapist: Well, that's good as it is important to get as much nourishment as possible. That's one thing that can really affect mood. Speaking of mood, how are you feeling in yourself? How would you describe your mood?

Anne: Depressed … really low, nearly all the time.

Therapist: Is there anything that helps lift your mood?

Anne:	Not a lot, talking to the children and … um I don't know. Sometimes if I do get myself out of the house … I just feel really low most of the time.
Therapist:	How low do you get? Do you ever feel like harming yourself?
Anne:	Yes, I'm ashamed to say I think about ending it all most days.
Therapist:	And how far does that get? Do you ever have any plans about how you might end things?
Anne:	Well, I've thought about taking a load of pills but I do know it's not a very effective way of doing it … and I just couldn't do it to the children … It's more the case that I'd like to die but I don't think I could ever do anything to actually finish it.
Therapist:	Those are very difficult feelings to struggle with on a daily basis, though. How are you managing to get through each day? What are you doing on a day-to-day basis?
Anne:	Hardly anything … I'm so embarrassed but I just can't get up the motivation to do anything … I get up … watch a bit of TV, force myself to eat lunch, watch more TV … basically, I'm just a useless lump … I'm so tired and I just can't be bothered to bother about anything …
Therapist:	What you're describing is really common for people with depression. … When people get depressed, they just don't feel like doing anything so they tend not to do very much but then they tell themselves off and feel guilty, which makes them feel even more depressed. … It's a vicious cycle really … We can talk more about how to break the cycle later.
Anne:	Well, I'm glad it's not just me and that there's a way to sort it out …
Therapist:	I just want to go back to some of the things you mentioned just now. You were saying you feel useless … do you have many thoughts like that?
Anne:	Oh yes … I'm thinking that all the time. I just feel like I'm a waste of space and useless.
Therapist:	Do any particular situations set off those kinds of thoughts?
Anne:	Hmmm … I think it every day … I think partly the fact that I'm not doing anything and feel so tired and slow adds to it. Also when I see my friends I feel like a waste of space … I haven't got anything to talk about … I just don't know what to say to them any more so I've started avoiding them because I can't cope with seeing them.
Therapist:	So it sounds as though that's another kind of cycle … Did you used to find it easy to talk to your friends?
Anne:	Oh yes … I mean it takes me a while to get to know someone new but with good friends I've always been able to chat, so it feels like a shock to feel like this … I feel as though I've lost all my confidence.
Therapist:	So in the past, you've had more confidence and been able to chat easily with people you know … Actually, it would be really helpful just to get a bit of a view of how things have been for you in the past and to hear a bit about your history so I can put things in context … Perhaps we could start right at the beginning … Were you born round here?
Anne:	Yes, although I went to live in London for a while when I went to university but I like it here so I came back and then stayed.
Therapist:	And what were things like while you were growing up … Did you live with a mum and dad?

Anne:	Yes, although Dad was away a lot with the navy. I got on well with him, though, when he was around … better than with Mum. She just wasn't affectionate at all. I do wonder now whether she was depressed. I never had any brothers or sisters and I can remember feeling lonely. Nan and Gramps were great, though, they were my dad's parents, really warm and lovely. I can remember being devastated when they died – I was about 14 at the time. They both died within a few weeks of each other. It was really so sad …
Therapist:	It sounds as though they were really important to you … It must have been tough when they died especially if they had such a special bond with you … How about school, what was that like?
Anne:	It was fine, I suppose … Actually that's not really true. I didn't find the work that bad, but I didn't really make friends at school. I sort of managed to be in a group but I was always on the outside a bit and Mum never allowed me to bring friends home … It was hard … things got better when I got to university …

Specific questions about depression and how it developed

- What does the depression feel like in your body?
- Where do you feel it?
- What kinds of thoughts do you experience about yourself, others and the world around you? [Can also give examples: 'Sometimes …']
- Are there times when you feel hopeless, as though you'll never get better?
- Do you ever feel like harming yourself? If, so how far does that go? Do you ever have plans about that? [See also risk assessment discussion below.]
- How were things when you were growing up?
- Do you remember how you felt about yourself as a child? And in later years?

NOTE: People who are depressed have often experienced trauma at some point in their lives or had experience of their needs not being met in some way. They may then have developed negative beliefs based on these experiences. Again this is a generalisation but it can be helpful to collect this information for the formulation. Guilt and shame can be important emotions.

NOTE: If people are showing any signs of low mood or depression it is important to ask about whether they have ever thought of harming themselves. There is a difference between self-harm as a coping strategy and self-harm with suicidal intent. For example, some people use self-harm, such as superficial cutting or burning, to release tension or as punishment if they feel bad about themselves. Other people take small overdoses of tablets in order to sleep or get 'time out'. In this context, self-harm is a coping strategy and, although it may help in the short term, it may not be helpful in the long term as it can lead to scarring (which may lower self-esteem) or, in the case of overdosing, to serious health problems.

Many people have suicidal thoughts but with no intent. It is important to ask about intent, as illustrated in the above case study. If someone does have a plan of how they might commit suicide, we would always advise you to seek supervision as soon as possible and inform the responsible medical officer. The action taken will depend on the individual case and we do not feel we can give further advice here. This is an important topic, especially within secondary mental health services where clients may have high-risk profiles and where careful assessment is vital. Policies and procedures can vary depending on the context of the service you are working in and we advise you read relevant policies and seek supervision.

Assessment Session Megan

Therapist:	As you know this is an assessment for cognitive behaviour therapy, or CBT for short … [as before – see Andy's assessment]
	So, what would be helpful is if you could start by letting me know what has been happening for you recently.
Megan:	Umm … It's so difficult to talk about … I'm so ashamed … and I don't know where to start … Umm.
Therapist:	Okay … it sounds like it's difficult to talk about … We are used to that … There's plenty of time … Would it help if I read out the referral letter your GP sent?
Megan:	Actually, that would help … Dr Z has been really kind … she helped me feel as though I wasn't the only one feeling like this …
Therapist:	Okay, this is the letter your GP sent …
	[*Therapist reads letter – see p. 17.*]
Megan:	[*Megan becomes very tearful*] I'm so ashamed …
Therapist:	It's okay, your GP was right, you're not alone … we see so many people who have exactly these sorts of thoughts about harming others and they are particularly common after giving birth.
Megan:	That makes me feel so much better … Dr Z said something along those lines but to hear someone else say it makes me feel as though it might really be true.
Therapist:	It'll help to get some more details on what's been happening for you. When did you first start having these thoughts?
Megan:	Well, it was pretty soon after Molly, my daughter, was born. I just felt so anxious all the time … Was she breathing? How she was feeding? … Everything was just so worrying and all the other mums in my ante-natal group seemed to managing alright … I just felt like a complete failure. How hard can it be to look after a small baby? I started to get all these thoughts … [*tearful*] really horrible thoughts …
Therapist:	I know it's hard, but would you be able to say what the thoughts were?
Megan:	I'm so ashamed … I've been having visions of hitting Molly, or strangling her … I'd never do it … but I still couldn't trust myself, so I had to get other people to help me out … The visions were just so horrible. I feel like I'm going mad. I just feel so much better when someone is with me …
Therapist:	Do you have someone with you for much of the time at the moment?

Megan:	Yes, mostly, Paul my husband although he's got to go to work or he'll lose his job … [*tearful*] … That's really worrying me. He's taken so much time off and his work are starting to get fed up with it. … My mum has come and stayed with me but she's always telling me what to do or how to do things differently.
Therapist:	So Paul's been spending a lot of time with you … What's he like?
Megan:	He's great, he's been so good. He spends so much time with Molly when he's at home and he seems to really enjoy it. He's been doing loads of nappy changing and feeding which has really helped me to cope, especially because I've been a bit frightened of being alone with Molly.
Therapist:	And how about your mum?
Megan:	Oh, I've had so many problems with Mum … Sometimes we get on really well but she's just always criticising me … always has done. She keeps telling me how to look after Molly 'properly' and keeps pointing out my mistakes, but it's not like I need anyone else to point them out … I know I'm not being a very good mum at the moment. I can't even go near Molly if I'm on my own … so I don't know if it's helpful to have Mum around.
Therapist:	Actually, it may sound a bit strange but it would be helpful to find out a bit more about how things were when you were growing up, including how your relationship with your mum was. Is that okay?
Megan:	Yes, that's fine. Mum's always been a bit edgy and she was so strict when we were growing up. It's been hard to please her really and I think she always favoured my sister. I'm the one who's always been the pain, the one who messes everything up.
Therapist:	Did you just live with your mum and your sister?
Megan:	No, Dad lived with us too … Well, I say that, but basically he really wasn't around that much and when he was, he was half-cut … he's a bit of a drinker. He and Mum have split up and I don't have much to do with him. He's okay though when he's sober and he's not critical like Mum. He's been to see Molly a bit so I think I might have more to do with him now … who knows?
Therapist:	And so has anyone else in the family had any similar difficulties?
Megan:	Well, I realise now that mum has done – I always thought her behaviour was a bit strange at times but now I think I know why. Her sister definitely had problems, she used to spend hours checking round the house …
Therapist:	So how would you describe life more generally as you were growing up?
Megan:	It's funny, 'cos at the time I just thought it was normal and that everything was fine but now I realise that things really weren't that good. It wasn't a happy time.
Therapist:	How was school?
Megan:	It was actually okay. I worked hard … actually I did quite well at school and I got quite a few GCSEs.
Therapist:	How about friends – did you get on with others at school?
Megan:	Yeah, I had quite a few friends at school. It was a reasonably good time … a bit of an escape from home.
Therapist:	And what about after you left school?
Megan:	I worked as a legal secretary – still doing that, actually. Well, I was before I had Molly. I really miss it now … can't believe I've just said that … whoever thought

I'd miss work? … I miss the company and the chat as well as just occupying my brain.

Therapist: It's quite a change, I imagine. Okay, sorry to shift around but can we jump back to the here and now and can I ask you a bit more about what it's like to have these thoughts?

Megan: Yeah, okay.

Therapist: When you get the thoughts, how does your body feel?

Megan: Sorry, I don't know what you mean.

Therapist: Well, sometimes when people get the sorts of distressing thoughts you've been describing, they can feel quite panicky and their hearts race, and so on.

Megan: Oh yes, I see what you mean … Yeah, my heart does race – I can actually hear it – and I feel all tense and sort of jittery. I've been feeling ever so tired as well but then I suppose I've just had a baby so it's not really surprising.

Therapist: Absolutely, it would be strange if you didn't feel tired at the moment and it's common to have all sorts of difficult thoughts and feelings just after a baby's been born – basically your life's turned topsy-turvy! Just listening to you, I'm aware that one of the ways you cope with these difficult thoughts is to make sure you have someone with you … Are there any other things you've been doing in order to cope?

Megan: Umm … I'm not sure … Well, I've phoned my health visitor a few times, actually quite a lot, she's probably fed up of me. She's really nice, though, but I do worry about bothering her and keep asking questions … Also, I suppose I've been washing my hands a lot – I've been worried about spreading germs to Molly so I've been washing a lot. It's hard to know what's normal really, 'cos it's important to be clean round babies isn't it?

Therapist: Definitely, and again sometimes it's hard to know what's normal when you've got a new baby in front of you, so lots of new parents struggle with this issue but it may be that it's just got a bit out of hand with you, so we need to help you rein things in a bit.

Megan: That would be great …

Specific questions about obsessional problems and how they developed

- What thoughts or images pop into your head?
- What do you feel this means about you or the world?
- Do you worry that, because you have had the thoughts, you will definitely carry the thoughts through?
- What sort of things do you do to bring the anxiety down?
- Do you perform any rituals, checking behaviours, or do you avoid any situations?
- How were things while you were growing up? Did you have to cope with any extra responsibilities as a child, such as caring for a relative?
- Do you remember being a conscientious child? Were you taught that it was important to be good?

NOTE: People who develop obsessional problems are often highly conscientious and therefore the intrusive thoughts or images they experience can be much more disturbing to them than a person who is less conscientious. This is partly why things can get 'out of hand' and start to become problematic. A person without obsessional tendencies may find it much easier to dismiss intrusive thoughts – 'Oh, that was a strange thought, never mind.' Important emotions may be guilt and anxiety. Obessional problems can also be used to fill time, to stop the person having the time to dwell on other difficult issues. So it can be helpful to ask what the person would be doing/thinking about if they did not have obsessional problems.

Summary

- The CBT interview can be employed to build up a formulation and start to understand the client's difficulties.
- Socratic questions help to guide discovery.
- Diary sheets help to build up information over time.
- Self-report questionnaires can be used as 'before and after' measures in order to observe change.
- Specific questions can be useful, depending on the presenting problem.

Further reading

Beck, A.T., Epstein, N., Brown, G. & Steer, R.A. (1988) 'An inventory for measuring clinical anxiety: psychometric properties', *Journal of Consulting and Clinical Psychology*, 56: 893–7.

Beck, A.T., Steer, R.A. & Brown, G.K. (1996) *Manual for the Beck Depression Inventory – II*. San Antonio, TX: Psychological Corporation.

Kirk, J. (1989) 'Cognitive-behavioural assessment', in K. Hawton, P.M. Salkovskis, J. Kirk & D.M. Clark (1989) *Cognitive Behaviour Therapy for Psychiatric Problems: A Practical Guide*. Oxford: Oxford University Press.

Padesky, C.A. (1993) 'Socratic questioning: changing minds or guiding discovery?', Key note address delivered at the European Congress of Behavioural and Cognitive Therapies, London, 24 September. www.padesky.com

Spitzer, R.L., Williams, J.B. & Kroenke, K. (1999) *Patient Health Questionaire – 9*. Copyright © Pfizer Inc.

Spitzer, R.L., Kroenke, K., Williams, J.B. & Lowe, B. (2006) 'A brief measure for assessing generalised anxiety disorder', *Archives of Internal Medicine*, 166 (10): 1092–7.

8

CBT Formulation

In this chapter we will explain what a cognitive-behavioural formulation is and why it is central to cognitive-behavioural therapy. We will then move on to look at the practical aspects of developing a formulation with your client and highlight some of the problems you might encounter when developing a formulation.

The cognitive-behavioural formulation (sometimes called the case conceptualisation) provides the overall picture of the development and maintenance of the client's problems. It enables the therapist to develop an understanding and individualised treatment plan based on the cognitive-behavioural model of psychological distress. As discussed in earlier chapters, the cognitive-behavioural model proposes that patterns of thinking and behaving develop through life. If predominantly negative thinking styles develop, a person is more vulnerable to the development of psychological problems as a consequence of certain life events or circumstances. Once psychological problems develop, they can be maintained by negative cycles of thoughts, emotions, physical sensations and behaviours. A cognitive-behavioural formulation must explain how and why the client's problems developed when they did and why the problems are persisting through patterns of thinking, feeling and behaving. Once this is understood, what needs to happen in order to break negative cycles becomes clear.

The functions of the cognitive-behavioural formulation

The cognitive-behavioural formulation is a tool which should be drawn upon throughout the course of therapy. It serves multiple functions, as outlined below.

Developing a shared understanding with the client

The formulation should always be shared with the client and if possible developed in collaboration with the client. Understanding the way the client sees the world and reaching a formulation are core therapist competencies as outlined by Roth and Pilling (2007). If the formulation makes sense to the client the rationale for treatment will be clear, resulting in better engagement with therapy. An important feature of CBT is the active involvement of the client and this starts with the formulation.

Increasing hope

Some people delay seeking help or disengage with therapy early on as they do not believe that things can be different. The CBT formulation gives a clear understanding and rationale for treatment, which can increase the client's hope that things can change. If the formulation makes sense to the client, and results in a belief that things can be different, it can have a positive effect on motivation and commitment to treatment.

Prioritisation of problems for treatment

The formulation helps to prioritise issues and problems for treatment. It helps the therapist and client to stay focused on these issues by providing a framework in which the therapy is contained. It can also remind the therapist and client of the goals and aims of therapy should the focus be lost. This function is particularly important for complex cases with multiple presenting problems, where the aims of therapy might be to address only some of the problems. It can be helpful to revisit the formulation with the client during the course of therapy, especially if it feels as though the therapy is losing focus or if new issues arise. As therapists, we find it useful to read over the formulation prior to each session as a reminder of the client's background and the treatment plan.

Overcoming therapist bias

Completion of a formulation can help to overcome potential bias in the therapist's goals by ensuring that all relevant factors for a particular client are considered. It is difficult for therapists to be completely 'unbiased' in the way that they approach clients' problems. Therapist bias arises for many reasons, including previous successful and unsuccessful therapy experiences as well as personal beliefs, attitudes, circumstances and experiences. It is difficult, if not impossible, to remove all therapist bias (we are, after all, human beings), but a formulation can help to reduce this bias, and at the least perhaps illustrate where our biases lie.

Communication

The formulation can also function as a useful communication tool for other professionals and/or the client's family or friends. Those close to the client often benefit from sharing the formulation with the client as it helps them to gain an insight into the problems that their friend or relative is experiencing. This is particularly useful if the family or 'system' around a person is inadvertently helping to maintain the problem.

Individualisation of treatment

The development of a formulation ensures that treatment offered is tailored exactly to the specific needs and circumstances of the individual client. This is one way in which a formulation differs from a diagnosis. No two people given the same diagnosis will experience exactly the same psychological distress for exactly the same reasons. When treating people psychologically it is therefore important that the therapy is tailored to the exact needs of the individual. The formulation is the tool that enables the therapist to develop this individualised understanding and treatment plan.

Predicting difficulties

The formulation can help to predict some of the difficulties that the client might experience during therapy. For example, if the formulation indicates that the client usually copes with difficult situations by avoiding them, it might be hard for the client to attend therapy sessions consistently. If the client has negative automatic thoughts about their own skills and competencies, they may lack the confidence to try out homework tasks. If the formulation highlights potential difficulties in therapy these can be discussed with the client and solutions can be generated.

Representing a formulation

Formulations can be represented in different ways, the important factor being that they make sense to both the therapist and client. They can be summarised in diagram form and the form of a letter. We have developed one way of organising and representing a formulation, illustrated in Figure 8.1. There is a blank copy of these formulation sheets in Appendix III and available to download from www.sagepub.co.uk/simmons

We hope the formulation sheet and maintenance cycle (see Appendix III) will help you to structure your thinking about formulation. Many other ways of representing formulation have been described. If you are interested in reading about other ways of structuring a cognitive-behavioural formulation/case conceptualisation we would suggest Dudley and Kuyken (2006) and Sanders and Wills (2005).

We find that the use of formulation sheets in therapy can help to provide clarity and structure to what is inevitably very complex and sensitive information. We usually

Figure 8.1 Sample formulation sheet

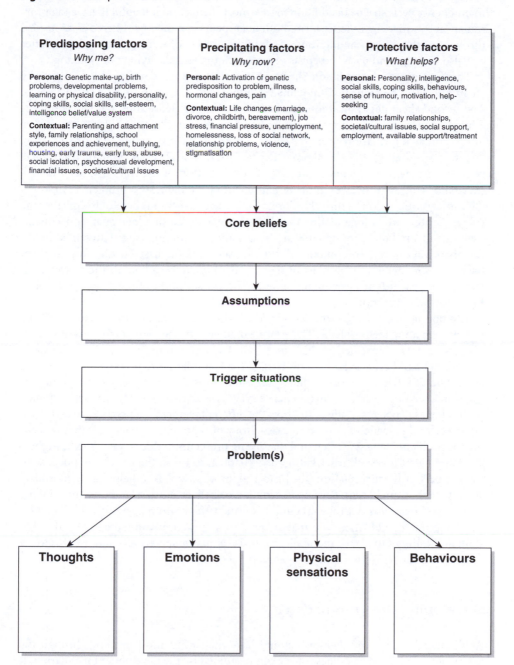

Predisposing factors
Why me?

Personal: Genetic make-up, birth problems, developmental problems, learning or physical disability, personality, coping skills, social skills, self-esteem, intelligence belief/value system

Contextual: Parenting and attachment style, family relationships, school experiences and achievement, bullying, housing, early trauma, early loss, abuse, social isolation, psychosexual development, financial issues, societal/cultural issues

Precipitating factors
Why now?

Personal: Activation of genetic predisposition to problem, illness, hormonal changes, pain

Contextual: Life changes (marriage, divorce, childbirth, bereavement), job stress, financial pressure, unemployment, homelessness, loss of social network, relationship problems, violence, stigmatisation

Protective factors
What helps?

Personal: Personality, intelligence, social skills, coping skills, behaviours, sense of humour, motivation, help-seeking

Contextual: family relationships, societal/cultural issues, social support, employment, available support/treatment

Core beliefs

Assumptions

Trigger situations

Problem(s)

Thoughts

Emotions

Physical sensations

Behaviours

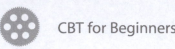

work on the formulation in session with the client making use of the formulation and maintenance cycle sheets. In addition to this, most clients find it helpful to have their formulation summarised in letter form. Both documents can then be referred to as needed throughout the therapy and beyond. We find the process of writing a formulation letter can also be helpful to us as therapists in consolidating and clarifying our thinking.

The first of our formulation sheets summarises historical information about the client and lists the identified thoughts, emotions, physical sensations and behaviours. The second sheet illustrates thoughts, emotions, physical sensations and behaviours as a maintenance cycle. The top half of the first formulation sheet considers historical or 'longitudinal' information about the client, sometimes called the three 'Ps', predisposing factors, precipitating factors and protective factors. A possible weak point of 'traditional' cognitive-behavioural theory is the lack of consideration of the roles of interpersonal, societal or cultural processes in the development of mental health problems. Although CBT interventions do not directly address these issues, we find it helpful to consider the role of context when formulating the client's problems, so that 'personal' and 'contextual' factors are both considered. Core beliefs and assumptions are represented below the historical information on our formulation sheet. As discussed earlier, you may not have this information at the start of therapy, if so it can be added to the formulation later on. We identify trigger situations and write a description of the problem(s) below the beliefs and assumptions.

The bottom part of the formulation sheet includes current or 'cross-sectional' information regarding the problems. This is broken down into the 'elements' of psychological distress that we identified earlier: thoughts, feelings (emotions), feelings (physical sensations) and behaviours. It is this part of the formulation that is essential to as well as unique to CBT. The cross-sectional information is then represented diagrammatically, on a second sheet. This 'maintenance cycle' is essentially the CBT model as applied to the client's problems. It illustrates how the different elements of psychological distress affect each other, which is a powerful visual way of representing what it is that is keeping the problem going. We often find that seeing problems in this way enables both therapist and client to see clearly what needs to happen to break the cycle. The purpose of the top part of the formulation (the historical information) is to help the client understand why they might have developed certain core beliefs and assumptions, thus linking their past experiences with the present. It is usually the bottom part of the formulation sheet and the maintenance cycle that are used more practically in therapy to start with. Roth and Pilling (2007) list the 'ability to devise a maintenance cycle and use this to set targets' as a core CBT therapist competency.

Developing the formulation

As discussed earlier, the therapist should have the formulation in mind through the assessment period, so that questioning can be guided by the developing formulation. It is not, however, essential that the formulation is complete before the active stage of therapy begins. Many clients do not divulge all their inner thoughts and feelings early on in therapy. The client's core beliefs and assumptions underlying negative automatic thoughts often emerge through the process of therapy as the client builds a trusting relationship with the therapist. If this is the case the deeper levels of cognitions can be discussed and added to the formulation as they emerge. The formulation should not be viewed as being 'correct' or 'set in stone'; it is more helpful if client and therapist view it as an 'initial hypothesis', which can be added to and changed through the process of CBT. If the formulation is considered fixed at the start of therapy, important information that is gleaned through the process of therapy will be missed. For example, how the client/therapist relationship develops can give vital clues about the person's interpersonal relationships, style of communication and personality. The results of behavioural and cognitive interventions will also provide further information and/or validation for the formulation. The formulation should therefore both inform the CBT intervention, and be modified by it. It is best viewed as 'fluid' and neither right or wrong, but rather a representation of the best understanding that therapist and client have at the time.

Predisposing factors (or 'why me?')

This includes any historical information about the person that could be related to the development of the problems. 'Personal' predisposing factors include genetics, birth and developmental problems, disability, personality, coping styles, social skills, self-esteem and intelligence. 'Contextual' factors include parenting and attachment style, family and school experiences, early traumas and societal or cultural issues. These are all factors which are hypothesised to increase a person's *vulnerability* to developing a particular problem.

Precipitating factors (or 'why now?')

This category includes factors that help to explain why the problem developed when it did. For clients who have had mental health problems for a long time, identifying precipitating factors will involve a consideration of what was going on in the person's life at the time the problems developed. 'Personal' precipitating factors include illness, hormonal changes, pain and the activation of genetic vulnerabilities. 'Contextual' factors can include life changes, job stress, financial pressure, unemployment, housing problems, relationship problems and loss of social support. If the client has been suffering from the problem for a long time, it can be useful to consider the 'why now' of seeking help. This can include factors such as feeling as though the problem has become unmanageable, pressure from family or friends, media information or an inability to achieve important life goals. An exploration of what prevented the person from seeking help in the past can give clues as to what apprehensions, fears or misinterpretations the person might have about therapy and what the barriers to change might be.

Protective factors

This is the positive bit. Client strengths and assets are sometimes overlooked in psychological therapy. It is, however, worthwhile spending time considering this with your client. It will help identify possible resources the client has available to him or her, in tackling the problem. This can include personal resources and resources from the client's relationships or environment. An important 'by-product' of this process is the raising of hope. It can help the client consider the positive aspects of themselves and their life at a time when negative issues and problems may be dominating. 'Personal' protective factors can include personality, intelligence, social skills, coping skills, sense of humour, motivation and help-seeking. Some examples of 'contextual' protective factors are positive and supportive relationships, employment and access to help.

Trigger factors

Trigger factors are things that can set the problem off. These differ from precipitating factors in that they refer to things that can stimulate the problem on a day-to-day basis, rather than what was going on at the time the problem first developed. If your client has had the problem for a long time, it might be difficult to identify trigger factors. This may be because the person is very effectively avoiding situations which could set the problem off.

Core beliefs

Core beliefs are the deepest level of cognition and, unlike thoughts, they are global rather than specifically about a certain situation or event. Examples include 'I am a failure' and 'The world is against me'. To use Padesky and Greenberger's (1995) garden analogy, core beliefs are the 'roots' that give rise to everyday thoughts. If somebody had negative core beliefs they are likely to generate many negative automatic thoughts. As discussed earlier, the client's core beliefs might not be apparent at the start of therapy and it is not essential to have this part of the formulation covered before therapy can progress. If this is the case, core beliefs can be added to the formulation later in therapy, as they are identified. There are some helpful techniques for eliciting core beliefs such as the 'downward arrow' technique. These are discussed in detail in Chapter 15.

Assumptions

These are sometimes called 'rules for living'. They serve the function of protecting people form their negative core beliefs. For example, a person with the core belief 'I am a failure' might develop the assumption 'I need to work a lot harder than anyone else or I will fail'. Like core beliefs, assumptions might not be apparent at the beginning of the therapy process, if so they can be added to the formulation later on. Identifying and working with assumptions is covered in Chapter 15.

Thoughts

Negative automatic thoughts (NATs) are the constant judgements that run through a person's mind. They can be about the self, other people or the world in general. They can be experienced as either words or images, and can be described as an internal running commentary on a person's experience. The cognitive-behavioural model proposes that the thoughts of people who are experiencing psychological distress will be comparatively more negative than the thoughts of psychologically healthy individuals. The thoughts are described as 'automatic' as they are not consciously generated by the person. NATs are related to core beliefs and assumptions (see Chapter 4). In order to develop a successful formulation and subsequent intervention NATs, should be identified as specifically as possible. Identifying and changing maladaptive NATs, assumptions and core beliefs is the cornerstone of CBT.

Emotions

The dominant emotional states experienced by the person are identified. If the client has difficulty in identifying emotional states some preparatory work on emotions may be necessary (see Chapter 17).

Physical sensations

Emotional states usually have physiological correlates. It is important that the therapist asks questions about these, as the client may not be relating physical sensations to the psychological problems they are experiencing, but rather seeing them as a separate physical issue. The therapist should ask questions about physical health and seek advice from a general practitioner to rule out a physical cause for the sensations if necessary. The physical manifestation of psychological problems is sometimes called 'somatisation'. The extent to which emotional distress is experienced physically varies between people. We find it helpful to move away from an either/or conceptualisation of psychological versus biological causality and instead look at how physical and emotional feelings can impact upon each other.

Behaviours

This part of the formulation identifies what a person actually does when they experience distress or discomfort. These behaviours are usually an attempt by the person either to cope with or to eliminate unpleasant emotional or physical feelings. Behaviours can be overt or very subtle, and include avoidance of situations or doing 'nothing'. Behaviours can also be cognitive – for example a person could carry out the *behaviour* of repeating a word over and over in their head. 'Safety' behaviours, which are discussed in more detail in the Chapters 7 and 10 should be included in this part of the formulation.

Reformulation

A common mistake that therapists make is to confine the use of the formulation to the early stages of therapy, but then fail to return to it as therapy progresses. If the formulation is used and modified throughout therapy there is less chance of losing focus, or of a divergence in goals of therapist and client. Consider bringing out the formulation sheets routinely in each session. If the therapy room has a table, the formulation can be placed on the table between therapist and client and referred to as needed during the session. It is useful to compare the outcome of the 'practice' tasks to the maintenance cycle, to consider where the intervention may have broken the cycle. The process of modifying a formulation to include new information learned in therapy is sometimes called 'reformulation'.

The best way to understand a formulation is to gain practical experience of developing one. Completed formulation sheets for our case studies are shown below in Figures 8.2b, 8.3b and 8.4b. We suggest that, before looking at these, you download the blank formulation sheets in Appendix III (from www.sagepub.co.uk/simmons) and have a go at formulating and completing maintenance cycles for Andy, Megan and Anne, based on the assessment information provided in Chapter 7.

Developing and sharing the formulation with the client

As discussed earlier, CBT is a therapy that requires active participation by the client. It is really important that the client is involved in the generation of the CBT formulation, and that the explanation provided by the formulation makes sense to the client. Below is an excerpt from a session with Andy which illustrates the collaborative development of a cognitive-behavioural formulation.

> *Therapist*:   So we have talked through some of the things that seem relevant to the development of the problem that you are experiencing. In order to make sense of it all, it can be helpful for us to develop what we call a formulation of your difficulties.

Andy: What's that?

Therapist: It's a bit like an overall picture that helps us to understand why you developed the problems when you did, what tends to trigger them off and what strengths and resources you have around and within you to draw upon.

Andy: So how will that help me to get better?

Therapist: Well, the formulation will also identify the different ways that the problem is affecting you, and will identify what is keeping the problem going. Once we have worked out what is keeping the problem going we can work out how we can start to change things.

Andy: Well my doctor has already told me that I have anxiety.

Therapist: Yes that's right, so now we need to work out why you developed the anxiety when you did, how it is affecting you, and why it has been difficult to change. A formulation should help us understand why you developed the problem that has been diagnosed as 'anxiety'.

Andy: Yes, I would like to understand a bit more about that because I haven't always felt like this. I don't see why I should have to feel like this when other people don't. Some days are better than others and I am not sure why.

Therapist: So perhaps completing the formulation will shed some light on this.
[*Shows Andy the formulation sheet*]
This is a sheet that we can use to help us organise the information for the formulation. Lets start at the top, with the 'why me?' box first. You mentioned that your mum suffered from anxiety?

Andy: Well yes, my mum has always been anxious, ever since I can remember: I remember her staying at home a lot, not wanting to go out, especially when there were lots of people around.

Therapist: And do you remember what you thought at the time?

Andy: Just that maybe you have to be careful.

Therapist: So maybe you developed some ideas about going out and being around other people through seeing your mum when you were little?

Andy: I suppose so. People also say we have similar personalities, we both like to do well at things, and get quite upset if we don't.

Therapist: Okay, so it sounds like both you and your mum might have quite high standards for yourselves and feel bad if you fall short of these?

Andy: Yes, I hadn't really thought about it before, but I was definitely expected to do well at school. I remember feeling really sick before tests at primary school, in case I did not come top in the class.

Therapist: The other thing that comes to mind is the bullying that you experienced at school.

Andy: Yes, I think that made me feel worried about doing the right thing. I didn't feel very confident when all that was going on.

Therapist: Okay, so let's list those things under 'why me?' as they might help to explain why you were vulnerable to developing this problem. Let's look at the next section, 'why now?'. This should help us to understand why the anxiety became a problem when it did, rather than at a different time in your life. Let's think about the things that were going on just before the anxiety became a problem.

Andy: I think there is an obvious thing there, the problems at work.

Therapist: Yes that seemed really significant. You also mentioned that you were not seeing so much of your friends and living alone for the first time. I wonder if there were fewer people around to talk to about your worries.

Andy: Yes, I was keeping it all inside, just trying to carry on.

Therapist: Okay, so I guess it does make sense that you became anxious at that time, you had lots of stress at work, and less support around you to help you cope with it.

Andy: Yes, looking back, quite a lot had changed.

Therapist: So now let's have a think about your strengths. From what you have told me about the bullying you experienced at school, you must have had a lot of strength and resilience to carry on going.

Andy: Yes, I don't like to give up. I think the other really good thing is that my family are being really supportive.

Therapist: Okay, so these things will be really important in helping you to overcome the anxiety. So now let's have a think about what triggers it off on a day-to-day basis. I remember last session you said that you found it really difficult to speak in groups.

Andy: Yes, that's definitely a trigger, but more generally I think it is just going into work, or even just thinking about going into work.

Therapist: Okay, so that's quite clear then, what sets it off on a day-to-day basis. So now let's move on to the next part of the formulation, where we identify how the problem manifests itself in thoughts, feelings, behaviours and physical sensations. Let's start with thoughts. Last session you told me about some negative thoughts that you experience in the trigger situations that we have identified.

Andy: Yes, I hate being in groups. I think that everyone will see me sweating; when it is worse I think I might collapse and make an idiot of myself.

Therapist: What makes you think you will collapse?

Andy: My heart beats so fast that I think I will have a heart attack.

Therapist: So those are really negative thoughts about what might happen. You also mentioned a physical sensation there, your heart beating fast. Last session you also mentioned that you sometimes experience chest pain, rapid breathing and sweating.

Andy: Yes, often, and I am really aware of it.

Therapist: So now let's identify how your emotions are affected. It seems that you have become low in mood?

Andy: Yes I have, and tense and nervous.

Therapist: So, finally, let's think about how the problem affects your behaviour. It seems that you tend to avoid the trigger situations.

Andy: Yes, I don't go out unless I have to, because I know that it will make me feel anxious.

It would of course take longer to get to this point in a 'real' session and there would be much more exploration involved. Sometimes, building the formulation can lead to quite lengthy discussions. Now the therapist moves on to the maintenance cycle part of the formulation. This is a key part of the formulation, as it indicates what is keeping the problem going and what the goals of treatment should be.

Therapist:	So now let's have a think about how these different elements of the problem may be affecting one another to keep the anxiety going. Let's take the example of going into a group of people at work. A typical thought that goes through your mind is that you will make a fool of yourself. How does that thought make you feel?
Andy:	Well, anxious I suppose, really nervous.
Therapist:	And do you notice any physical feelings when you think the thought 'I will make a fool of myself'?
Andy:	Oh yes, loads, that's the awful thing I can feel my heart beating fast, I start to sweat and I can feel my neck going red, then I feel even more anxious.
Therapist:	So thinking that thought has definite implications for how you feel physically. The physical sensations then lead to you feeling more anxious. When you think the thought and feel the emotional and physical feelings that are brought on by it, what do you do?
Andy:	Well there is no way I could go into the meeting then. I know for sure I will make a fool of myself because I am sweating, I am red, I can't breathe, so I don't go, I make an excuse.
Therapist:	And what do you imagine would have happened if you had gone?
Andy:	It would have been an awful, terrible embarrassing disaster.
Therapist:	So you never find out what it actually would have been like, but assume that it would have been bad. I suppose that assumption then just adds weight to the initial thought that we started with, that you would make a fool of yourself.
Andy:	Yes, I suppose it does. I just dread the next time even more.

After going through the maintenance cycle part of the formulation, it can be helpful to go through the cycle again, replacing the negative thought with a positive thought, to illustrate hypothetically the consequences of a positive thought on subsequent emotions, physical sensations and behaviours. If you are starting with behavioural work, then consider working through the cycle, replacing the behaviour with a different behaviour to show how this can break a negative cycle.

After discussing the maintenance cycle with the client, we find it helpful to draw potential CBT interventions on to the maintenance cycle. This gives a visual link between the understanding of the problems that has been reached through the formulation process, and how cognitive and behavioural interventions can help (an example of this type of diagram is given in Figure 3.4 on p. 24). This personalises the treatment and shows the client how CBT could help with their own, specific problems. If the client has a good understanding of how exactly the interventions will help with their own individual problems, they are likely to have more confidence in the treatment.

Completed formulation sheets and maintenance cycles for our case studies are shown below in Figures 8.2b, 8.3b and 8.4b. These are followed by a sample goal-summary formulation letter for Andy.

Figure 8.2a   Anne's formulation

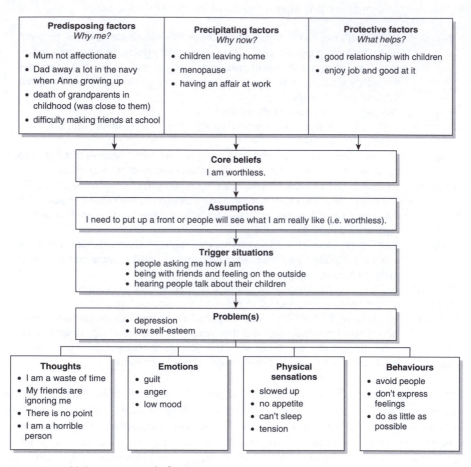

Predisposing factors *Why me?*	Precipitating factors *Why now?*	Protective factors *What helps?*
• Mum not affectionate • Dad away a lot in the navy when Anne growing up • death of grandparents in childhood (was close to them) • difficulty making friends at school	• children leaving home • menopause • having an affair at work	• good relationship with children • enjoy job and good at it

Core beliefs
I am worthless.

Assumptions
I need to put up a front or people will see what I am really like (i.e. worthless).

Trigger situations
• people asking me how I am
• being with friends and feeling on the outside
• hearing people talk about their children

Problem(s)
• depression
• low self-esteem

Thoughts	Emotions	Physical sensations	Behaviours
• I am a waste of time • My friends are ignoring me • There is no point • I am a horrible person	• guilt • anger • low mood	• slowed up • no appetite • can't sleep • tension	• avoid people • don't express feelings • do as little as possible

Figure 8.2b   Maintenance cycle for Anne

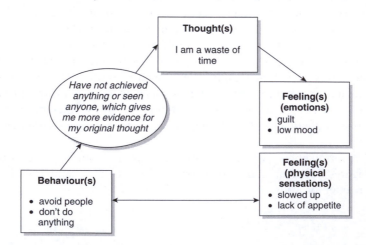

Thought(s)

I am a waste of time

Have not achieved anything or seen anyone, which gives me more evidence for my original thought

Feeling(s) (emotions)
• guilt
• low mood

Feeling(s) (physical sensations)
• slowed up
• lack of appetite

Behaviour(s)
• avoid people
• don't do anything

Figure 8.3a Megan's formulation

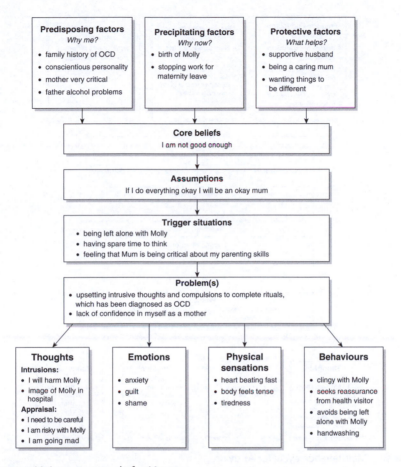

Predisposing factors	Precipitating factors	Protective factors
Why me?	*Why now?*	*What helps?*
• family history of OCD	• birth of Molly	• supportive husband
• conscientious personality	• stopping work for	• being a caring mum
• mother very critical	maternity leave	• wanting things to
• father alcohol problems		be different

Core beliefs
I am not good enough

Assumptions
If I do everything okay I will be an okay mum

Trigger situations
• being left alone with Molly
• having spare time to think
• feeling that Mum is being critical about my parenting skills

Problem(s)
• upsetting intrusive thoughts and compulsions to complete rituals, which has been diagnosed as OCD
• lack of confidence in myself as a mother

Thoughts	Emotions	Physical sensations	Behaviours
Intrusions:	• anxiety	• heart beating fast	• clingy with Molly
• I will harm Molly	• guilt	• body feels tense	• seeks reassurance
• image of Molly in hospital	• shame	• tiredness	from health visitor
Appraisal:			• avoids being left alone with Molly
• I need to be careful			• handwashing
• I am risky with Molly			
• I am going mad			

Figure 8.3b Maintenance cycle for Megan

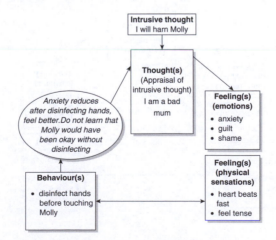

Intrusive thought
I will harm Molly

Thought(s)
(Appraisal of intrusive thought)
I am a bad mum

Feeling(s)
(emotions)
• anxiety
• guilt
• shame

Anxiety reduces after disinfecting hands, feel better. Do not learn that Molly would have been okay without disinfecting

Feeling(s)
(physical sensations)
• heart beats fast
• feel tense

Behaviour(s)
• disinfect hands before touching Molly

Figure 8.4a   Andy's formulation

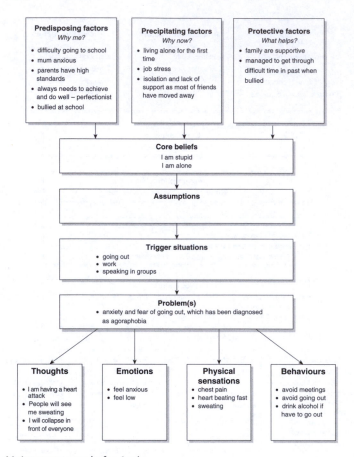

Figure 8.4b   Maintenance cycle for Andy

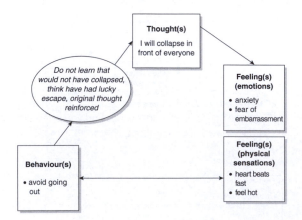

Sample formulation letter

Dear Andy,

This letter aims to summarise the understanding that we have reached of the problems that you are currently experiencing and the goals that we have set to address these problems.

You came to therapy because of problems that you had experienced at work and a fear of going out that had developed. You were referred by your GP who had diagnosed you with 'agoraphobia'. You briefly discussed cognitive-behavioural therapy with your doctor and felt that it might be helpful to you. When we first met together we discussed in detail how cognitive-behaviour therapy helps people. We talked about the cognitive-behavioural 'model' of distress and how 'vicious cycles' can develop. You felt that this way of understanding things made sense in relation to the problems you are experiencing.

We talked about some of the things that might have made you 'vulnerable' to developing anxiety problems, such as your family history of anxiety, the experiences of bullying at school and the high standards that you recognise in yourself and your parents. We then looked at why you might have started to feel anxious at the time you did. At the time, you had experienced lots of change and stress in your life. You were living away from home for the first time, most of your friends had moved away and you were feeling a bit isolated. In addition, you were experiencing a substantial amount of stress in your job. We talked about some of your strengths, such as the support you receive from your family, and the fact that you have been able to get through very difficult times in the past.

We talked about how early experiences influence the 'core beliefs' that people develop about themselves, other people and the world in general. We identified some of the negative 'core beliefs' that you hold about yourself, such as 'I am stupid' and 'I will end up alone.' We then noticed some of the 'rules' that you live by in order to manage these 'core beliefs'; you have the assumptions 'I must get things right' (then others won't think I am stupid) and 'I have to work extra hard' (because I am more stupid than others). You have lots of positive beliefs about yourself, such as being a good person and having a good sense of humour, but it is the negative beliefs that are causing problems, so it is these that we have focused on.

Next we looked at the everyday thoughts (negative automatic thoughts) that you are experiencing and noticed how these are related to your core beliefs and assumptions. These included things like 'I will collapse in front of everyone', 'I am having a heart attack' and 'people will see me sweating'. We looked at how thoughts, emotions, physical sensations and behaviours all interact to 'maintain' the problems that you are experiencing. The negative thoughts tend to make you feel low and anxious and you often experience physical sensations such as chest pain and rapid heart-beat. As a result, you avoid going into situations that you think will make you feel anxious, and if you cannot avoid them you drink alcohol. These behaviours tend to reinforce your initial thoughts, as you assume that if you had not avoided the situation, your predictions would have been right. We drew out this pattern as a diagram using examples of negative thoughts that you noticed (the vicious cycle or maintenance cycle). This showed us possible places that we could break the cycle.

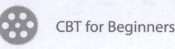

After developing this understanding of what was going on we moved on to set some goals. You were able to identify some general goals that you wanted to work towards such as going out, feeling calmer and more confident. We set some specific goals based on cognitive-behavioural techniques that would help us achieve these general goals and we have recorded these on your goals sheet.

You are hopeful that things can be different and are committed to working on the goals that we have set in therapy. We realise that there will be a lot of hard work on your part and changing things requires lots of practice and trying things out. We have agreed that we will review how things are going every four sessions to check that our understanding of things still makes sense and to monitor your progress. I look forward to continuing to work with you on this, Andy.

Yours sincerely,

The therapist

Common problems with formulation

We will now describe some common problems that we have encountered in the process of developing a formulation collaboratively with the client, and suggest some solutions to the problems.

A lack of collaboration

This can arise as a result of expectations of the client or therapist or both. If the client sees the therapist as the expert, then there may be an expectation that the therapist will have all the answers. The therapist needs to resist this position in CBT in order to explore the issues collaboratively with the client. It might be necessary to recap on the CBT philosophy of 'collaborative empiricism', for example, as follows:

Therapist: So shall we have a think about how some of the issues that were going on at the time might have affected your mood?
Anne: I don't know, you are the expert; I was hoping that you would be able to tell me that.
Therapist: Well, I do know about depression and how CBT can help. Although I have worked with people with depression before I have not worked with you before. No two people have exactly the same histories and everybody's experience of depression is different. I do not want to make any assumptions about your experience of depression and why it might have developed.
Anne: So basically you don't know and you can't help.
Therapist: That's not what I meant. I am hoping that we can build an understanding together. I know a bit about depression and CBT but you are the bigger expert on *you*.

| Anne: | I suppose so – so what do we do then? |
| Therapist: | Let's have a think about the things that were going on in your life just before you started to feel depressed, you mentioned that… |

In this example the therapist resists taking on the role of 'expert' and encourages the client to participate in the formulation process.

The client has a 'medical model' of illness

This is a relatively common problem that should be addressed right at the start of therapy when the client is educated about the CBT model. We find that even if this is the case, it can arise again in the formulation stage, as health beliefs can be powerful. As discussed earlier, we feel it is important to avoid a debate over whether problems are physical *or* psychological. The CBT model proposes that physical and emotional feelings can affect each other. Health beliefs vary between individuals, cultures and age groups. Here is an example from a session with a client with anxiety.

Client:	My heart was just beating so fast I could have had a heart attack. It just wasn't right, I could have had a heart attack.
Therapist:	What was going through your mind before you noticed your heart beating fast?
Client:	You just think it's all in my mind, don't you?
Therapist:	No, not at all. I asked that question because I know that the thinking processes, which take place in the brain, can lead to physical changes in other parts of the body, so I was interested in the link between your thoughts and the changes in the rest of your body.

There is flexibility within the CBT model regarding the degree to which physiological correlates of emotions are discussed. If your client presents to therapy with a very 'biological' understanding of their mental health difficulties, this can be accommodated. The important issue is that the physical sensations are linked to the thoughts, emotions and behaviours in the maintenance cycle.

The client does not want to discuss the past

As discussed earlier, historical information is useful for helping the client to understand why their problems have developed. It is not, however, vital for developing a maintenance cycle, which is the essential part of the formulation for planning the intervention. It can help to explain to the client that the important part of their history is how certain factors influenced the way they see themselves and the world in general. Another approach is to explore some of the negative thoughts and assumptions the client might hold about what talking about the past will mean to them. If your client is very reluctant to talk about the past you can consider starting to work on the maintenance cycle without this information, as current NATs are all that is needed. As the client starts to feel more comfortable in therapy, they might feel more able to explore some of the core beliefs and assumptions that they hold, and why these developed. This can be a more natural link to talking about past experiences.

The formulation does not help develop a treatment plan

We often find that if the formulation does not indicate what would help, it is not based in CBT theory. Sometimes there is too much emphasis on historical information and a lack of emphasis on the maintenance cycle. It can be helpful to go back to the CBT model and relate the assessment information to it, preferably with the help of a supervisor. Another possibility is that there is a piece of the jigsaw missing. It might be that the client is not ready to divulge certain information, or is even unaware of certain things. One solution to this problem is to spend more time on the formulation stage. If it is suspected that there is important information missing from the formulation we find that it can sometimes be helpful to be open about this with the client. For example:

> *Therapist*: So that is the understanding that we have reached so far. This is only our third meeting and since we don't know each other that well yet, I am just wondering about how easy you have found discussing things today.
>
> *Client*: It's been okay, a bit strange I suppose, talking about these kinds of things as you are more or less a stranger, but it hasn't been as difficult as I thought it would be.
>
> *Therapist*: Yes, it can be difficult to talk about personal things, especially at the start of therapy. I would not expect you to necessarily feel able to talk about everything that you feel is important straight away. I would not want you to feel you have to mention things that you feel uncomfortable talking about.
>
> *Client*: I guess it might get a bit easier with time?
>
> *Therapist*: Yes, it probably will. How much of the important things do you feel you have been able talk about so far would you say?
>
> *Client*: Quite a lot, well most of it actually. There is just one thing really…
>
> *Therapist*: I don't want you to feel that you have to talk about that thing if it does not feel comfortable at the moment, but I think that it is good that we are both aware that there is one important thing that we have not talked about…

The therapist could go on here to explore whether there is anything that would make it easier for the client to talk about the problem. We have found that confidentiality issues, feeling disloyal to another person, feeling ashamed and fear of burdening the therapist are common reasons for clients not disclosing information.

The formulation is either too complex or too simplistic

The formulation needs to be detailed enough to hypothesise about the development and maintenance of the client's problems without being unnecessarily complex. The most straightforward explanation of the client's difficulties should be developed. This usually means focusing on the role of thoughts, feelings, physical sensations and behaviours in maintaining the client's difficulties. Using unnecessarily complicated CBT theory and language is a common mistake made by therapists. The basic CBT model is simple, yet our client's problems are not. The cognitive behavioural formulation is of course a simplified picture of the client's problems and this should be explained. It does not aim to include every aspect of the client's life, but focuses on the key issues which related to the development and maintenance of the presenting problems.

Butler (1998) suggests testing a formulation by asking the questions outlined below:

- Does it make theoretical sense?
- Does it fit with the evidence?
- Does it account for predisposing, precipitating and maintaining factors?
- Do other people think it fits? (client, other professionals, family)
- Can it be used to predict difficulties?
- Can you work out how to test the predictions? (by selecting interventions, etc.)
- Does the past history fit?
- Does treatment progress as expected?

Considering group differences in formulation

The role of society and culture should be considered when developing a CBT formulation so that the ensuing treatment plan is sensitive to these issues. Our aim is not to cover this topic in detail here, but to outline the main issues to consider when developing a formulation with your client. There are three main areas. Firstly, there is the role of factors such as gender, sexuality, society and culture in the *development* of psychological problems; that is, the contribution that being part of a certain 'group' might have made to predisposing and precipitating factors. An example could be the role that low socio-economic status and poverty could play in the development of problems. Secondly, there is the issue of how being part of a certain 'group' might influence the client's *understanding* of the causality of mental health problems. This is an important point to consider when developing a shared formulation with the client, since if the therapist is from a different cultural background, he or she may have a completely different aetiological model. As discussed earlier, it is vital that the formulation makes sense to the client so that the rationale for treatment is understood. For example, in some cultural and religious groups some mental illnesses are thought to relate to possession by spirits. If the therapist has not been exposed to these health beliefs this could be missed in the formulation, which would lead to the therapist and client holding different understandings of the client's problems. The third consideration is the degree to which membership of certain groups might influence the degree of *stigmatisation* or *acceptance* by the group as a result of experiencing mental health problems. Ng Chee Hong (1997) describes strong mental health stigma in traditional Chinese culture, which can damage the family name. In contrast Fabrega (1991) and Dols (1987) found no evidence of stigma attached to mental illness in traditional Islamic societies.

If you are aware of cultural or societal differences between you and your client we suggest that you enquire about the issues we outlined above, using Socratic dialogue (see Chapter 7) and make use of supervision to explore the issues. It can be helpful to read about mental health issues in different groups and societies, but this is not a substitute for discussing the issues with the client. It should not be assumed that just because a person has experienced a certain culture or group, they necessarily hold the dominant beliefs and values of that culture or group.

Summary

- The main function of a CBT formulation is the development of a cognitive-behavioural understanding of the client's problems that enables a treatment plan to be developed.
- It is important that the formulation makes sense to the client and it should be developed in collaboration with the client.
- The formulation should be used and modified throughout therapy as new information emerges.
- Group and cultural differences should be considered in the process of developing a formulation.

Further reading

Crisp A.H. (ed.) (2004) *Every Family in the Land: Understanding Prejudice and Discrimination against People with Mental Illness.* London: Royal Society of Medicine Press.

Johnstone, L. & Dallos, D. (eds) (2006) *Formulation in Psychology and Psychotherapy: Making Sense of People's Problems.* Hove: Routledge.

Sanders, D. & Wills, F. (2005) *Cognitive Therapy: An Introduction* (pp. 24–53). London: SAGE.

Wells (2006) *Case Formulation in Cognitive Behaviour Therapy: The Treatment of Challenging and Complex Cases.* New York: Routledge.

9

Setting Therapy Goals

The whole process of therapy and setting therapy goals can feel a bit like being in a foreign land with a foreign language. Greenberger and Padesky (1995) use the Lewis Carroll story *Alice in Wonderland* to illustrate this process – specifically the moment at which Alice, facing a fork in the road, encounters the Cheshire cat and asks him which fork to take. He responds by asking her where she wishes to go. Alice, never having been to Wonderland before, says she has no idea where she would like to go. The Cheshire cat cheerfully exclaims that it does not really matter which way she goes in that case.

Greenberger and Padesky (1995) note that therapy can feel a lot like being in a strange place, not knowing the rules and where it is possible to get to. However, they note that in order to make the best use of therapy time, it is actually important to know where you are going and how you might get there. Working with the client and facilitating them to set goals is therefore a fundamental element of CBT and also one of the core competencies discussed by Roth and Pilling (2007). Goals are usually developed in a collaborative way over a number of sessions, using the formulation and the client's ideas. The therapist facilitates an exploration of the problems the client has presented and enables the client to then choose goals that are focused towards change. It is important that the goals that are chosen are a priority for the client or they will not be motivated to work on these goals.

Goals work best when they are:

- graded
- specific
- positive
- measurable
- realistic
- time-limited

Graded goals

It is important for clients to be able to manage the first few tasks with relative ease so they get a sense of achievement and feel spurred on to tackle more complex tasks.

Specific goals

Goals need to be specific enough that the client knows when they have been achieved. 'I want to be more assertive' is too global and makes it difficult to assess when the goal has been achieved, whereas 'I want to be assertive enough to take a top back to a shop' is very specific.

Positive goals

Goals need to be presented in a positive way so that the client is moving towards the goal rather than away from a particular difficulty. Therefore 'I don't want to feel depressed any more' is a goal, but it makes it difficult for the client to work towards anything.

Measurable goals

Goals need to be measurable in order to record progress over time. Practice diaries can be used, along with rating scales and noticing changes in behaviour. The intervention chapters cover rating scales and the use of diary sheets in more detail.

Realistic goals

Clients need to feel that the goals are realistic enough to be achievable. Goals that seem too difficult will cause clients to feel panicky and their motivation will drop. It may be that the client can make achievable goals and then, as these are achieved, they can think about more difficult goals.

Time-limited goals

It helps to give each goal a time limit. 'I'll go into a supermarket and walk up one aisle on Tuesday' is very different from 'I'll go into a supermarket and walk up one aisle sometime this month.' (Do also note the specificity of this goal!)

Goal setting is usually the next step after the formulation has been discussed with the client. It is an ongoing process throughout treatment sessions. As the client manages the first goals, further ones can be discussed.

The above list is all very well but, in practice, setting goals with clients can be a really tricky process! It can be helpful to get the client to come up with some general goals and then think about the steps they may need to take in order to achieve these goals – this can help to identify specific goals. The following dialogue with Andy might help to illustrate this process and suggest questions to ask in order to help a client set some realistic, achievable goals.

Goal setting with Andy:

Therapist:	Having discussed the formulation, one of the next steps is often to set some goals for the therapy. This helps us both to keep on track and to think about how we can plan the sessions so you get the most out of them.
Andy:	Okay, that sounds fine to me … I mean really I just want to get better and stop worrying all the time … I just never used to be like this.
Therapist:	So we need to think about what needs to happen in order for you to get to that point …
Andy:	I really just want to be back to normal …
Therapist:	Okay, well that's a helpful start. What does back to normal mean to you?
Andy:	I just don't want to be anxious any more, I'm fed up of feeling anxious all the time.
Therapist:	I guess I should say at this point that some anxiety is normal and it's impossible to get rid of anxiety altogether – strange as it sounds, it is there for a reason and we can talk about why we get anxious in a later session … but it sounds as though you want your anxiety levels to get back to how they used to be, meaning that they were manageable before.
Andy:	That's it, yes … I just want to get back to how I used to be.
Therapist:	So what sorts of things are you unable to do now because of the anxiety?
Andy:	Working, that's the biggest thing.
Therapist:	So it sounds as though that's a really big goal for you … What else are you missing out on?
Andy:	Just going out, seeing friends … you know, I can't even go into the supermarket on my own any more – I find that so embarrassing – the supermarket. I feel like a 5-year-old child!
Therapist:	You don't know how common that is actually … most of the people I see hate the supermarket and avoid it as much as possible … something to do with the lighting, the queues and the fact that the exit is often hard to get to … What do you worry about in the supermarket?
Andy:	Yep, those things and I think I worry about getting anxious and that I'll get a panic attack and that people will stare at me and see me sweating and maybe I'll collapse …
Therapist:	Okay, so going to the supermarket might be a goal … and it sounds like going out generally might be a goal … Where might you go?
Andy:	To the pub with friends, on the bus and tube, shops, back to tennis – I've stopped going there, hmm just to walk down the road … You know, I can't even

open my front door without feeling anxious now and I can't pick up the tele-phone, I leave it to go on to answerphone …

Therapist:	What's the worry with picking the phone up?
Andy:	I think just having to speak to people and explain that I can't go out – I'm embarrassed.
Therapist:	So, might it be helpful to have a story to tell people about what's going on for you?
Andy:	What? Make one up?
Therapist:	Well, sort of … Sometimes people find it helpful to prepare a bit so they don't feel quite as uncomfortable and can decide how much to tell different people.
Andy:	Actually that would be really helpful because I know I'd tell some people more than others.
Therapist:	Okay, so it sounds as though you've got quite a lot of different goals in mind … I've been scribbling away as we've been talking, so would it be helpful for us to try and work out a bit of a plan?
Andy:	Yes, that would be good.
Therapist:	So, as we've talked about before, it's important to try out more manageable goals first, so if going out is a general goal, would opening the front door and then closing it again be the first step?
Andy:	I guess so … Is that an okay goal? It sounds a bit easy.
Therapist:	Yes, it's absolutely fine … If you were to do that twice daily for the next week, it would really help you to get started … What might be next? Walking to the gate and back?
Andy:	Yes, then I could walk to the nearest lamp-post.
Therapist:	Great, and what might be next?
Andy:	The next lamp-post.
Therapist:	Yes, you could continue along like that … What would be the next step up then after lamp-posts?
Andy:	There's a little shop I could try going into but I'm finding queues very hard at the moment.
Therapist:	Well, could you go in, have a wander round and then leave?
Andy:	Oh, I'm not sure about that …
Therapist:	What might be the problem with that?
Andy:	I don't know … hmm … well, it's a bit weird isn't it? Just to walk round and not buy anything from such a small shop?
Therapist:	I don't know, I think I do it a fair bit but I know it can be a problem for some people … What might be your worry thoughts about it?
Andy:	I think I'd worry they might think I was stealing …
Therapist:	Okay, that makes sense then … that's quite a common worry … so we might need to make a note of that as we can do some work on those sorts of thoughts. *[Goals about working on negative/worry thoughts can be written down at the same time in this way.]*
Andy:	I think that would probably be useful.
Therapist:	We're writing down some very concrete goals about what you would like to be doing differently and we've just talked about thoughts, but I guess it's also important to think about how to cope with the panic attacks you've been experiencing and we can do that alongside working on the other goals – do you think you would find that helpful?

Andy: Oh yes, if there is some way of controlling what's happening to my body a bit that would be so helpful.

Therapist: Okay, so learning some coping strategies and also some education about what happens to the body when you panic would help …

The above excerpt is an illustration of how goals can be discussed. There are many ways of having this conversation, but it is essentially a collaborative exercise between client and therapist and forms the basis upon which the therapy sessions are organised. Andy's initial goals might look like this:

General goals	Specific goals
To go out	To open front door
	To walk to gate
	To walk to nearest lamp-post
	To walk to second lamp-post
	To walk to corner shop and not buy
To feel calmer	To learn relaxation and breathing techniques
	To learn about anxiety
	To learn distraction
To identify and challenge negative thoughts	To identify worry thoughts
	To tackle worry thoughts about people looking at me
To feel more confident	To feel more confident with friends
	To have more confidence when going into shops

Andy is obviously wanting to go back to work and this can certainly be noted down as a future goal. However, to begin with, it can be helpful just to concentrate on noting down the initial goals in detail.

Similar conversations could take place with Anne and Megan. The initial goals in depression are often focused on behavioural goals such as activity monitoring and scheduling (see Chapter 11 for full explanations of these terms) because trying to challenge thoughts in someone who is not doing anything can be very difficult. The person is likely to be having a lot of negative thoughts about the fact that their activity levels are so low and it would be hard to challenge this. The maintenance part of the formulation can be discussed, particularly focusing on 'the low activity cycle' (see Figure 11.4 on p. 109). The person could be asked about what they used to do in terms of activities before they became depressed and what they might imagine themselves doing in the future if the depression went away. A graded approach is useful and, if the person is able to list some activities, these could then be broken down into smaller, more manageable steps.

Anne is having difficulty sleeping and so getting some structure into her day and tackling the sleep issue would be important goals to discuss. Anne is clearly experiencing many negative thoughts and it would be useful to have a conversation about working on these thoughts. Other issues specific to Anne include the guilt she is experiencing with regard to the affair she had. She may need to process some of these feelings and come to terms with them. This is unlikely to be a strictly CBT intervention and may be tackled in a number of ways, depending on the concerns Anne has been left with because of the affair. She may just need to talk about what happened or to explore the pros and cons of telling Jack or to forgive herself at some level. It seems, from the formulation, that Anne may have experienced a loss in role in terms of the fact that her children have left home. This hypothesis can be explored later in the therapy process and Anne may need to process this loss, but also look at how she can forge other roles for herself. Anne's initial goals might look like this:

General goals	Specific goals
Investigate activity levels	Monitor activity levels
	Activity scheduling
	Monitor mood
	Repair sleep pattern
To work on self-esteem	To identify and challenge negative thoughts about self
	To gradually start having more contact with friends and to tackle resultant negative thoughts as they arise
	Experiment with expressing feelings
Process issues regarding the affair	Discuss the affair
	Pros and cons of telling Jack
	Self-forgiveness
	Exploring preventative methods for the future and how she can improve her relationship with Jack
Explore loss of role	Processing the loss of role
	Forging new roles

Note that the last two general goals are not 'set in stone'. It is fine to note things down but not have these as firm goals, as goals often change through the process of therapy. A particular issue for depressed clients is the lack of motivation they often experience at the start of therapy and it can be difficult for some depressed clients to identify any goals. Therapists might have to take a more directive approach in some instances when helping clients to identify goals.

The initial goals for people with obsessive problems tend to be behavioural goals focusing on cutting down on rituals, checking and reassurance seeking. Avoidances can also be tackled in a graded way. Obsessive compulsive behaviours (i.e. checking/ rituals, etc.) tend to be extensive by the time the person has sought help and may feel overwhelming to therapists without a lot of experience in this area. It can therefore be helpful in the first instance to focus on one small area (e.g. lounge or car) or one behaviour. Megan's reassurance seeking is extensive and also means that she is losing confidence in her ability to parent Molly. Therefore one of the first goals might be for Megan to monitor her levels of reassurance seeking using a diary sheet. (Note: for some people with obsessive problems, keeping a diary can become another ritual so it is useful to check this out – this will be discussed in more depth in Chapter 11). She can then cut down on this reassurance seeking on a gradual basis (see Chapter 11 for an explanation of how this can be achieved). Education about the CBT model and discussing maintenance cycles can be very helpful with people who experience obsessive (also known as intrusive) thoughts. Thought challenging may also be helpful – thought challenging with people with obsessive compulsive problems is usually different from challenging with people with other disorders, and this is explained in more depth in the Chapter 14. Megan seems to have some self-critical thoughts and may have some low self-esteem. This can be investigated more thoroughly through the course of therapy and it might be that future goals would be about tackling negative core beliefs. Megan's relationship with her mother is difficult and she may find it useful to explore the interactions they have together and experiment with reacting differently. She may also wish to learn some assertiveness techniques. Megan's initial goals might look like this:

General goals	Specific goals
Investigate current checking/reassurance seeking	Use diary sheets to monitor reassurance seeking Cut down on reassurance seeking Later focus on monitoring and cutting down on other behaviours
Learn about maintenance cycles for obsessive problems	Examples of maintenance cycles Normalising intrusive thoughts Work on thoughts specific to obsessive problems
Work on self-esteem	Identify negative core beliefs Work on changing core beliefs
Explore relationship with mother	Explore interactions between Megan and her mother ?Experiment with interacting differently with her mother. ?Learn some assertiveness skills

Summary

- Facilitating clients to set goals for themselves is a fundamental element of CBT.
- Goals work best when they are:

  - graded
  - specific
  - positive
  - measurable
  - realistic
  - time-limited

Further reading

Greenberger, D. & Padesky, C. (1995) *Clinician's Guide to Mind over Mood.* New York: Guildford Press.

Sanders, D. & Wills, F. (2005) *Cognitive Therapy: An Introduction.* London: SAGE.

10

Coping Strategies

Helping a client to identify coping strategies is probably the most useful place to start once the formulation has been discussed and goals have been identified. Many of the coping strategies in this chapter are aimed at tackling the physical symptoms experienced and building up coping strategies in this way can be one of the first steps towards breaking the maintenance cycles discussed in the formulation chapter (see p. 75). It can be useful for clients to be able to think about the coping strategies they have already been using and what helps and what doesn't help. As discussed in other parts of this book, some 'coping strategies' may be useful in the short term but they may actually keep the problem going in the longer term and thus may not be helpful ongoing strategies. For example, it is common for clients to mask feelings of anxiety by using alcohol and, while this may ease the anxiety in the short term, it doesn't solve the root of the problem and may give the client an alcohol problem on top of an anxiety problem.

Some clients use 'safety behaviours' which are coping strategies, but they may also be keeping the problem going. Safety behaviours are particularly prevalent in people with anxiety problems. They are very common in people with social phobia. Safety behaviours may help the person to enter a feared situation but only by using certain props or strategies – for example alcohol. Another safety behaviour that might be used by a person who goes out to dinner (so they are not avoiding going out) is to grip their knife and fork very tightly so that their hands do not shake. Using this strategy might help in the short term but it also adds to the idea that the person would not cope if they just held their utensils in the usual way. Thus safety behaviours can maintain anxiety in the same way as complete avoidance, although the avoidant behaviour is much more subtle. Clinicians often wonder at which point they should help clients tackle safety behaviours. The general rule is that if the person has to use safety behaviours to go into certain situations, then so be it (although too much alcohol should be discouraged). The safety behaviours can be tackled once the person is successfully entering previously feared situations. It is important that the therapist is able to identify safety behaviours as this is a core competency for CBT as outlined by Roth and Pilling (2007). These behaviours, however, are not always obvious in the first instance.

It can be helpful to get clients to identify their own coping strategies before teaching new strategies. The following dialogue with Anne illustrates how coping strategies can be identified:

Therapist: It's useful to try and identify how you've been coping with your difficulties so far before we talk about developing any new ways of coping.

Anne: Okay, but I've just been getting through really. I'm not sure it could really be called coping.

Therapist: Well, getting through can be very difficult when you feel low and depressed, so the fact that you are 'getting through' is important. Do you feel as though there is anything that helps you to get through?

Anne: Hmm … talking to my children is helpful but it's so much more difficult now they've left home. My daughter being in Australia makes it pretty expensive although we have now just set things up on the internet so that has made it a bit better …

Therapist: What is it about talking to your children that is helpful?

Anne: Well, they distract me from my thoughts. I can ask them all about themselves and not have to think about me and all the things I'm not managing at the moment … yeah …

Therapist: So it helps to talk to your children … What else helps you to cope?

Anne: Well drinking wine is a great help but I don't suppose that's part of the treatment is it?

Therapist: Wine's one of those things that's helpful in the short term but you are right, it is not helpful in the long term because it's a depressant so it can lower the mood. Also it numbs thoughts and feelings so it works as an avoidance strategy – do you remember the maintenance cycles we discussed and how avoidance keeps difficulties going?

Anne: Yes, I know what you mean and it is something I would like to cut down on. I don't drink a lot of alcohol but it's regular, most evenings.

Therapist: We can add that to the list of goals. How about other coping strategies?

Anne: Going to work helps actually … I don't think I'm too bad at my job and I can hide my depression there most of the time.

Therapist: So it sounds as though it would be important to continue going to work rather than taking time out. … Any other strategies that are helpful or that have been helpful in the past … for example, some people like to relax in certain ways?

Anne: I used to go swimming but I've felt so tired recently that I've not felt like going. I used to read a lot but my concentration is so bad that I've not been able to read. I used to have a massage every couple of weeks but I just haven't felt like going. That was good at the time though … I suppose I used to do quite a lot, thinking about it. I've given quite a lot up haven't I?

Therapist: People often find it really hard to keep these sorts of strategies going when they feel depressed because when people are depressed they don't feel like doing anything. They then tend to do a lot less, which leads to them thinking thoughts such as 'I should be doing more, I'm useless', and they feel guilty which makes the depression even worse. It's a vicious cycle and the only way to break it is to force yourself to do some things very gradually. It can be very hard at first but usually helps most people. We'll be talking about this more in later meetings. It does seem as though there are already helpful strategies you can go back to. Can you think of any more?

Anne: Don't think so … hang on I used to go to yoga which helped …

Therapist: That's good to hear as we'll also be talking about something called mindfulness which is a bit like meditation and yoga also uses some of the same principles. There are quite a few coping strategies that we'll be discussing …

Below are a number of strategies that can be discussed with clients and that they can practise at home between sessions. These strategies work most effectively if the client practises them when they are relaxed or feeling in a reasonable mood. They will not be able to employ them when feeling stressed/anxious until they are very used to using them when feeling more relaxed.

Psycho-education

Psycho-education essentially means educating clients about CBT, psychology and symptoms. Although this is not strictly a coping strategy, the recognition of symptoms and realising what is happening to the body can act as a coping strategy. Psycho-education occurs throughout the therapy process, although it generally occurs in more depth at the beginning of therapy. The process of going through the formulation is often an opportunity to educate clients about how their difficulties have developed and are being maintained. Socratic questioning can be used in this process but it is also necessary to impart information in a more didactic way on occasion. Going through the maintenance cycles often gives the best opportunity to discuss different symptoms and also to let clients know which symptoms are common to many people.

Psycho-education about physical symptoms often occurs at the same time as discussions about coping strategies. It can be important for clients to learn that when they are depressed, their body will feel tired and their sleep and appetite are likely to be disturbed. They can be encouraged to try and eat three meals a day even if they are not hungry and to introduce healthy, nutritious foods into their diets as well as trying to build up the size of their meals over time until they reach the normal amounts of food. A good sleep routine is important and, if clients are 'napping' during the day, they can be asked about what effect they feel this might have. A routine before bedtime can be helpful and having a hot milky drink as well as reading or watching something relaxing before going to bed can be useful.

Clients who experience anxiety will sometimes not realise the impact that anxiety can have on the body and can find their symptoms very frightening. It can therefore be very powerful to discover that anxiety can have such a big impact. Clients can learn that when they have anxious thoughts, adrenaline is released from the adrenal glands and that causes their breathing to quicken as well as their heart rate, and other symptoms, such as sweating, appear. These symptoms occur for a reason to help the body to prepare for 'flight or flight'

(much more useful in caveman days rather than now, when we tend to be more scared in social situations!). The breathing quickens in order to get more oxygen into the body and the heart races to pump blood to the muscles so they can react if required. Muscles tense in readiness for running away or fighting. However, if you are not running away or fighting, the body is then left to cope with a whole load of symptoms which can feel very frightening. Breathing quickly can cause dizziness, as too much oxygen is breathed in and the balance of gases is disturbed. People can then become focused on the symptoms and start worrying about them, which can lead to further anxiety and symptoms. Some of the coping strategies below, such as breathing exercises and progressive muscle relaxation, can help clients to gain control over some of these physical sensations.

Breathing techniques

When people feel stressed and anxious, they tend to breathe too quickly. This can either happen to the extent where the person is breathing so quickly it actually leads to a panic attack, or over-breathing (breathing too fast and too deeply) can be more prolonged but less severe, which can also cause physical discomfort of a less acute nature.

In both of the above cases, breathing techniques can be practised so that the person is better able to control their breathing when required. The main task is to slow down the breathing and allow it to be controlled and relaxed. This takes practice and the client will need to practise the techniques regularly before they will actually be of use in a situation where they feel anxious. This is a key point, as people often try to use the techniques at the height of their stress and they can then be very disappointed when they do not work.

The following dialogue extract with Andy will help to illustrate how to explain breathing techniques to a client:

Therapist: We're going to spend some time discussing breathing techniques today, as breathing too quickly can lead to physical symptoms and sometimes a panic attack. Do you remember we discussed breathing when we talked about what happens to the body during panic?

Andy: Yes, and I remember from biology lessons as well. It's just so hard trying to control your body when you're having a panic attack. It seems to have a mind of its own.

Therapist: Actually, that's one of the important points about learning breathing techniques. It's really important to practise them when you're feeling calm so that you get used to using them and will be able to put them in to practice during a panic. If you try to use them during a panic before you've practised them, they just won't work. So I want you to just to sit back in a comfortable position in your chair and close your eyes if you want to … If you feel safer leaving your eyes open, just focus on a spot on the wall … Just try to relax your muscles as much as possible and place one hand on your chest and one hand just below your ribs. … Breathe in gently through your nose now and hopefully you will feel your hand move forward, meaning you are breathing deeply. … Breathe out now through your mouth … and in … slowly and gently … imagining just below your ribs is a big red balloon, inflating and deflating … Try and keep movement in the chest to a minimum as breathing from the chest is generally shallow breathing and this can cause physical discomfort. … Keep this regular rhythm going … slow, deep and gentle breaths, aiming for about eight to twelve breaths a minute with breathing in and out counting as one breath … Just keep this gentle rhythm going now [let the client continue for a minute or two] … It may take a while to get used to this new rhythm but, when you have, you will find that your breathing is generally more relaxed … okay, when you are ready, become aware of your surroundings again and open your eyes. … How was that?

Andy: Okay, a bit strange but not too bad.

Therapist: It does become much more comfortable with practice, and the more you practise the more your breathing will feel gentle and comfortable at other times. You will also be able to employ this breathing technique if you feel yourself going into panic mode …

The client can be asked to practise the breathing once a day for 5–10 minutes to help them to get used to the new way of breathing. See Davis et al. (1988) for further reading on breathing exercises.

Relaxation techniques

There are many different kinds of relaxation techniques. Some involve lying down, closing the eyes and imagining a really lovely or safe place and using all the senses to give reality to the scene. Other relaxation techniques are more active and involve the client tensing and relaxing various parts of their body. This type of relaxation is called progressive muscle relaxation and can be described to the client, as in the following dialogue. Again, Andy is used in this example as progressive muscle relaxation is most useful with clients who are experiencing anxiety and stress.

Therapist: We're going to discuss something called progressive muscle relaxation today, now you feel more comfortable using the breathing techniques. This relaxation technique involves tensing and relaxing the muscles of the body in turn. The reason for doing this is that when we are stressed, our muscles tend to be tense all the time and we don't even notice how tense we are.

Andy: I certainly know that I tend to be really tense a lot of the time and I get a lot of neck and back pain.

Therapist: That's really common especially for people who experience anxiety problems. We can go through this exercise in the same way as we did for the breathing, with you trying it out in the session. So if you sit back in the chair so you feel comfortable … close your eyes if you want to … Now just practise the slow breathing … in through your nose and out through your mouth … slowly and gently … imagining the bit beneath your ribs inflating and deflating like a red balloon … Now point your left foot and hold for three … and relax … Now the right foot for three … and relax … Bend your left foot up to the ceiling for three and relax …

The relaxation continues in the same vein until all the muscles of the body have been tensed and relaxed: feet, calves, thighs, buttocks, stomach, biceps, forearms, hands, neck and face. Clients need to practise when they are feeling relaxed so they can employ it when required in more stressful situations. Some therapists make tapes of this routine for their clients to listen to but relaxation tapes are easy to purchase in a variety of book and music shops or over the internet. See Davis et al. (1988) for more information on relaxation exercises.

Grounding techniques

Grounding techniques are just that, techniques to 'ground' someone. When people get very anxious they can feel numb and as though they are losing contact with their environment. So grounding techniques can help to bring the anxiety levels down and help the person to get in contact with the environment again. Other ways to describe this feeling are: a dreamlike state; things not feeling real; feeling floaty and 'fuzzy'. The following list of techniques can help clients:

1   Tell yourself that the reason you are feeling so bad is because you feel anxious. Recognising anxious feelings is the first step in learning how to cope with them.

2   Start to ground yourself:

  • Stamp your feet.
  • Use a 'grounding' object – a comforting object that you carry around with you and squeeze when you are feeling in distress to bring you back to the present, e.g. a rounded stone, a small soft toy or a lavender bag, etc.
  • Use breathing/relaxation techniques.
  • Make contact with yourself: notice how parts of the body feel, starting with the feet and working upwards. Do you feel hot? Cold? Numb? Energetic? Restless? You can also try just touching parts of your body or shaking your body in order to try and get in contact with yourself.
  • Develop a grounding image: rehearse a calming image, one which helps you to feel in control and safe such as a peaceful garden, a beach scene or a walk through the countryside. It is useful to practise summoning this image when you are feeling relaxed, as this will make it much easier to use when you are feeling panicky.
  • Develop a grounding phrase: this might be a few words or a phrase to remind you that you are surviving in the present. Examples might be 'I am in Bristol, it is Tuesday today', or 'I am strong and will go on surviving.' Some people actually write these kinds of statements down on pieces of card and keep them in their pockets for 'emergencies'.

3   Make contact with the environment. Use each of the senses to get in contact with the environment around you:

  • Sight: use your eyes to make contact with the world. Look at the different colours around as well as the shapes and light and shade.
  • Hearing: listen to the sounds you hear, including voices, traffic noise, birds singing, etc.
  • Touch: use your sense of touch to make contact with the ground, the chair you are sitting on, plants, etc. Notice the temperature and any different textures around you.

- Taste: try sucking a sweet or having a warming drink.
- Smell: use your nose to smell what's around you, including car exhausts, flowers and perfumes.

Distraction techniques

Distraction techniques can be very helpful in a number of situations especially for very anxious clients who are starting to tackle their avoidance of situations. Distraction is helpful at times, but not when it becomes the person's only coping strategy – if someone is constantly distracting themselves in order to stave off anxiety, it will be difficult for them to be present in a situation and start to enjoy it. Thus, distraction techniques can help people to start tackling their avoidance but it needs to be used in moderation. Below is a list of distraction techniques:

- Counting – e.g. counting back in 3s from 200; counting backwards from 100.
- Counting cars (or anything else) – e.g. counting the number of red cars you see go past or the number of people wearing boots (this could be inappropriate for people with obsessive compulsive tendencies).
- Visualisation – thinking of a lovely place – really imagining it with all the senses.
- Remembering a pleasant memory – in lots of detail.
- Focusing on breathing slowly.

Mindfulness

Mindfulness is a technique that is often used with people with depression and other mental health problems. Indeed, it is the mainstay of some therapy for depression. There is limited space for a full discussion of mindfulness here and further reading is recommended (see p. 100). However, in brief, mindfulness means paying attention in a particular way: *in the moment* and *non-judgementally*. Imagine you are on a train on the way home from visiting some friends. You may be looking out of the window. What are you thinking about?… Chances are you are remembering the weekend and/or thinking about what you might be doing later or what you might eat for tea. How often do you look out of the window and really *see* what is outside? How often are you *in the moment*, observing what is happening right now? Even if you feel you really are fully observing what is outside, how often do negative/unhelpful thoughts pop into your head? A lot, probably! Mindfulness is about being in the moment, using the senses to become aware of what is happening right now. Negative thoughts might pop into the head on a regular basis but the aim is to notice them and then turn the attention back to the task in hand, which is to be in the moment. Examples of mindfulness exercises might be:

- observing the colours in a room
- listening to sounds
- listening to a piece of music

- observing one's breathing
- touching a rough piece of material, etc.

The exercises can be tried for a few minutes while in sessions and clients can be debriefed afterwards. They will often be judgemental of their ability to stay focused on the mindfulness task but it is important to discuss negative thoughts and reiterate that it is fine to have negative thoughts but that the task is to notice the thoughts and then bring the attention back to the mindfulness task. Gaining benefit from this exercise may take time and clients will often have to practise it on a daily basis before they notice the benefits of mindfulness.

Mindfulness is a particularly useful skill for clients presenting with obsessional problems. Intrusive thoughts are a key feature of obsessive compulsive disorder and usually cause the client significant distress. As discussed in Chapter 12, evaluation of the client's thoughts, along with psycho-education about intrusive thoughts, are the main cognitive strategies for obsessional problems. Mindfulness can, however, also be helpful in the early stages of therapy, to enable the client to 'notice' and 'let go' of unwanted intrusive thoughts instead of focusing on them.

Summary

- Helping a client to identify and develop some coping strategies can be a useful place to start after the formulation has been discussed.
- Beware of safety behaviours which maintain the problem.
- Breathing techniques can help people to slow their breathing down and are especially useful for those people with panic attacks.
- Progressive muscle relaxation is particularly helpful for people who are tense and anxious.
- Grounding techniques are quick and easy to learn and easily employed in difficult situations once they are practised.
- Mindfulness is only mentioned briefly here, but some consider it to be a therapy in its own right. See Further reading below.

Further reading

Davis, M., Robbins Eshelman, E. & McKay, M. (1988) *The Relaxation and Stress Reduction Workbook*. Oakland, CA: New Harbinger Publications.

Hawton, K., Salkovskis, P.M., Kirk, J. & Clark, D.M (1989) *Cognitive Behaviour Therapy for Psychiatric Problems: A Practical Guide*. Oxford: Oxford University Press.

Kennerly, H. (1997) *Overcoming Anxiety*. London: Robinson.

Segal, Z.V., Williams, J.M.G. & Teasdale, J.D. (2002) *Mindfulness-based Cognitive Therapy for Depression: A New Approach to Preventing Relapse*. New York: Guilford Press.

11

Behavioural Interventions

In terms of the formulation maintenance cycles, behavioural interventions are strategies which help clients to target *the behaviours* that might be keeping the maintenance cycles going (see p. 24). Behavioural exposure strategies are most helpful for clients with anxiety and obsessive compulsive problems, whereas activity monitoring and scheduling strategies are most helpful for clients with depression. Obviously, many clients may have anxiety and depression, so a mixture of techniques can be used and the formulation can guide which techniques might be most helpful to start with. It can be important to seek supervision to guide these kinds of dilemmas.

Behavioural exposure

Behavioural exposure essentially means helping the client to face up to situations they have been avoiding, usually because of anxiety. As has been discussed throughout the book, avoidance is a commonly used coping strategy – we all do it! It helps us in the short term and generally lowers anxiety levels. However, it maintains the idea that the person would not have coped if they had actually faced up to the situation. The client is then left thinking that they cannot cope the next time they come across the same situation, so they avoid it again, strengthening the idea that they cannot cope in such situations. Behavioural exposure is most commonly used with clients who experience anxiety, predominantly phobias. However, it is also often used to tackle obsessive problems and may also be used in depression where clients have used avoidance as a way of coping.

The therapist's job, then, is to educate the client about how this cycle works. The therapist and client review the maintenance cycles obtained during the formulation phase (see Chapter 8). The therapist reminds the client how avoidance maintains the problem and they start to discuss how this avoidance can gradually be reduced. Clients can sometimes feel quite panicky at this point and it is important to give them information that tackling the avoidance is a slow process and that they are always in charge of choosing the pace and the goals to be addressed.

The next step is for the therapist and client to work together to identify all the things the client has been avoiding. A 'graded hierarchy', also known as a 'ladder', can then be developed by placing these avoidances into a list. The easiest avoidance/goal to tackle is usually placed at the bottom of the ladder or hierarchy (or the top depending on what feels most comfortable to you and the client) – then you can work up or down in sequence, each avoidance/goal getting gradually more challenging as you go up (or down) the ladder. There are several important issues to consider when making goals:

1   The first goal at the bottom of the hierarchy needs to be manageable enough for the client to be able to achieve it without difficulty. This will give them confidence and a feeling that they want to try the next goal.
2   Each goal should be given a rating from 0–10 (where 0 is 'zero anxiety' and 10 is the 'most anxiety ever felt').
3   Goals need to be specific – for example, 'walking to the nearest lamp-post' would be better than 'walking outside'. This means that the client knows exactly when they have achieved the goal.
4   Each goal on the hierarchy needs to be very *slightly* more difficult than the last goals – jumps that are too big are discouraging.
5   The client needs to be educated to practise each goal until they feel comfortable, before moving on to the next goal. It is most effective if the client allows anxiety levels for each task to fall to 2/3 out of 10 before moving on to the next task.
6   Clients can sometimes be put off trying tasks because they feel some anxiety. It is important, therefore, to educate them that it is normal and also quite important to feel some anxiety as it helps them to learn that they can get through situations despite feeling anxious. They also find out that the anxiety is reduced each time they go into the situation because they get used to it.
7   Goal practice must be regular. Clients sometimes try out a situation and then do not repeat it for a few weeks. However, during this time, the person forgets they managed to cope last time they tried going into the situation and the anxiety builds again. Regular practice is very, very important!

Andy should be encouraged to keep practising the first few steps (even if he thinks they are very easy) until he feels ready to walk to the local shop. He can then practise walking to the local shop until his anxiety levels have gone down to 2/3. Then he can move on to the next step. Of course, in the real world, clients often have to face unexpected situations that are much higher up their hierarchy. The client can be encouraged to cope with these situations as best they can, but not to worry too much if they do not feel confident in these situations, as they are trying to gain confidence while doing the easier goals. When the client has reached the top goal on the hierarchy, a new hierarchy can be made.

Clients often have setbacks along the way. Setbacks or 'blips' are an important part of recovery and, although it can be frightening for clients when they panic after a period

Figure 11.1 Example of a graded hierarchy for Andy

Fear of going out	Rating scale (0–10)
1. Go outside front door	0.5
2. Go outside the front door – to gate	0.5
3. Walk to nearest lamp-post	1
4. Walk to nearest shop	4
5. Go into the shop and walk round	5
6. Buy an item and stand in the queue	6
7. Drive to town, park and then drive home	6
8. Drive to town, park and walk to nearest shop	7
9. Drive to town, park, go to nearest shop and go in	7.5
10. Drive to town, go to nearest shop, buy item	8
11. Go to town, walk round a few shops, buy some items	8.5
12. Go to local pub with friends, have a few drinks	9
13. Go to local pub with friends, just have soft drinks	10
14. Attend a family gathering	10

of no panics (or get a patch of low mood after mood has improved), it is helpful for them to have these setbacks so they can learn to recover from them. If a client has a setback, they can be encouraged to move back down a few steps on the hierarchy. Setbacks are covered in more detail in Chapter 19. There is also a detailed setback handout in Appendix XV which can be given to clients.

Once the hierarchy has been devised, the client can be given a practice diary to note down their goals on a daily basis. If they make a note of their changing anxiety levels day by day, it helps them to know when to move on the next step (when anxiety levels go down to 2/3) and also allows them to see the progress they are making.

Special strategies for clients with obsessive compulsive problems: Exposure with Response Prevention (ERP)

Clients with obsessive problems may be exposed to anxiety in treatment in a slightly different way. As well as cutting down on avoidance, treatment involves reducing checking behaviours and reassurance-seeking (see maintenance cycles for Megan, p. 77) while the client exposes him or herself to anxiety in a variety of ways. This is known as exposure with response prevention (ERP).

Clients with obsessive compulsive problems are usually extremely worried about exposing themselves to their feared situations without having their usual rituals/reassurance-seeking behaviours available. They need to be warned that when they first expose themselves to

Figure 11.2 Example of Andy's practice record

			Anxiety rating (0–10)	
Date	Task	Before	During	After
22/7/5	Going out of front door	5	5	2
23/7/5	Going out of front door	5	4	1
24/7/5	Going out of front door	3	3	1
25/7/5	Going out of front door	2	1	1
26/7/5	Walking to front gate	6	6	4
27/7/5	Walking to front gate	5	5	3
28/7/5	Walking to front gate	4	3	2
29/7/5	Walking to front gate	4	3	1
30/7/5	Walking to front gate	2	1	1
31/7/5	Walk to near lamp-post	9	8	5
1/8/5	Walk to near lamp-post	7	7	4
2/8/5	Walk to near lamp-post	6	5	4
3/8/5	Walk to near lamp-post	5	5	3

the feared situations without rituals/reassurance-seeking, their anxiety (or sometimes other emotions) will become very high and may remain high for a couple of hours, sometimes more. However, the anxiety cannot remain high and eventually levels off and comes down. The person begins to learn that they can cope without a ritual in that particular situation and they may then be ready to move on to tackling a new situation (although they will need to keep practising the previous scenario as well). Again, remind clients that they can take this process at their own pace. The next step is for the therapist and client to work together to identify the checks the clients make, the situations they are avoiding and what reassurance they ask for. Checking behaviour/avoidances/reassurance-seeking in clients with obsessional problems can be substantial! It can be helpful to start in just one or two areas of the client's life, such as the lounge or the car, etc. A hierarchy can be made in the same way as described earlier for Andy and the goal-setting points (Chapter 9, pp. 85–6) can also be used as a guide. In addition, the hierarchy can include exposure to previously avoided situations as well as tackling rituals and reassurances.

Sometimes clients ritualise by using covert (internal or hidden) rituals, such as saying rhymes; repeating phrases; saying prayers; balancing the intrusive thought with a 'good' thought or image; counting using good numbers, etc. Covert rituals can be spotted because they will lower the client's level of anxiety. They can be dealt with in the same way as behavioural rituals.

Example hierarchy for Megan

Situations/triggers	Rating scale (0–10)
1 Spending time with Molly, husband present	2
2 Spending time with Molly, husband next room	3
3 Cooking, using knives, husband with Molly	4
4 Spending time with Molly, health visitor present	5
5 Reducing phone calls to health visitor by one each week	5
6 One hour a day with no reassurance-seeking from husband	6
7 Reduce checking on Molly at night by one	7
8 Cooking using knives, Molly in room, husband next door	8
9 Going for a walk with Molly and husband	8
10 Going for a walk with Molly, husband 10 metres behind	9

The hierarchy can then be used as a guide to making more specific goals and mini-hierarchies. For example, Megan can start working on the first couple of situations on the list, both of which have been situations that she has avoided but that she does not feel too anxious about. It is good to start off with 'easier' situations so the client can achieve success. Some of the other items on the hierarchy may need to be broken down into smaller 'mini-goals/lists'. Try the exercise below to make a mini-hierarchy/list for Megan:

Exercise – building a mini-hierarchy for Megan regarding reassurance-seeking

Try building a hierarchy about reassurance-seeking for Megan. See if you can fill in the gaps on Figure 11.3, with the first goal being to cut down by one the number of times she phones the health visitor each week, with the final goal to have just the agreed contact with the health visitor. You can also fill in some goals for reassurance-seeking with her family. There are no right or wrong answers. When you build a hierarchy in therapy, it is important to work in collaboration with the client and try and find small steps together.

Exercise – building a graded hierarchy for Megan

As the client manages to achieve the above goals, a new 'mini-hierarchy/list' can be developed. The client can choose one or two goals at the top (or bottom) of the mini-hierarchy (i.e. the 'easier' goals, depending on which way up you build the list – it really doesn't matter) to try between sessions. It is important to give the client information about what to expect when tackling goals on the hierarchy as it can be very difficult to

Figure 11.3 Exercise – building a graded hierarchy for Megan

Goals	Rating scale (0–10)
1. Phone the health visitor once less often in the week.	_____
2. Phone health visitor three times less often in the week.	_____
3. Phone health visitor three times less often and have one hour each day without asking mum/husband questions	_____
4. _____	_____
5. _____	_____
6. _____	_____
7. _____	_____
8. _____	_____
9. _____	_____
10. _____	_____
11. _____	_____
12. _____	_____
13. _____	_____
14. To have 'normal' contact with health visitor and half a day without asking mum/husband questions	_____

cut down on obsessive-compulsive type behaviours. The behaviours are so successful at bringing down anxiety levels that it can be a real challenge for clients to expose themselves to the anxiety by cutting down on the behaviours.

The client needs to be reminded regularly of the obsessive compulsive cycle, that when a trigger situation occurs they will experience intrusive thoughts. In Megan's case, she has the thought 'I might harm Molly', and then because she has had that thought she thinks she might actually harm Molly (thought–action fusion – see Chapter 12) which leads to her feel extremely anxious. She finds that asking for reassurance reduces the anxiety very effectively. However, she doesn't learn to cope with the anxiety by herself and this strengthens the idea that she can only cope by asking for reassurance. Megan can be reminded of this cycle and talked though what would happen if she cut down on one phone call to the health visitor. In the usual scenario, Megan might have the thought, 'I'm going to harm Molly', then 'because I've had that thought, it means I'll actually do it', so she would get highly anxious and cope by phoning the health visitor which would bring the anxiety down. If she delayed phoning the health visitor for two hours, the anxiety would stay very high for a period of time. However, for most people, it would gradually reduce and she would learn that she could cope without the phone call. This period of time can be agonising for a lot of clients, especially when they are first starting out with this form of exposure. It is important to inform them of this and say that it will get much easier over time and with each goal they successfully tackle. Some clients with obsessive problems can successfully make use of goal sheets to help them to keep track of ritual/avoidance/reassurance reduction. See Appendix IV for

examples of record sheets that can be used with clients with obsessive compulsive problems. It is important to recognise that record sheets may not be useful for all clients with
obsessional problems as, for some clients, using record sheets can just be additional rituals. This is something to be vigilant about.

Reassurance-seeking can be difficult for families of obsessional clients to cope with.
It can sometimes be much easier for family members to just give the reassurance, as not
doing so can seem to increase anxiety in the short term and cause arguments and upset.
Therefore, it may be useful to have a session with the family and also to liaise with others involved, such as GPs and health visitors. It may be useful to share the maintenance
cycle of the formulation and discuss how to answer the client's constant questions without giving reassurance. An example of something Megan's husband could say is: 'I know
you are working to cut down on questions over the next hour so I can't answer that
question just yet.' The client will need to be open about their goals as some reassurance
will still be given in the first instance.

Behavioural experiments (or tests)

A behavioural experiment is where a client sets themself a goal but sees it as an experiment
rather than a goal that has to be achieved in a successful way. Therefore, whatever the outcome, the client learns something about how they cope in a particular situation. Most
often, the experiment is for the client to try doing something they have been avoiding and
then just to 'see what happens' – hence the expression 'experiment'. Behavioural exposure
tasks can usefully be framed as experiments, especially at the beginning of therapy when the
client does not have much experience of trying out tasks between sessions.

Experiments can be useful because they help to take the 'failure aspect' out of the
equation. Clients can often feel as though they have failed if they go into a situation but
become so panicky that they have to leave. However, with behavioural experiments,
leaving a situation does not mean failure; it simply means an opportunity to learn and,
perhaps, to do things differently the next time. Experiments can be very useful especially
at the beginning of therapy, giving the client the opportunity to test out ideas and to
realise that their feared situations may not be as bad as they were imagining. Experiments
allow an exploration of thought processes before, during and after the experiment and
can sometimes give evidence against negative thoughts.

Examples

Andy has been experiencing panic attacks. His thoughts during these attacks are: 'I'm
having a heart attack' and 'I'll collapse in front of everyone.' He avoids going out and he
also avoids all exercise – even walking up stairs very slowly because any increase in
heart-rate/breathing leads him to have thoughts like 'I'm having a heart attack', and

these thoughts can lead to a panic attack. The experiment he could try is to do some exercise in the therapist's office to test the theory that the symptoms are dangerous. He could test alternative thoughts that the symptoms are due to exercise – if so, the symptoms should lessen if he stops exercising.

Anne has started to avoid her friends as she feels that she has nothing to say to them and has also started to believe that they are ignoring her. They have been phoning her less often but this may be because she hardly ever takes up the offer of meeting them. An experiment might be that she could phone one of her friends and have a five-minute telephone conversation. She could then identify any positive or negative thoughts that arise as a result of the conversation. Experiments such as these provide good information about a person's thinking processes and this can be used for thought challenging (see Chapter 14)

Megan asks for lots of reassurance from both her family and her health visitor. As reassurance-seeking maintains the problem, one of the treatment principles is to help the person cut down on their reassurance-seeking, thus exposing themselves to the anxiety. This is discussed further in the 'behavioural exposure' section. In this section, the first goal for Megan is to cut down the number of times she phones the health visitor each week by one. So this goal could be framed as a behavioural experiment. In this instance, Megan can conduct the goal as an experiment, letting go of the outcome and just seeing what happens. Negative thoughts can be collected and noted down as these may be useful to add information to the formulation and to use in later thought challenging.

Further examples of behavioural experiments

- Giving someone a compliment.
- Making a mistake.
- Doing things less than perfectly.
- Smiling at other people rather than frowning.
- Going to the local shop and not buying anything.

One of the experiments above – smiling at people rather than frowning – can be particularly useful for people with anger problems. So many people with anger problems get into a negative cycle where they feel angry, so their facial expressions are negative. Other people tend to pick up on this and frown back. The 'angry' person, in their turn, picks up on this and has negative thoughts that everyone is against him/her, thus perpetuating the cycle. One way to break this cycle is try a behavioural experiment: smiling at a few people can produce dramatic results for a person who is always frowning!

Activity monitoring and scheduling

Activity monitoring and scheduling can be very helpful for people who are depressed. It basically means helping someone to monitor their activities and plan in a schedule of activities. This is something that becomes extremely difficult for depressed people to do. Some of the main symptoms of depression include: tiredness, a lack of energy, lethargy,

Figure 11.4   Example of a vicious cycle

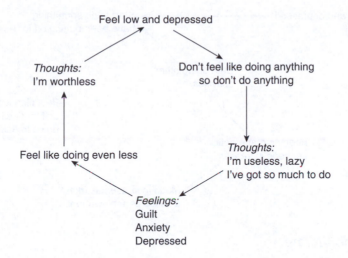

lack of motivation and general 'lowness'. It is very hard for people who are depressed to think of doing more – how can you do more if you feel so tired? Depression is exceptionally powerful in making people feel as though they cannot do anything at all. As the lack of motivation increases, almost all tasks feel overwhelming to the extent where it feels safer to do nothing at all. As the depressed person does less, they start to have negative thoughts about themselves, leading to feelings of guilt and shame – this in turn makes them feel worse. Additionally, by doing less, they are usually cutting themselves off from things that might previously have given them pleasure and stimulation. For an example of a vicious cycle, see Figure 11.4. This is just the same as the maintenance cycles shown earlier but shown here in a slightly different form, i.e. it goes round a couple of times.

This cycle could occur in lots of different forms, but the essential message is that the depressed person becomes trapped. They feel overwhelmed by small tasks and then criticise themselves for not doing anything, which makes them feel guilty and worthless, leading to further lethargic feelings. Many people compare the amount they are able to do now they are depressed with what they used to be able to do when they were feeling fine, which leads them to have negative thoughts such as 'I should be able to do that, I used to be able to do so much more' – making them feel even more worthless.

Many people think that they have somehow to summon up the motivation before they are able to become more active, and they have thoughts such as, 'I don't feel like doing that now, maybe I'll be more in the mood later.' Unfortunately, it is unlikely that the person will feel differently later. This is because motivation and the will to do something actually tends to come *after* the person has made themselves do something, even if it is something that seems very small in comparison to what the person 'used' to be able to do. This 'positive activity' cycle is illustrated in Figure 11.5. Again this is just the same as earlier maintenance cycles but in a different form.

Figure 11.5 The positive activity cycle

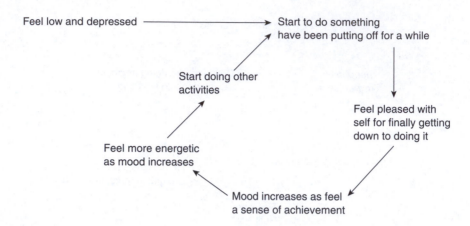

Activity monitoring

The first step of activity monitoring is for clients to be given the above information – this is key. The next step is for them to monitor current levels of activity. The client can be educated into the model by explaining that activity monitoring helps to see what he/she is doing each day and whether any activities help to lift the mood or give them a sense of achievement. Some clients can feel ashamed about the amount they are doing and it can be useful to go through examples to help them see that having a shower and eating breakfast are actually activities worth writing down. They may also be doing more than they thought they were.

An example of an activity record sheet can be found in Appendix V (see also Figure 11.6). For each hour the client can be encouraged to make an entry, even if it is sleeping or watching TV. The next task is to rate each activity for the amount of pleasure gained and the amount of achievement felt. It can be difficult for some clients to notice these aspects at all and may take some practice. While filling in an activity record, the client can be asked to rate the amount of pleasure they felt on a 0–10 scale and told not to worry if the numbers are very low but to try to differentiate between the amount of pleasure for each activity. The same can be done for level of achievement felt. The main goal is to show that some activities will be more effective in lifting mood. It can help some people to rate their mood every day on a 0–10 scale and try and see if activity has an effect on mood. Obviously there are many variables that have an effect on mood but one of them is likely to be activity level.

At the next session, the activity record can be reviewed with the client. Hopefully, there will be at least some activities that rise above zero for both pleasure and achievement.

The next step is to start helping the client to add in or schedule activities for the next week. This can happen slowly, as adding in too many activities can leave the client feeling pressurised and may make them feel worse. One way of starting to schedule

Figure 11.6   Activity monitoring sheet

(NB: See Appendix VI for a blank sheet)

Days / Time	Monday Mood = 2	Tuesday Mood = 3
9–10 a.m.	Sleeping P = 1 A = 2	Sleeping P = 1 A = 2
10–11 a.m.	Sleeping P = 1 A = 0	Sleeping P = 1 A = 1
11–12 noon	Ate breakfast in front of TV P = 1 A = 3	Had shower P = 1 A = 5
12–1 p.m.	Washed up P = 0 A = 4	Ate breakfast P = 1 A = 3
1–2 p.m.	Watched TV P = 3 A = 1	Read magazine P = 2 A = 3

Key: P = Pleasure
          A = Achievement

activities is for the client to make a list of potentially pleasurable activities and also of activities that may give a sense of achievement. This can seem like an overwhelming task, especially for those who are very depressed, so it may help just to write down a couple of activities that could be tried the next week – they need to be fairly achievable tasks. It can be helpful to decide when these tasks will be conducted so plans can be made and help can be enlisted from friends if required.

NB: A more basic activity record sheet can be used for some clients (Appendix VI) as the more detailed sheet can be overwhelming for some clients, especially if they are very depressed.

Excerpt from a session with Anne focusing on activity monitoring and scheduling

The first part of the extract focuses on discussing the concept of activity monitoring and giving Anne a rationale for filling in record sheets. The second extract focuses on activity scheduling.

Therapist:	Do you remember when we were discussing your formulation, we spent some time talking about the effect that activity has on mood?
Anne:	Vaguely, but I don't remember that much, sorry.
Therapist:	That's okay, we can spend some time on it today … I just wondered what happens to your mood when you have a day doing nothing?
Anne:	Well, I'm not doing much at all at the moment and my mood tends to be very low. I suppose I have more time to think about all the things that are going wrong and time to dwell on negative things … but I just can't seem to get the motivation together to do anything … I don't feel like doing anything and I can't seem to make myself. Then I just feel so lazy. Then I feel really guilty and ashamed of myself so I feel worse …
Therapist:	This is a common pattern in depression. People who are depressed tend to feel like doing nothing and so they don't do very much or only do the boring tasks that have to be done. This leaves them with negative thoughts such as 'I haven't achieved anything, I'm useless', and 'I'm worthless, can't even do simple tasks', and then this leads to even lower mood … and so the cycle continues.
Anne:	Well, that pretty much sums it up but I really can't get myself to do anything. What do I do about that?
Therapist:	That's the really difficult bit. It's so hard to make yourself take that first step when you feel exhausted. Do you worry that you will make yourself feel even more tired?
Anne:	Yes, I think that's definitely one of the reasons for avoiding things a bit. I feel tired and so I say to myself that if I do anything at all, I will feel even worse. So I tend to try and get some rest during the day so I will feel better.
Therapist:	And does that work?
Anne:	No, it doesn't I don't think because I just feel guilty for having a rest and feel really lazy for doing it.
Therapist:	Can you think back to any times where you have forced yourself to do something and felt better afterwards?
Anne:	I suppose so … a bit better anyway. I guess I feel a bit better if I get at least some chores done … but I should be able to do those things … they never used to be an effort … so I don't feel that much better.
Therapist:	I'm just noticing some of the thoughts you have while you're doing the chores and it sounds like you're comparing what you're able to do now with what you used to be able to do before you got depressed. Is that right?
Anne:	Oh yeah … I do that all the time … all the time. I think it makes me feel worse and even more useless.
Therapist:	Do you think those kinds of thoughts stop you from doing the things you used to find easy?
Anne:	Yes, because when I try and do things and can't, it reminds me of what I used to be able to do.
Therapist:	What you're describing is very commonly experienced by people who are depressed. Thoughts like 'I used to be able to make dinner so easily, so why can't I do it now?' and 'That's not an achievement; anyone should be able to do a pile of ironing' can really undermine anything you do manage to do.

Anne: That sounds pretty familiar, that's what I tend to do all the time. It's so hard, though. I used to be able to do so much that I feel frustrated with myself constantly now. I really don't know how to get myself out of this.

Therapist: Well, one of the first steps is to start monitoring your current levels of activity. This gives us the chance to see if anything you are doing helps to lift your mood. I'll just show you a monitoring sheet … On these sheets anything counts as activity. Sleeping is an activity, as is eating breakfast and having a shower. Shall we fill in a day together as an example?

Anne: Okay then, but I really haven't been doing much … it's actually really embarrassing, I feel like such a lazy person.

Therapist: People often worry about this bit but in some ways it can make the next stage, where you add in activities, easier as anything you add in is progress.

Anne: I suppose that's true.

Therapist: So how about yesterday? Shall we take it from 8 a.m.?

Anne: Well that's pretty easy. I got hardly any sleep the night before, so I slept until about 11.30.

Therapist: Sleeping counts as an activity so we'll put sleeping into each of those squares. It can be helpful to rate the amount of pleasure you felt from each activity on a 0–10 scale and also the amount of achievement on a 0–10 scale.

Anne: Well, I suppose I felt a little achievement in sleeping as I find it hard to sleep. It would have been better to sleep at night, though. I'll give it a 1 for achievement and probably a 1 for pleasure as well. Is that right?

Therapist: Yes that sounds fine. Did you get up when you woke up or did you stay in bed a while longer?

Anne: I stayed in bed until about one. I kept thinking about getting up but just couldn't seem to. When I got up, I made myself eat some breakfast/lunch which I suppose is an achievement as I find it hard to do. I didn't manage to have a shower, which would have been good as I think that makes me feel a little bit better. I then sat on the sofa watching TV.

Therapist: Okay, I've written those things down. How long were you watching TV for?

Anne: Pretty much all afternoon … till about 5 … then I finally got off the sofa and made some toast for tea. I phoned a friend at about 6.

Therapist: And can we do some ratings for all those activities … what about having breakfast/lunch?

Anne: Well, that was an achievement and I'd give it a 4 for achievement but I didn't enjoy eating it, so maybe 1 for pleasure …

The above conversation might continue along the same lines for a while. The client could be given an activity monitoring diary to take home and fill in for the next session. It can be helpful to ask the client to rate their general mood on a 0–10 scale at the end of each day, which may help to identify which activities lift mood (although obviously activity is only one aspect which has an effect on mood). Clients often worry about how to fill in the record sheets 'properly' and it may be important to pre-empt this by discussing it with clients first and asking them about any concerns they might have. Make it clear that the form does not have to be neat, spelling really doesn't matter, and so on.

The extract below could be taken from the next session with Anne. She will have had a couple of weeks to fill in the record sheets and will be bringing the sheets back to discuss. The next step would be activity scheduling which is discussed in the dialogue.

Therapist:	So I see you've brought along the record sheets we discussed last time. Have you had a chance to fill them in at all?
Anne:	Well, sort of. I'm really not sure whether I've done them right.
Therapist:	We can just have a look over them. The main thing is that they make sense to you and enough sense to me that we can discuss them together.
	[*Client and therapist look over record sheets together.*]
Therapist:	So, looking at the day after we last met to start with … it looks as though that was a bit busier than I thought it would be from our discussions last time.
Anne:	Yes, I actually tried to do much more for the first few days because I was embarrassed about how little I was doing.
Therapist:	So the first few days were very busy by the looks of things … you've been getting up earlier and you've been shopping and swimming …
Anne:	Yes, I did manage it for the first few days and it did seem to make me feel a lot better and I felt like I'd been able to achieve a lot but I just couldn't keep it up.
Therapist:	Well, I'm really impressed you gave it such a go and it's good that for a few days it did help to improve your mood … . What do you think happened then?
Anne:	I think I did a bit too much and couldn't keep it going. I went back to what I was doing before and felt even worse because I thought I should be doing more … . I suppose I need to do something in between the two …
Therapist:	Yes, I was thinking the same thing … It seems as though you've now found out that doing a bit more can help your mood but it's a case of getting some balance so you don't exhaust yourself … . Maybe getting up an hour earlier every other day rather than every day … . Shall we have a look through the next fortnight's record sheets and just plan in some activities so that you have them written down and planned in advance?
Anne:	Yes, that sounds like a good plan and it might stop me from overdoing it …
Therapist:	So just thinking about tomorrow … what sort of time do you want to get up?
Anne:	I'll say about 12 to actually get up out of bed and maybe I'll try and have a shower and breakfast. I could pop to the local shop tomorrow, and then I'll leave it there and do what I normally do.
Therapist:	Great, that sounds realistic and manageable, so maybe the day after could be just like a normal day with no added extras. What do you reckon?
Anne:	Yes, that sounds fine …
Therapist:	How about the day after, do you want to get up an hour earlier again?
Anne:	Yes and I'll make sure I have a shower and breakfast and … hmm … maybe I'll go swimming.
Therapist:	Sounds good, so a quiet day the day after?
Anne:	Yup …

The above conversation could continue along the same lines or the therapist could use their judgement and leave the client to plan the rest of the record sheet themselves. A problem which often arises during activity scheduling is that clients feel they should be doing much more or they dismiss improvements because they feel they used to be able to do a lot more before their problems started. These 'negative thoughts' can be captured and challenged (see Chapters 13 and 14).

Summary

- Behavioural exposure is most useful with people who are anxious and have started to use avoidance as a coping strategy.
- Behavioural experiments are a way of trying out tasks without failing – every outcome is an opportunity for learning.
- Activity scheduling is most useful with depressed people.
- However, these strategies can be useful for many different types of problems.
- Psycho-education with regards to positive and negative activity cycles is an important first step.
- Activity monitoring then helps to gain an understanding of what the person might already be doing and what helps/doesn't help.
- Activity scheduling can be very helpful but it is important to note if the client is having any negative thoughts as these may impede progress. See Chapters 13 and 14 for how to manage negative thoughts.

Further reading

Kennerly, H. (1997) *Overcoming Anxiety.* London: Robinson.

Moore, R.G. & Garland, A. (2003) *Cognitive Therapy for Chronic and Persistent Depression,* Clinical Psychology series. Chichester: Wiley.

Pedrick, C. & Hyman, B. (2005) *The OCD Workbook: Your Guide to Breaking Free from Obsessive-Compulsive Disorder.* Oakland, CA: New Harbinger Publications.

12

Cognitive Interventions:
Psycho-education about Thoughts and Beliefs

The first stage in working with negative automatic thoughts is to identify them. This may be relatively easy for some clients, but more difficult for others. In order to correctly identify cognitions your client needs to understand what a 'thought' is, and (probably more importantly) what it is not. Once negative automatic thoughts can be identified, they can be evaluated and alternative ways of looking at things can be developed. In this chapter we will cover psycho-education about thoughts and beliefs.

Psycho-education about thoughts and beliefs

The difference between a thought and a fact

For many people thoughts are so frequent and strongly held that they feel like facts. It is in our nature as human beings to believe that our beliefs are true (otherwise we would not believe them!) but people suffering from depression, anxiety or obsessional problems are prone to very strongly held, rigid and fixed beliefs. People who are suffering from severe depression are particularly likely to confuse a thought with a fact. It is therefore worthwhile spending some time exploring the nature of thoughts and beliefs with your client before starting the work on identifying and evaluating unhelpful thoughts. Have a discussion with your client about the difference between *believing* something to be true and something *actually* being true. In order to illustrate this point we have found it helpful to start with non-negative examples. Most people presenting for therapy will answer 'no' when asked by the therapist: 'If I believe that I have a fabulous singing voice, does that mean that I definitely have a fabulous singing voice?' – some in fact finding it ridiculous or amusing to think that this thought implies fact. Once you have made the point using a couple of positive examples, move on to examples of negative thoughts. Most people will be less biased when thinking of other people's situations compared to their own. It is therefore best to start with 'third-party' examples, such as, 'If Rosie believes that the reason her neighbour cancelled dinner is that she does not like her, does this mean that Rosie's neighbour definitely does not like her?' Talk through a few 'third-party' examples before moving on to examples of your client's own negative thoughts. The important point to come out of this work is that a thought does not *necessarily* imply fact. Be careful not to imply that a thought *definitely* does not imply fact.

Psycho-education on this point is particularly important when working with people with obsessive compulsive disorder (OCD). This is because a common feature of OCD is that the person feels very distressed about having had a thought that is unacceptable to them. We will cover psycho-education about obsessional thoughts in more detail later.

The function of thoughts and beliefs

So if thoughts and beliefs do not *necessarily* reflect the reality of a situation, why do we develop them? This is a useful question to explore with your client. In order to be able to function as human beings we need to make assumptions to predict what will happen in a given situation. If we did not do this we would have to treat each new situation naively as if it were the first time we had encountered that type of situation; we could not generalise from other similar situations that we might previously have encountered. This would be extremely tedious and time-consuming so we develop assumptions and beliefs to help us take 'short cuts'. The problem is that as a result we sometimes get these assumptions wrong. Here is an everyday example. I am sitting on a chair at my desk and notice a book that I would like to look at on a shelf above my desk. I stand up to reach the book, flick through, read what I need to read and then, without looking, sit back down on my chair. During this process I have made an assumption that my chair will still be there when I sit back down. However, *thinking* that my chair will be there and it *actually* being there are not the same thing. I was caught out once when a colleague entered the room, saw me standing up, did not realise I was using the chair and moved it. In order never to make this mistake again I would have to check that the chair was there, by looking or feeling for it before sitting down (and I did for some time!). We need to have assumptions and beliefs about the world around us in order to function effectively and efficiently and it is not the aim of CBT to remove them – which would be impossible and undesirable anyway. The aim of CBT is to remove the negative *bias* in these thoughts, assumptions and beliefs, not to remove them altogether. We are usually unaware of bias because we naturally assume that what we believe is a good reflection of reality. If we are depressed or anxious our cognitions are particularly likely to be biased to be a more negative reflection of reality. As discussed earlier in the book, we are more likely to develop negative core beliefs, assumptions and thoughts if we have experienced lots of negative events in the past, but this negative bias might not be appropriate for current or future situations (see Chapter 4).

What gets in the way of reality and our thoughts?

You will have oriented your client to the CBT model earlier in therapy (see Chapter 3) so they should already understand the different elements of the CBT maintenance cycle and how different thoughts can have different consequences for feelings and behaviours. This should be reiterated and the client's understanding of thoughts and beliefs should be developed further, prior to starting thought identification and evaluation work. It is useful to discuss how our thoughts are influenced by our *interpretation* of an event or situation and the meanings that we attach to them. As our thoughts are 'automatic' we are not usually consciously aware of this process.

In order to illustrate this point it might be helpful to talk through some hypothetical examples with your client. Here are some that we use.

The parents

Naomi and Martin have an 18-year-old daughter Isobel. Isobel has gone out with her friends and has promised her parents that she will be home by midnight. Naomi and Martin go to bed at 11.30 p.m. and listen for Isobel arriving home. Midnight passes and Isobel has not arrived home, so her parents continue to listen out for her. At 1.30 a.m. they hear the front door close and Isobel creeping up the stairs. Martin feels angry, but Naomi feels overjoyed. This is because Naomi and Martin have interpreted the situation differently, resulting in different NATs and subsequent emotions. Martin thought: 'She is so inconsiderate, how dare she worry us by not getting home on time', whereas Naomi thought: 'She has not come home – something bad might have happened to her'.

The train

Three friends are travelling on a crowded train from Leeds to Bristol. The train stops in a tunnel without warning, close to the station in Bristol. After five minutes a voice comes over the intercom and says 'We apologise for this delay, which is due to unforeseen circumstances.' The three friends experience different emotions when the train stops.

Figure 12.1   Maintenance cycle for Vicky

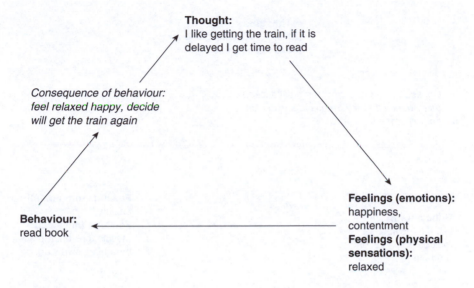

Thought:
I like getting the train, if it is delayed I get time to read

Consequence of behaviour: feel relaxed happy, decide will get the train again

Behaviour:
read book

Feelings (emotions):
happiness, contentment
Feelings (physical sensations):
relaxed

Vicky feels happy, Louise feels angry and Dawn feels anxious. This is because the friends have different thoughts about the situation. Vicky thinks: 'I like the train. I get a chance to read and I can finish my magazine.' Louise thinks: 'These tickets cost a fortune, the trains are never on time and they don't even bother to tell us what the problem is.' Dawn thinks: 'There is a problem with the train – it is not safe.'

In both of these examples the situations are the same for the people involved. It cannot therefore be the situation alone that is responsible for the different thoughts and subsequent feelings that each individual experiences. It is the *interpretations* of the situations that result in the different thoughts and emotions for the individuals involved. We cannot assume that our thoughts are fact because they are subject to the *interpretations* that we make.

We will now look at how Vicky's and Dawn's thoughts impact on subsequent emotions, physical sensations and behaviours in the CBT maintenance cycles illustrated in Figures 12.1 and 12.2.

The maintenance cycles for both Dawn and Vicky show how the feelings and behaviours resulting from the initial thought serve to reinforce that thought. This is how what is often called a 'vicious cycle' begins.

Additional psycho-education for individuals with obsessional problems

Clients presenting with obsessional problems will need some further psycho-education about the nature of their thoughts. Obsessional thoughts are unwanted, repetitive

Figure 12.2 Maintenance cycle for Dawn

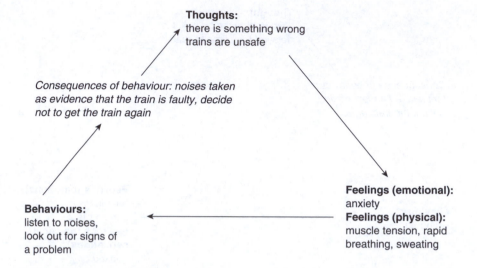

Thoughts:
there is something wrong
trains are unsafe

Consequences of behaviour: noises taken
as evidence that the train is faulty, decide
not to get the train again

Behaviours:
listen to noises,
look out for signs of
a problem

Feelings (emotional):
anxiety
Feelings (physical):
muscle tension, rapid
breathing, sweating

thoughts (or images) that come into a person's mind against their will. These 'intrusive' thoughts are experienced as very distressing because the content of the thought is unacceptable and/or shocking to the person. Common examples include: 'I left the cooker on; the house will burn down and kill the neighbours', 'I have spread disease', 'I might have hit a pedestrian while driving', 'I have harmed the baby'.

Everybody experiences intrusive thoughts at times; one theory suggests that as humans we have evolved to experience intrusive thoughts as random alerts to potential risks and threats in the environment. These are ignored most of the time as they are irrelevant. In people who develop obsessional problems the thoughts are not dismissed as irrelevant but instead a meaning is attached to having had the intrusive thought. It is this 'thought about the thought' or 'appraisal' that determines whether or not the experience of the intrusive thought leads to distress and ultimately the development of obsessional problems.

It is important to stress the point that a person who has an intrusive thought about doing something unacceptable is no more likely to do the unacceptable thing than somebody who has not had the intrusive thought. It is this point that people with obsessional problems often fail to realise. They assume that the fact they have thought the thought (or seen the image) must mean something terrible about themselves as people. In the extreme this is called 'thought–action fusion'. The person thinks that having had the thought is as bad (or almost as bad) as having done the act. For example, a new mother who has a thought about harming her baby sees herself as a 'bad mother' who harms her baby.

As discussed earlier, it is the 'appraisal' of the 'intrusive' thought that constitutes the NAT for individuals with obsessional problems, rather than the intrusive thought itself.

To illustrate this point here is a scenario involving an intrusive thought that is very common in the general population.

The church

Sarah and Bradley are getting married. Silence falls in the church as the clergyman asks: 'Does anyone know of any reason why these two people should not be joined together in holy matrimony, speak now or forever hold your peace'. All four bridesmaids experience an intrusive thought at this point. They think a thought along the lines of 'I am going to shout out "yes"'. They see images of themselves standing up and shouting out while the bride, groom and congregation look on in horror. The four bridesmaids all have different appraisals of this thought. Amal thinks: 'I could stand up and say that, but of course I am not going to!' Rebecca thinks: 'How funny, I wonder if anyone else thought the same thing.' Eloise thinks: 'That was a random, meaningless, intrusive thought', and Karen thinks: 'How terrible of me to want to do something so awful on my friend's special day'. None of the bridesmaids actually did stand up and shout 'yes' and Karen (who experienced the most negative appraisal) was no more likely to do it than the others. Karen did, however, experience the most distress as a consequence of her appraisal of the intrusive thought.

This example illustrates the point that it is not the intrusive thought itself that causes the person distress, but the meaning that is attached to it. It is therefore this appraisal of the intrusive thought rather than the intrusive thought itself that needs evaluation using cognitive strategies.

Summary

- Thoughts, assumptions and beliefs do not necessarily reflect fact.
- Thoughts, beliefs and assumptions serve functions.
- Our thoughts about a given situation depend on our interpretation of the situation. This is why different people can have different thoughts about the same situation.
- Most people experience intrusive thoughts at times.
- Thinking about doing something does not mean that you will do it.
- Negative thoughts and beliefs are common for people suffering from depression, anxiety and obsessional problems.
- CBT aims to correct the negative bias in the thought processes of people suffering from mental health problems.

13

Cognitive Interventions:
Identifying Negative Automatic Thoughts (NATs)

Most of our thoughts are not pondered on, or even brought into conscious awareness, so identifying negative automatic thoughts can be difficult. Even if thoughts are thought about, if they imply fact (as discussed earlier) they are unlikely to be questioned. Before moving on to thought evaluation, the client will therefore need to learn how to spot the NATs in their thinking.

Identification of NATs is the essential first step to changing thinking processes through cognitive techniques, but it can cause problems. When clients are asked to identify and record NATs they will be consciously attending to the NATs more than usual. A risk of this focus on the negative is that the client can start to feel even more negative or hopeless. A drop in mood is a particularly high risk for clients presenting with depression. It is therefore important that the client learns the skills needed to evaluate and challenge NATs soon after they have learnt the skills needed to recognise them. This can be a problem if the client or therapist is unavailable (takes a holiday, for example) after the work on identifying NATs, so forward planning is advisable. Although unpleasant for the client, a negative change in emotions through focusing on NATs can be made use of in therapy. The experience can be used to illustrate the effect that NATs have on emotions and behaviour by using the CBT maintenance cycle. Here is an excerpt from a session with Anne, when this is discussed in the homework review:

Therapist: So how did you get on with recording your negative automatic thoughts during the week?
Anne: Well, I noticed that I was having lots of them, all the time really. I wrote some down here. [*Passes therapist a thought record sheet*]
Therapist: Thank you, let's have a look. [*Anne and therapist look at the record sheet*] So you were having lots of thoughts along the lines of being lazy, there being no point in doing anything and your friends not wanting to see you?

Anne:	Yes, among others. Once I started recording them I realised that I was having them all the time.
Therapist:	It sounds like that was a bit of a surprise.
Anne:	Yes it was. I hadn't realised how negative I have become.
Therapist:	And how did it feel to notice all these negative thoughts?
Anne:	Awful, I just felt terrible thinking about it. I mean, I know they must have been there all the time, but it really made me think about how dreadful things are.
Therapist:	So focusing on the negative thoughts seems to have affected your mood?
Anne:	Yes, I think it did, I think I would just rather not think about it.
Therapist:	Yes I can see how difficult it has been for you. As we discussed before when we talked about how CBT works, after identifying the thoughts the next stage is to work out what to do with them in order to reduce the distress that they cause.
Anne:	That would be good.
Therapist:	It is interesting that focusing on the negative automatic thoughts has led you to feel even more low. I suppose that shows us what an impact they can have on how you feel emotionally.
Anne:	Yes, they certainly seemed to affect my mood.
Therapist:	And it does make sense that focusing on the negative makes you feel worse.
Anne:	Yes, I can see that now. I have just realised how negative I am all the time. I wish I wasn't, but it is all true.
Therapist:	It seems important then that we move on to look at some strategies for dealing with the thoughts, now that you are able to identify the NATs that you are having.
Anne:	I suppose so. I don't want to keep feeling like this.

As might have been predicted, focusing on the NATs leads to deterioration in Anne's mood. The therapist empathises with this, and then explains what has happened within a CBT framework. It is important that the client understands the rationale for recording NATs – that it is a necessary first step to changing thinking, otherwise there is a risk that he or she will lose motivation.

How to help clients elicit NATS

We will now discuss some techniques which can be used to help clients elicit NATs.

Discussion of recent situations

The client is asked to recall a specific recent difficult situation or event, which should be focused on and described in as much detail as possible. The therapist should ask first about the client's emotional response to the situation, as this can help the client to access the specific NATs.

Use of imagery

In some cases the real potency of a NAT is revealed through enquiry about mental images. If the client is having trouble accessing the NAT verbally, or if the negativity of a thought associated with a situation does not seem in proportion to the level of distress reported, it can be helpful to ask about mental images. If negative images are identified, then the therapist can make use of the imagery strategies for changing negative cognitions discussed later on.

Here is an excerpt from a session with Andy where the therapist identifies negative images:

> *Therapist*: So you were on the bus and you started feeling really panicky and had a strong urge to get off the bus?
> *Andy*: Yes, I suddenly felt really really anxious.
> *Therapist*: Can you remember what went through your mind at the time?
> *Andy*: I just thought 'I have to get off the bus now.'
> *Therapist*: And anything before that?
> *Andy*: No, not really. I think I might have wondered whether people were looking at me.
> *Therapist*: Can you remember why you thought that people would be looking at you?
> *Andy*: I am not sure; I can't really remember what I was thinking.
> *Therapist*: Do you remember getting any images at the time, for example of yourself, or something happening?
> *Andy*: I'm not quite sure. What do you mean?
> *Therapist*: Well sometimes people see a picture in their mind of themselves, or what might happen in a certain situation.
> *Andy*: Oh I see what you mean. I think I saw myself going red and sweating – yes, that's what went through my mind, and then I imagined people looking at me and then moving away.

In this example the therapist enquires about images, as the NATs Andy identifies do not seem negative enough to explain the extremely powerful emotions that he experienced. The therapist could go on to use imagery techniques, for example imagining a different outcome.

The worst case scenario

This is a useful technique for eliciting the negative component of the automatic thought. Sometimes the client will describe a thought that is not, in itself, negative. It is rather the meaning behind the statement that is negative. Examples of these thoughts include:

- The telephone is ringing.
- He is going away for the weekend.
- She hasn't taken her shoes off.

If the therapist prompts by asking 'What is the worst thing that could happen if X, Y, Z?' or 'What does it mean if this is true?', then the actual negative belief can be elicited. For example:

- The telephone is ringing. → I will sound stupid.
- He is going away for the weekend. → He is going to leave me.
- She hasn't taken her shoes off. → She does not respect me.

Using role play to explore situations

This is a useful technique for when thoughts and emotions associated with specific situations are not easily elicited from memory. The therapist and client enact a situation in session and the therapist stops at key points to ask the client how they are feeling or what they are thinking. The therapist should be aware that re-enacting difficult situations can be a powerful emotional experience for the client. It is important that the client is prepared for this, and there is enough time allowed at the end of the session for client and therapist to 'de-role'.

Diary keeping

It is harder to access thoughts and emotions connected with specific situations after the situation has passed. The therapist should ask the client to keep a diary or record sheet between sessions, so that important events can be remembered and discussed in therapy. As mentioned earlier, clients with obsessional problems usually experience an intrusive thought and a subsequent appraisal of the thought (the appraisal being the target of cognitive interventions). The record sheet for these clients is therefore modified to take this into account. Examples of completed thought record sheets for Anne, Andy and Megan are shown in Figures 13.1, 13.2 and 13.3. Although it is not essential, we find that recording emotions, physical sensations and behaviours in addition to NATs is useful, as the information can then be used to illustrate the maintenance cycle. If you feel that recording this amount of information would 'burden' your client too much (and perhaps result in reduced compliance) you can use the simpler thought record sheet (as in Figure 13.1), and then explore associated emotions, physical sensations and behaviours in the homework review part of the next session. The therapist should complete the record sheet first with the client in a therapy session before asking the client to use it between sessions as a homework task. Blank versions of all three of our examples of thought record sheets are provided in the appendices.

When the client first starts to record NATs and images alone it can be helpful for them to have a list of questions handy as an aid to identifying the thought or image. Here is a

Figure 13.1 Thought record sheet for Anne (basic)

Date	Situation	Emotion(s)	Thoughts and/or images
	Where were you? Who was there? What were you doing? When?	*What did you feel at the time? How strongly did you feel it? (0–10)*	*How strongly do you believe the thought? (0–10)*
	Monday morning, lying in bed Jack had gone to work	(1) Guilty – 9.5 (2) Disgusted with myself – 9 (3) Low – 8	(1) I am lazy – 10 (2) I am useless – 9 (3) I am pathetic – 10

Figure 13.2 Thought record sheet for Andy (detailed)

Date	Situation	Emotion(s)	Thoughts and/or images	Physical sensations	Behaviours
	Where were you? Who was there? What were you doing? When?	*What did you feel at the time? How strongly did you feel it (0–10)*	*How strongly do you believe the thought? (0–10)*	*Did you notice any changes in your body at the time?*	*What did you do after experiencing the NAT?*
	On the bus going into town	Anxious – 9.5 Embarrassed – 8.5 Image of myself sweating and going red, people staring and moving away	I have to get off the bus – 9	Heart beat fast, started to feel hot, hands went tense, started breathing quickly	Got off the bus

list of suggested questions. (We have included this in Appendix VIII as a handout that can be given to clients.)

- What was going through your mind before you felt guilty/anxious/sad?
- What does this say about you if it is true?
- What were/are you afraid might happen?
- What would be the worst thing that could happen if it is true?
- What does this mean about what the other person thinks about you?
- What does this mean about the other person (or people in general)?
- What images do you have about the situation?

Thinking biases

Negative thoughts can be put into categories according to their meaning. These categories are sometimes called 'thinking errors', 'twisted thinking' or 'cognitive distortions'.

Figure 13.3   Thought record sheet for Megan (obsessive compulsive disorder)

Date	Situation	Intrusive thought/ image	Appraisals	Emotion(s) sensations	Physical	Behaviours
	Where were you? Who was there? What were you doing? When?	What was the thought or image that came into your mind?	What was your thought about the intrusive thought?	What did you feel at the time? How Strongly did you feel it? (0–10)	Did you notice any changes in your body at the time?	What did you do after experiencing the NAT?
	At home alone with Molly Heard her crying in her cot	I thought 'I will harm Molly if I touch her'	'I am dangerous' 'I am a bad mother' 'I shouldn't be left alone with her'	Anxious – 7 Low – 6 Guilty – 8	Felt my heart beating fast	Washed my hands ten times then went to Molly

We will refer to them as 'thinking biases'. It is not essential to work on thinking biases in CBT, but if you do it can give the client a useful short cut to identifying and challenging NATs. Numerous categories of thinking biases have been described in the CBT literature. In Figure 13.4 we have outlined some of the most common thinking biases and given examples of NATs for each. We have also included this in the Appendix IX as a handout for clients. We find that the most useful thing about this work is that it helps clients to spot patterns in their thinking. It is less important that the thoughts are allocated to exactly the right category. There is after all some overlap between the categories, and some thoughts fit into multiple categories. Different people are 'prone' to different thinking biases, but we find that most clients easily recognise at least two or three thinking biases that are common in their own thinking. Identification of a thinking error alone can instigate a challenge to the negative thought.

Psycho-education around thinking errors

Have a general discussion with your client about these different thinking errors, covering the following points:

- We all have thinking biases. However, people with mental health problems probably have them more often.
- Some thinking errors are more common in certain problems. Social anxiety, for example, is often accompanied by mind-reading, and obsessional problems by personalisation and black-and-white thinking. Depression is frequently accompanied by fortune-telling.
- Being aware of the common categories of thinking errors can help people to identify and challenge NATs.

Figure 13.4 Thinking biases

Catastrophising
When the worst possible outcome is predicted and magnified
If I make a mistake I will lose my job.
I can feel my heart beating fast, I am going to die.

Mind-reading
Guessing another person's thoughts
They thought I looked stupid.
She didn't really want to meet up with me.

Fortune-telling
Predicting a bleak future, without evidence for it
There is no point, I will just fail at it.
I am always going to be like this.
No one will ever love me.

All-or-nothing (black-and-white) thinking
Only seeing the extremes, being unable to see the 'grey' area
If I don't get 100 per cent I am a failure.
If he doesn't phone me every day he doesn't love me.

Discounting the positive
When positives are viewed as worthless or meaningless
He was just saying that to be nice.
Anyone could have done that.
NB: Look out for 'yes buts' in response to positive information.

Overgeneralisation
A single negative event is viewed as affecting everything, or as a signal that everything will go wrong
The bus didn't turn up. Everything is going wrong.
I burnt the cake. The whole party is a disaster.

Personalisation
Feeling responsible when not at fault
It's my fault no one is enjoying themselves.
They cancelled the trip because they don't want to go with me.

Next, move on to discuss specific thinking biases:

Catastrophising

This is when the consequences of a negative event are predicated to be disastrous. Often the outcome is not as bad as predicted, or the negative consequences can be easily resolved through problem solving strategies.

Mind-reading

Discuss how we can never know fully what another person is thinking. We can guess what they may be thinking by using their behaviour and body language as clues, but these are just guesses and prone to mistakes. There is always more than one explanation for a particular action or behaviour that we witness in another.

Fortune-telling

Fortune-telling is a particularly damaging thinking error. This is because, if we strongly believe something will happen, we can (non-intentionally) behave in ways to make it more likely to happen. This is a well-known psychological effect called a 'self-fulfilling prophecy'. Discuss how none of us can really predict the future (if we could, we could make a lot at the bookies!).

All-or-northing (black and white) thinking

This is when thinking becomes polarised into extreme positives or negatives. Have a discussion with your client about the 'grey area' in between the extremes. Do they often find it hard to see this grey area?

Discounting the positive

This can be a hard to spot. Look out for 'yes buts' when discussing positive experiences or successes with your client. Explain how positive information does not 'fit' with a generally negative mental state, and is therefore 'disqualified', as if it can't be true. Would the client have the same attitude if they were thinking about somebody else's experiences?

Overgeneralisation

We cannot assume that because something happens once it will always happen. Similarly, we cannot assume that because something negative happens in one context it will happen in other contexts. Sometimes it can make us feel more in control to believe that we *know* that something will always be the case, but we rarely do.

Personalisation

Most situations or events are not the sole responsibility or fault of one person. Like overgeneralisation, feelings of control may be important in the development of these types of beliefs. Although personalisation often leads to feelings of guilt or shame, it can also give the person a sense of control over things; if you are responsible, you can do something about it.

As part of orienting your client to different categories of thinking error, you can use a practical exercise that we often use when teaching CBT, explained in Appendix X. You will notice that NATs can sometimes fall into more than one of these categories. It is the conversation around the thinking biases that is the really useful part of this exercise. Do not worry if you are unable to 'pigeon hole' certain NATs into a thinking bias category.

After reviewing the common types of 'thinking biases', identify some of the client's recent NATs and discuss which thinking-bias categories they fall into. We have illustrated an example of this type of conversation for Andy:

Therapist:	So those are some common ways that our thinking can become distorted. It sounds like you recognise some of them in your own thinking.
Andy:	Yes, I think I do some of them a lot, without realising.
Therapist:	Let's think of some specific examples. Earlier you were telling me about a thought that you often had when the phone rang when you were working.
Andy:	Yes, I thought that it would be my boss. I thought that he would ask me to do a presentation and I would make a fool of myself.
Therapist:	So the thought was 'I will make a fool of myself' when the phone rang?
Andy	Yes, that's right.
Therapist	So, looking at the different categories of thinking error, what type of thinking biases might have been relevant to the thought 'I will make a fool of myself'?
Andy:	[*Looks through sheet*] I am not sure really…um…
Therapist:	Well it sounds as though you thought you knew at the time what would happen in a presentation.
Andy:	Yes, well no, at the time it felt as though I definitely *knew* what would happen if I did the presentation.
Therapist:	Okay, so looking back did you really know as a fact, what would happen.
Andy:	No, I suppose not. I was making a prediction about what would happen.
Therapist:	So it sounds like you were 'fortune-telling'?
Andy:	Yes, I think I was.
Therapist:	Let's see, what else might have been happening to your thoughts. When the phone rang you thought 'It's my boss, he wants me to do a presentation'?
Andy:	That's right.
Therapist:	So it sounds like you were 'fortune-telling' that it would be your boss, and also 'mind-reading' what your boss would be thinking?
Andy	Yes, it could have been anyone – the phone has the same ring whoever calls! It is not always my boss. In fact it is rarely my boss, and even if it had been he could have been calling for anything.
Therapist:	So now let's think a bit more about your other thoughts at the time you thought 'I will make a fool of myself'. What would be the worst thing about making a fool of yourself?
Andy:	At the time I was thinking that I might lose my job.
Therapist:	Do you think that thought would fit into any of the categories of thinking bias that we have discussed?

Andy: [*Looks through thinking error sheet*] Perhaps I was catastrophising at the time. It probably was unlikely that I would lose my job, and I think I was 'fortune-telling' what would happen.

In this example Andy and the therapist identify which thinking biases Andy was making in his NATs. The therapist could go on to have a discussion with Andy about whether he feels that these biases are a common feature of his thinking. If the client seems to respond well to the thinking bias work, and it helps them to make sense of their NATs, it can be helpful to incorporate a column for 'thinking errors' into the thought record sheet and thought evaluation sheets that will be discussed later. Blank versions of these forms are provided in the Appendices, which are available to download from www.sage pub.co.uk/simmons

Summary

- Identification of negative automatic thoughts is the first stage to evaluating NATs.
- Focusing on NATs can affect mood – it is therefore important to move on promptly in therapy to evaluating NATs.
- Role play, discussion of recent events, imagining the worst case scenario, use of imagery and diary keeping can all help the client elicit NATs.
- The NAT for people with OCD is usually the appraisal of an intrusive thought.
- NATs can take the form of images.
- Having a list of questions can help clients identify NATs.
- NATs can be grouped into categories of different thinking biases.
- Spotting thinking biases can help client's recognise NATs.
- A list of responses to the client's common thinking biases can help challenge NATs.

14

Cognitive Interventions:
Evaluation of Negative Automatic Thoughts
or 'Thought Challenging'

The technique of evaluating of NATs (sometimes known as 'thought challenging') is the primary cognitive strategy in CBT. It is based on the idea that people who are experiencing psychological distress have distorted patterns of thinking. Their thoughts are not a true reflection of reality, but are biased towards a more negative reflection of reality. As discussed earlier, thinking can be distorted in different ways, and some of these 'thinking biases' are particularly common in people experiencing mental health problems. Thought evaluation is a cognitive technique that aims to correct the negative bias in thought processes. This then leads to more positive feelings and behaviours.

NAT evaluation should first be learnt and practised in session with the therapist. Once the client has the necessary skills, NATS can be recorded and evaluated as homework practice between sessions. Pertinent or problematic examples can then be discussed in session with the therapist.

Deciding which NATs to focus on

As session time is limited it is important to focus on NATS that are central to the client's problems. If several NATS are elicited in a conversation you will need to decide which thoughts to focus on in session. In order to do this it is helpful to revisit the formulation, therapy goals and session agenda. Below are some questions to consider when deciding whether or not to focus on a particular NAT.

Does the thought seem relevant to the formulation of the client's problems?

Remember that the formulation provides the understanding of the problem and structure for therapy. Can you see how the NAT would fit into a CBT maintenance cycle?

Does the thought relate to a problem that was not identified during assessment and formulation?

If this is the case, the issue might need to be incorporated into the formulation. Alternatively, the thought might relate to a separate problem or issue that would be best addressed outside the therapy, or in a different stage of therapy. A very practical problem such as not having enough time to get important jobs done, could be dealt with through other support systems, or through problem solving techniques (see Chapter 16).

Will addressing the thought help you and the client meet the goals of the session?

To answer this question, go back to the session agenda. It is not usually possible to cover all issues in one session, especially for clients with complex or multiple problems. It is important that the session retains a focus. If the thought does not seem related to the agenda topics, gently remind the client of them. If the thought seems very important you can offer to alter the agenda based on the new issue that has been raised, for example, 'It sounds as though that thought was very distressing for you. We had planned to focus on thoughts around failing this week, but should we review the agenda in light of this thought?' If the issue seems less pressing, you can discuss putting it on the agenda for the following session, for example, 'That sounds like an important negative thought. We had decided to focus on thoughts around failure for today's session, but should we put it on the agenda for next week?'

Is the thought distorted or dysfunctional?

Is there evidence of thinking bias in the client's thought? The client might have some negative thoughts that are not particularly biased or causing undue problems. If this is the case, then there is less of an argument for focusing on them. The thought might reflect reality – it would after all be abnormal if everything around us was positive. If it seems as though the thought is an accurate interpretation of reality, yet is causing significant distress, see Chapters 10 and 16 on coping strategies and problem solving.

Does the thought cause emotional distress?

The most important NATs to focus on are the ones that cause emotional distress. You can look for physical signs of an emotional impact of the thought, such as changes in breathing, speech and facial expression. If unsure about the emotional impact that the thought had at the time, you can ask the client 'How did this thought make you feel?' If you feel that your client is unable to access or describe emotions associated with the thought see Chapter 17 on working with emotions.

Does the client believe the thought?

NATs that are strongly believed are likely to have more impact on emotions and behaviours than thoughts that are less strongly held. Ask the client: 'How strongly did you believe the thought at the time – let's say from 0–10 with 0 being not at all, to 10 being totally?' People with obsessional problems are, however, often plagued by shocking unwanted thoughts that they do not rationally believe, yet which they respond to because of the high levels of emotion elicited. As discussed in Chapter 12, it is the appraisal of the intrusive thought rather than the intrusive thought itself that needs evaluation. In these cases, the therapist should look for how strongly held the appraisal is when deciding whether to focus on it. For example: 'So you had an intrusive image of yourself smothering the baby and then thought "I am a bad mother because I thought about harming my child"? How strongly did were believe that you were a bad mother at the time?'

Evaluating negative automatic thoughts

This is often called 'thought challenging' but we believe this label can be misleading. CBT does not aim to directly challenge thoughts, assuming they are 'wrong', as this can have the effect of strengthening the NAT and underlying core belief. Although you might have suspicions, you will not know whether or not the NATs are biased when you first start working on them with your client. What CBT does aim to do is explore NATs to find out if they are biased; if found to be so, then alternative ways of thinking are developed. It is important that the therapist takes a non-judgemental stance rather than assuming that the thoughts are biased or 'wrong' from the outset. One way of evaluating NATs is for the therapist and client to consider evidence both for the thought and against the thought. Only direct factual evidence should be used in the evaluation. The client might initially put forward feelings or other NATs as evidence supporting the NAT, but these do not count as evidence. We often say: 'Would that stand up in court as evidence?' The example below for Andy illustrates the process of generating evidence for and against a NAT and some of the difficulties that can arise.

> *Therapist*: So when you were thinking about the presentation you had the thought 'I will lose my job'. When we thought about this some more you identified the thought: 'I am no good at my job.'
>
> *Andy*: Yes, that's right.

Therapist:	And how strongly did you believe that thought at the time – let's say from 0–10?
Andy:	I would say 10. There was no question, I knew it was true.
Therapist:	And how strongly do you believe the thought now?
Andy:	Not quite as strongly, but I still think it is true, probably about 8.
Therapist:	So you still believe quite strongly that you are no good at your job. How does it make you feel when you think this thought?
Andy:	Really anxious, panicky and then hopeless, I suppose.
Therapist:	And what do you feel like doing when you feel like this? [*The therapist starts to relate Andy's experiences to the CBT maintenance cycle.*]
Andy:	Not going in, phoning in sick, as I have done a few times before I went on long term sick leave from work.
Therapist:	And what do you end up thinking when you phone in sick?
Andy:	Well, that I am no good at my job. I can't even get to the office, so how can I be any good at the job?
Therapist:	Okay, so the thought is leading to feelings and behaviours which actually reinforce your initial thought that you are no good at your job? [*Therapist summarises the maintenance cycle.*]
Andy:	Yes, I don't know what to do about it though, I just feel stuck.
Therapist:	Well, as we discussed before, when we are feeling anxious or low our thoughts can become more negative. I don't know whether or not you are no good at your job, perhaps we should look at the evidence for and against it. What evidence do you have that you are no good at your job?
Andy:	Well I just know it, I feel it inside. [*Here the client describes a feeling that something is the case rather than direct evidence.*]
Therapist:	So what you are describing is a feeling that you are no good at your job. What is the evidence that the feeling is based on?
Andy:	Well, as I said, I am always phoning in sick.
Therapist:	Yes and we discussed how that stems from the initial thought that you are no good at your job. It is not evidence in itself that you are no good. What we are looking for here is direct evidence that you are no good at your job.
Andy:	Well, my work just isn't good enough, Pete's is always better. I should be able to work quicker as well. [*Here the client lists more negative automatic thoughts as evidence for the target thought. Would the thought :'Pete is always better'. stand up in court?*]
Therapist:	What you are describing are more negative thoughts about your work, so I don't think that we can count them as direct evidence. I am not sure whether these thoughts are accurate or not. We could explore them a bit later on, but for now let's try and stick to finding direct evidence for the thought 'I am no good at my job'.
Andy:	I am not sure then really. I can't think of anything.
Therapist:	Let's turn to the evidence against the thought now. What direct evidence do you have against the thought 'I am no good at my job?'
Andy:	Well, most of the feedback I got from my boss in the annual review was good.
Therapist:	And could this have been the case if you were no good at the job?
Andy:	Well no, I suppose he wouldn't have had much good to say.
Therapist:	Can you think of any other evidence?

Andy:	Well, I have been promoted a couple of times, and my performance indicators were in the top 10 per cent.
Therapist:	That sounds like very direct evidence. We have just spent a short time on this, but how would you rate your belief now, after considering the evidence for and against it? [*Therapist asks for a re-rating of the belief conviction.*]
Andy:	Less strong – maybe about three.
Therapist:	And how do you feel?
Andy:	A bit more hopeful, less anxious about it really.

Thought evaluation sheets are the tools that we use for the thought evaluation process. These should be completed together with the client in session to start with. Once the client understands what is needed, the evaluation sheets can be completed by the client between sessions and then reviewed with the therapist in session. An example of a completed thought evaluation sheet for Andy's example above is shown in Figure 14.1 and there are blank thought evaluation sheets in Appendix XI that are available to download from www.sagepub.co.uk/simmons

We will now discuss each column of the thought evaluation sheet and suggest some tips for helping the client fill it in.

Situation

Get the client to describe where they were and what they were doing at the time that they experienced the NAT. What was the environment like? Was it noisy, crowded, hot? Who were they with? Friends? Family? Colleagues, strangers? Alone? What time of day was it?

Emotions

Get the client to describe the emotions they felt at the time (see Chapter 17 for preparatory work on emotions for clients who find it difficult to identify or label emotions). Get the client to rate the emotions for intensity, agreeing the scaling of this with the client. We often use 0 = 'very mild', to 10 = 'the strongest I have ever felt it'.

Thoughts and/or images

Get the client to list the different thoughts or images they had at the time. Be careful that interpretations of thoughts are not given instead of actual thoughts (NB except for clients with obsessional problems where it is the appraisal that is worked on as the NAT, rather than the intrusive thought). The thoughts are rated for the strength of belief in

Figure 14.1   Thought evaluation sheet for Andy

Date	Situation	Emotion(s)	Thoughts and/or images	Evidence for the thought	Evidence against the thought	Alternative (balanced) thoughts
	Where were you? Who was there? What were you doing? When?	*What did you feel at the time? How strongly did you feel it? (0–10)*	*How strongly do you believe the thought? (0–10)*	*What direct evidence do you have to support it?*	*What direct evidence do you have against it?*	*Rate how strongly you believe this alternative (0–10)*
	Tuesday evening at about 7 p.m. At home, on my own Thinking about presentation	Anxiety – 8	I am no good at my job – 8 Image of myself messing presentation up, people laughing	I phone in sick [*this was later 'disqualified' as not direct evidence supporting the thought*]	Good feedback from boss Performance indicators in top 10%	Although I sometimes avoid going to work because of anxiety, I am actually very good at my job – 7

them. Again, agree the method of scaling this with the client. We find that 0 = 'do not believe at all' to 10 = 'believe completely' usually works well.

Evidence for the thought

Only direct evidence that supports the thought should be listed here. Be wary of other NATs that the client puts forward as evidence.

Evidence against the thought

This includes anything that contradicts or is inconsistent with the NAT. Be aware of the thinking bias of 'disqualifying the positive' when looking for evidence against the thought.

Alternative (balanced thoughts)

After reviewing the evidence for and against the NAT an alternative or more balanced thought is generated.

We have listed some questions below that can be used in the generation of alternative thoughts. It can be helpful for the client to have a list of these questions handy when evaluating thoughts, so we have provided them as a handout in Appendix XII. We find the third question on this list, about advice to a friend, particularly helpful.

Questions to ask when evaluating NATs

- Am I only noticing the 'down' side of things?
- Am I expecting myself to be perfect?
- What would I say to one of my friends if they were thinking like this?
- What would one of my closest friends say about this?
- Am I assuming that my way of looking at things is the only way?
- Am I assuming that my way of looking at things is the right way?
- Am I blaming myself for something that is not my fault?
- Am I judging myself more harshly than I would judge others?
- What are the pros and cons of thinking this thought?
- Am I feeling hopeless about the possibility of changing things?
- What is the evidence for the thought?
- Am I making any thinking errors? (go through thinking errors sheet)
- Do I often think like this when in a certain state of mind?
- When I am feeling different do I think differently about things?
- Are there certain situations or times when I see things differently?
- Are there any experiences I have had that contradict this thought?

Variations on the thought evaluation sheet

There are many variations on the evaluation record sheet in the CBT literature. We find there is a balance to strike when designing a sheet that is simple enough to be 'user-friendly', yet captures all the relevant information. Another evaluation sheet that we often use is shown below and filled out for one of Anne's examples (Figure 14.2).

This evaluation sheet does not ask for 'evidence for' and 'evidence against' the NAT, just for an alternative thought. This is particularly useful for clients who are suffering from severe depression. These clients often have very entrenched negative automatic thoughts and are likely to attend selectively to negative information and events while 'filtering out' positive things. This means that they can usually generate lots of 'evidence for', but very little 'evidence against'. The risk is that the client will return to the next therapy session with the 'evidence for' column bursting with examples but the 'evidence against' column blank. Seeing a list of evidence like this can actually serve to strengthen beliefs. Although the therapist can help the client to attend to the positive in session, the homework practice might prove difficult to start with. If the client has been depressed

Figure 14.2   Thought evaluation sheet for Anne

Date	Situation	Emotion(s)	Negative automatic thoughts and/ or images	Alternative thoughts/ images	Outcome
	Where were you? Who was there? What were you doing? When?	What did you feel at the time? How strongly did you feel it? (0–10)	How strongly do you believe the thought? (0–10)	What are your new balanced thoughts and/or images? How strongly do you believe them? (0–10)	1. Re-rate NAT 2. Re-rate emotions
	Lying in bed	(1) Guilty – 10 (2) Disgusted – 9.5 (3) Sad – 7	I am lazy – 10	I am having difficulty motivating myself. I need to set small manageable goals – 9	NAT – 5 Emotions (1) 4 (2) 6 (3) 6

for a long time the 'maintenance cycle' is likely to have been reinforced, providing the client with 'actual' evidence that things are really bad. In these cases it is important that the therapist orientates the client well to the maintenance cycle, so that negative behaviours and consequences are understood as part of this self-perpetuating cycle, rather than something intrinsically negative about the client or their life.

Another version of the thought evaluation sheet includes a column for 'thinking bias'. This is particularly useful if your client is 'prone' to making certain thinking errors. The client can generate a list of responses to their common thinking errors, which can be used in the alternative thoughts/images column. We have included an evaluation sheet of this type in Appendix XI.

A modified version of the thought evaluation sheet should be used for clients presenting with obsessive compulsive problems. This is because information is needed on the intrusive thought and subsequent appraisal of the intrusive thought. We have illustrated a completed thought evaluation of this type for Megan (see Figure 14.3).

Clients with very strongly held negative beliefs can find it difficult to accept the idea that their own thoughts or beliefs do not necessarily reflect reality. They may understand the examples outlined above, but insist that their own beliefs are in fact 'true'. In these cases it is important that the therapist does not get caught in a battle where they are trying to convince the client that their belief is not true. This can have the effect of actually strengthening the client's belief. Instead, the therapist should take a neutral stance – for example, 'I don't know whether this is true or not, but it might be interesting

Figure 14.3   Thought evaluation sheet for Megan

Date	Situation	Emotion(s)	Intrusive thought/ image	Appraisal of intrusive thought (NAT)	Alternative thoughts/ images about intrusive thought	Outcome
	Where were you? Who was there? What were you doing? When?	*What did you feel at the time? How strongly did you feel it? (0–10)*		*How strongly do you believe the thought? (0–10)*	*What are your new balanced thoughts and/or images?How strongly do you believe them? (0–10)*	1. *Re-rate NAT* 2. *Re-rate emotions*
	At home with Molly She wanted me to pick her up	Anxious – 8	Image of Molly seriously ill in hospital	I could give her something nasty if I touch her without disinfecting my hands – 7	I could not give her anything by touching her – 9 Anyway, they say that it is bad for children to be in a too clean or sterile environment – 8	Anxious – 2

to explore this a bit further…' If the client is intent on proving that their beliefs are in fact correct, it can be useful to avoid the whole 'true or false' debate and instead focus on whether a thought is helpful or not. This can be illustrated by working through the thought using the CBT maintenance cycle to illustrate the impact that thinking the thought can have on subsequent emotions, physical sensations and behaviours. Here is an excerpt from an early session with Anne to illustrate this point:

Anne: I haven't done anything that we discussed since we last met because I am so lazy.

Therapist: How has your mood been? It sounds like it has been difficult to motivate yourself?

Anne: I have felt awful. I wish I wasn't so lazy.

Therapist: When people are feeling low and depressed it can be really hard to get motivated. It can seem like there is no point. Have you felt like this?

Anne: Yes I suppose I have, but I think that is just because I am a totally lazy person, not because of anything else. Other people wouldn't just sit around like I have.

Therapist: Are there any times that you can think of when you have not felt like this about yourself?

Anne: No, not recently. There is just no excuse.

Therapist:	What would your daughter Jess say to you if you said that you were thinking you were lazy?
Anne:	I don't know – what could she say? It's a fact, I haven't done anything that I had planned to because I am too lazy. [*The therapist realises that the thought is too rigid to be challenged at this point in therapy, so changes the focus to the impact of the thought on Anne's emotions and subsequent behaviours.*]
Therapist:	You seem to believe very strongly that you have been lazy. How would you rate the strength of this thought?
Anne:	100 per cent. It's true and there is nothing anyone can say to make me feel better. [*becomes tearful*]
Therapist:	I notice that as we have been focusing on this thought you have become upset.
Anne:	Yes, I just feel like a waste of space, I don't know why you are bothering.
Therapist:	So have you noticed that your mood has dropped in the past when you have thought that you are lazy?
Anne:	[*Thinks*] Yes I suppose it does not make me feel great.
Therapist:	Perhaps we could look at how this thought affects you, using the diagram we looked at last time.
Anne:	Okay.
Therapist:	So when you think the thought "I am lazy" you feel low [*Starts to draw maintenance cycle on piece of paper.*]
Anne:	Yes.
Therapist:	Do you notice any other emotions?
Anne:	I feel guilty and disgusted with myself.
Therapist:	So you feel low, guilty and disgusted. Do you notice any physical feelings in your body?
Anne:	Um, I don't know really. I sometimes feel sick, don't feel like eating, oh and really really tired.
Therapist:	And what do you do when you experience these emotions?
Anne:	I just stay in bed. [*Therapist draws in this part of the maintenance cycle.*]
Therapist:	Anything else?
Anne:	Well, last week I cancelled seeing my friends. I didn't deserve to go and couldn't be bothered anyway.
Therapist:	Okay, now let's think how these behaviours affect you. What happens when you stay in bed?
Anne:	Well I suppose I know for certain then that I am a lazy waste of time.
Therapist:	And when you cancel plans with your friends?
Anne:	I felt guilty for letting them down. I can't even manage to spend time with them any more, that's really awful. [*Therapist finishes drawing out the CBT maintenance cycle on a sheet of paper (see Figure 14.4).*]
Therapist:	So when you think the thought 'I am lazy', you tend to feel sad, guilty and disgusted with yourself. When you feel like this you cope by cancelling arrangements and staying in bed. By doing this you generate more evidence for the belief 'I am lazy'?
Anne:	Yes that's what happens. I am stuck in this awful cycle with it and can't get out of it.

Figure 14.4 Anne's maintenance cycle for the NAT 'I am lazy'

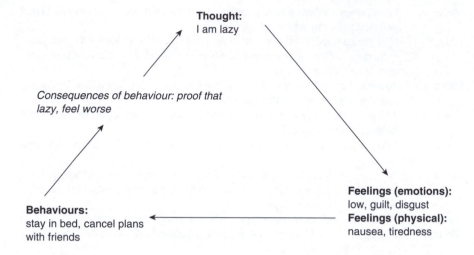

As with many severely depressed people, some of Anne's beliefs are too rigid and entrenched to be evaluated at the start of therapy. Anne is more likely to benefit from techniques to distract her from the thought at this stage (see Chapter 10 on coping strategies) and behavioural strategies. If Anne starts to experience some success (for example through activity monitoring and scheduling; see Chapter 11) she will have some direct evidence to challenge her beliefs when she moves on to cognitive work with the therapist.

Generating alternative images

This technique is particularly helpful for clients who tend to experience NATs in the form of visual images. We will not cover this subject in detail here; Beck (1995) has a good chapter on working with imagery and we would recommend this for further reading. In summary, imagery work can include:

- **Psycho-education about mental images**
  Normalise the experience of having mental images. In the same way that thoughts do not necessarily imply fact, images do not necessarily reflect reality, or what will happen.
- **Following the image to completion**
  This should help identify what the client's biggest fears are. It can be considered the imagery equivalent of using the 'downward arrow' technique to access core beliefs (p. 150).
- **Imagining a different outcome**
  This involves generating an image and then following it through, deliberately changing it to create a positive outcome. Examples of this could be imagining coping well in a difficult situation, or a catastrophe not happening.

Additional strategies for obsessional problems

As discussed earlier, there are some differences between CBT for obsessional problems and CBT for anxiety and depression due to the role of intrusive thoughts in the development and maintenance of obsessional problems. The appraisal of the obsessive thought can be worked on in the same way as NATs for anxiety and depression, but addressing the obsessional thought directly requires some different strategies. Strategies for dealing with intrusive thoughts directly that have been described in the literature include habituation exercises, thought-stopping techniques and mindfulness exercises (mindfulness techniques are discussed on pp. 99 and 144). These techniques could fit into the chapter on behavioural interventions but we decided that, as they are strategies that deal directly with exposure to thoughts, we would place them in this chapter.

Intrusive thought-habituation techniques

As discussed earlier, intrusive thoughts are often accompanied by strong negative emotions such as fear and anxiety. Habituating to these intrusive thoughts literally means exposing oneself to the thoughts until the brain has had a chance to get used to them, and thus the strong emotions lessen. Repeating a feared thought over and over causes the thought to lose its power and the body therefore ceases to become 'over-aroused' by the thought. There are a number of different techniques that can be used to try and habituate to intrusive thoughts:

1. *Written exposure*
    This essentially involves writing the thought down on a piece of paper until the level of anxiety (or sometimes other emotions such as guilt) drops to about 2 or 3 out of 10. Sometimes the thought has to be written down about fifty times or more before the emotions are brought down to a more comfortable level. It is important to refrain from using any rituals, avoidances or reassurance-seeking while doing this task. Once one thought has been tackled, another one can be targeted.
2. *Loop-tape exposure*
    Loop-tape exposure involves using a tape recorder to record the thought by repeating it over and over about thirty to fifty times. The tape should then be listened to over and over until the level of anxiety (or sometimes other emotions such as guilt) drops to about 2 or 3 out of 10. Again, it is important to refrain from rituals, etc., in order to gain benefit from the task.

The objective of the above two habituation techniques is to help the client begin to experience their intrusive thoughts while experiencing less frightening emotions. These two techniques can help clients to learn that intrusive thoughts are just thoughts and they will lose their power and become less frequent once the client stops trying quite so hard to control them. Some less experienced clinicians can feel nervous about trying these techniques as clients can feel quite stressed at the idea of seeing their thoughts on paper. Again, we stress the importance of seeking supervision for all aspects of the therapy process.

Thought-stopping techniques

Thought-stopping techniques involve generating the intrusive thought and then stopping the thought, usually by shouting 'stop' out loud and then replacing the intrusive thought with a more pleasant image. This is usually practised in therapy sessions and then between sessions. The goal is usually for the client to move from verbalising 'stop' out loud, to thinking 'stop'. Research into thought-stopping shows very mixed results (James & Blackburn 1995), and is not advocated by all researchers and practitioners. A problem of this strategy is that it can increase avoidance and fear of the intrusive thought.

Mindfulness techniques

Mindfulness has been discussed in more depth in Chapter 10. However, in brief, mindfulness means paying attention in a particular way: *in the moment* and *non-judgementally*. Mindfulness is about being in the moment, using the senses to become aware of what is happening right now. Intrusive thoughts might pop into the head on a regular basis but the task is to notice them and then turn the attention back to the task in hand which is to be in the moment. Look back to Chapter 10 for some examples of mindfulness exercises. It is about labelling the thoughts as 'intrusive thoughts' (some people even visualise the thoughts being scooped into the back of a lorry and being driven off) and then turning the attention back to the task of being in the moment. The exercises can be tried for a few minutes in sessions and clients can be debriefed afterwards. They will often be judgemental of their ability to stay focused on the mindfulness task. Remind clients that it is normal to have intrusive thoughts but that the task is to notice the thoughts and then bring the attention back to the mindfulness task. Gaining benefit may take time and clients will often have to practise it on a daily basis (for a maximum of five minutes to start with) before they notice the benefits of mindfulness.

As discussed earlier, psycho-education around the nature of intrusive thoughts and normalisation of the experience of intrusive thoughts is an important and effective part of CBT for obsessional problems, the rationale being that the more intrusive thoughts are feared and/or avoided, the more prominent they become. In addition, it is the appraisal of the intrusive thought rather than the intrusive thought itself that is considered to be the biggest factor in the maintenance of the obsessional problem. Psycho-education around intrusive thoughts and subsequent appraisals, cognitive techniques aimed to challenge appraisals and behavioural strategies that target subsequent rituals are the techniques that are usually very helpful for obsessional problems.

Covert rituals

The behavioural rituals that clients use to bring down the level of anxiety associated with intrusive thoughts were discussed in Chapter 11. However, sometimes clients ritualise by using covert (internal or hidden) rituals such as saying rhymes; repeating phrases; saying prayers; balancing the intrusive thought with a 'good' thought or image; counting, using good numbers, etc. Covert rituals can be spotted because they will lower the client's level of anxiety. They can be dealt with in the same way as behavioural rituals.

Responsibility charts

Overvalued ideas of responsibility are often a feature of OCD. As discussed previously, people with OCD often make 'personalisation' thinking biases, believing that they are to blame for events that they did not have any control over. Compulsive rituals can serve to temporarily reduce feelings of guilt and shame if the person feels that, by carrying them out, they are fulfilling their responsibility to avert a problem. Rituals can also temporarily reduce anxiety by increasing the person's sense of control over the feared event. Problems with cognitions relating to responsibility (and subsequent feelings of guilt and shame) can also be a feature of depression and anxiety problems, but are particularly common in OCD.

A responsibility chart is a useful and practical way of challenging negative automatic thoughts relating to responsibility and blame. The purpose of the chart is to introduce the idea that there are usually several factors contributing to a particular event or situation. The client is given a blank sheet with a circle on it. The situation or event is defined at the top of the sheet. The client is then asked to think about all the people, circumstances and aspects of the situation or event which have contributed to it. These are listed on the sheet. The client is then asked to divide the circle into segments, with each person/circumstance/aspect taking a proportion of the circle that represents its importance in contributing to the situation. The client's own contribution to the situation or event should be assigned last, so that it is not given a disproportionally large chunk of the chart. A blank responsibility chart is provided in Appendix XIII.

The dialogue below and Figure 14.5 illustrate the completion of a responsibility chart with Megan.

Therapist: [*Looking at thought record sheet*] So you were troubled by the thought 'If Molly gets ill it will be my fault'?
Megan: Yes I just kept thinking it all the time and imagined her being really unwell. That's why I had to keep cleaning the kitchen floor over and over.

Therapist:	So you were thinking that you would be to blame if Molly became ill. Do you think it would be your entire fault?
Megan:	Yes, I mean I'm her mother; it's my responsibility to make sure that she is well.
Therapist:	It sounds like this is an important thing for us to work on. How about we do an exercise on this, to look at the factors that might be involved if Molly were to become ill.
Megan:	Okay.
Therapist:	Here is a sheet of paper; we are going to divide up the circle to represent the things that might be involved in Molly becoming ill. Firstly, let's write the situation on the top of the sheet. What type of illness were you thinking about when you recorded the thought?
Megan:	I was imagining her having a cold.
Therapist:	Okay, now underneath let's list all the factors that would be involved in Molly getting a cold.
Megan:	Well me for a start, not keeping the house clean enough and not giving her good enough food for her immune system.
Therapist:	Right, so you feel that you play a part. Of course you would never, ever want to, but let's just imagine, could you make Molly have a cold if you chose to?
Megan:	Well, no, I couldn't.
Therapist:	So there must be some other things involved in getting a cold.
Megan:	Oh I see what you mean, well there is the virus to start with. There has to be a virus to get a cold.
Therapist:	Yes – anything else?
Megan:	Well I suppose they are more common at certain times of year and the kids all seem to get them at the same time.
Therapist:	So that's two more factors – the time of year and other children having colds?
Megan:	Yes, that's right. Now I am thinking that I have to be responsible to stop her getting the cold virus, though.
Therapist:	I suppose there is not much you can do about the time of year. What about catching colds from others?
Megan:	Hmm, I suppose there is not a lot I can do about that. I wouldn't want her to be a prisoner. When I get a cold, though, I make sure that I cover my mouth when sneezing and throw away tissues, so that it is less likely to spread.
Therapist:	So perhaps another factor might be people coughing, sneezing, etc.?
Megan:	Yes, but I suppose I can't be responsible for that. I can't stop them, especially if I am not even there. [*Looks worried*]
Therapist:	You look a bit worried. It is quite common to feel anxious when looking at responsibility. Accepting that you are not totally responsible for a situation can also mean that you feel as though you have less control over it and can't do so much about it.
Megan:	Yes I do feel a bit anxious now, but I feel anxious having to do all the cleaning rituals anyway. It's never enough.
Therapist:	Let's move on to the chart. Let's take the contributory factors that we have just identified and assign them a proportion of the circle, then we will look at your part....
	[*Megan and therapist go on to divide the pie chart up.*]

Figure 14.5   Megan's responsibility chart

Responsibility thought:

If Molly were to get a cold it would be all my fault.

Contributing factors:

the cold virus
time of year
other people around molly having colds
coughs and sneezes
me

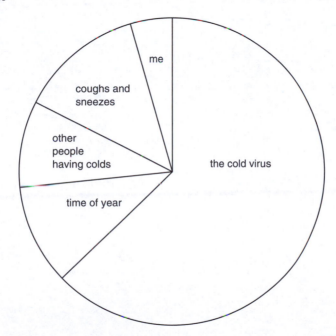

Summary

- Focus on thoughts that are related to the formulation of the client's difficulties and are causing distress.
- Be wary of directly challenging very strongly held NATs. Instead explore alternative possibilities or focus on the effect of the thought on the maintenance cycle.
- Use thought evaluation sheets initially in session and then as homework.
- Consider using imagery techniques, which can be helpful for clients who often experience NATs in the form of mental images.
- Consider using responsibility charts for individuals with OCD.

Further reading

Beck, J.S. (1995) *Cognitive Therapy: Basics and Beyond.* New York: Guilford Press.

James, I.A. & Blackburn, I.M. (1995) 'Cognitive therapy with obsessive compulsive disorder', *The British Journal of Psychiatry,* 166: 444–50.

Sanders, D. & Wills, F. (2005) *Cognitive Therapy: An Introduction.* (pp. 24–53). London: SAGE.

15

Cognitive Interventions:
Working with Assumptions and Core Beliefs

This chapter introduces the concept of working with assumptions (or 'rules for living') and core beliefs. We decided to keep this fairly brief as this is an introductory book. However, there is scope for writing whole books on this topic and, indeed, our Further Reading list points towards helpful reading material. Working with assumptions and core beliefs usually occurs later in the therapy approach after the more straightforward interventions, described in earlier chapters, have been implemented. For clients with minor mental health problems, the more straightforward interventions should be adequate. However, some clients and presenting issues require input at a deeper level. Sanders and Wills (2005: 154) suggest that core belief/assumption work is conducted in the following situations:

1   When there is clear trauma emerging from early and/or previous experience.
2   With deeper 'themes' emerging strongly in the client's material.
3   When early attempts to achieve some symptom relief have definitely not worked.
4   When the client requests some longer-term therapy focused on early experience.

Working with assumptions and core beliefs tends to require more therapeutic skill, partly because beliefs at a deeper level are more ingrained and therefore more difficult to change, but also because clients with a lot of negative core beliefs are likely to be more complex to work with. As we have discussed throughout the book, supervision is vital – especially for therapists who are starting to work with this approach.

Core beliefs and assumptions were introduced in Chapter 4. They tend to be developed through childhood and elaborated on during a person's life. The 'child's toy' example (Chapter 4) is a very helpful way of describing the development of core beliefs. As a brief recap, core beliefs tend to be developed according to a person's experiences in childhood. Thus, in very simple terms, if a person has a lot of good experiences in childhood, they tend to develop positive beliefs about the world, themselves and other people. However, negative experiences in childhood tend to lead to the development of more negative beliefs about the world, themselves and other people. The person then tends to 'screen' information according to their beliefs, and thus the beliefs get stronger.

Core beliefs are the deepest level of cognition and they are global and absolute beliefs, rather than being conditional on certain terms. Examples include statements such as 'I am worthless', or 'The world is against me.' Core beliefs differ from automatic thoughts in being global rather than specific: for example, 'Everyone hates me', rather than 'Ian hates me.' Core beliefs may be latent. In addition, some people may have many negative beliefs, which, if their lives are going very well, may get triggered rarely. Their positive beliefs then have the opportunity to become more prominent and impact more on their thoughts, feelings and behaviour. This helps to explain why certain events tend to trigger episodes of mental health problems: certain events may trigger the person's negative beliefs and they may then start filtering in information according to these negative beliefs.

Assumptions, sometimes known as 'rules for living' are also developed in childhood. They are most easy to notice when put into words and are usually defined by 'if … then …' phrases (e.g. '*If* I make a mistake, *then* I will be a complete failure') or 'should'/'must/must not' statements ('I *should* always be able to cope well'). 'Rules for living' are developed as a way of 'protecting' people from their negative core beliefs. For example, a person with a core belief about failure may strive to make sure they don't fail and they may have the following 'rule for living': 'I must not make any mistakes or I will be a complete failure.' In this way, people are constantly striving to make sure they don't trigger negative core beliefs.

Spotting core beliefs and assumptions

The first step in working with assumptions and core beliefs is to start spotting them. They may become evident as the therapist is working with automatic thoughts. Some thoughts are very hard to challenge and this may be because they are actually core beliefs. During the course of therapy, while working with negative thoughts and behavioural interventions, it is helpful for the therapist to be vigilant for information that might give clues as to the client's rules/assumptions and core beliefs. This information can be noted down and added to the initial formulation. As noted earlier, the formulation is a constantly evolving 'picture' of a person's difficulties and thus may change over time. If the client has kept thought diaries or records over time, then recurrent thoughts may give indications as to core beliefs and assumptions and these can be added to the formulation sheet as they arise.

Identifying beliefs using the downward arrow technique

Once negative thoughts are identified, the 'downward arrow technique' (Burns 1980) can be used to tease out the 'rules' and beliefs underlying the person's negative

Figure 15.1   Andy: downward arrow

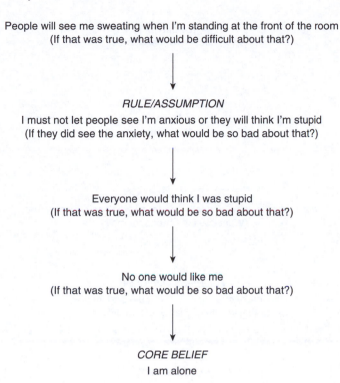

People will see me sweating when I'm standing at the front of the room
(If that was true, what would be difficult about that?)

RULE/ASSUMPTION
I must not let people see I'm anxious or they will think I'm stupid
(If they did see the anxiety, what would be so bad about that?)

Everyone would think I was stupid
(If that was true, what would be so bad about that?)

No one would like me
(If that was true, what would be so bad about that?)

CORE BELIEF
I am alone

thoughts about themselves, other people and the world. The following questions can be useful:

    What's so bad about that?
    What does this mean about me?
    What would be so difficult about that?
    What does this mean about other people?
    What does this mean about the world?

In the example in Figure 15.1, 'I am alone' seems to be the core belief. There may be more than one core belief present here and it may be the case that Andy also believes 'I am stupid.'

Sometimes therapists worry about getting exactly to the *right* beliefs (i.e. the ones that are causing the person most difficulties) instantly. This is not always possible and it may take a lot of gentle exploration before core beliefs can be identified.

Figures 15.2 and 15.3 show examples for the other two clients we have been following. In Anne's example, she makes the assumption that her friends will realise she is a fraud if she is unable to keep talking to them in the 'normal way' and this assumption can be tested using behavioural experiments (see p. 107).

Figure 15.2   Megan: downward arrow

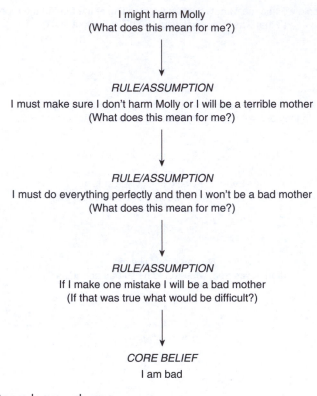

I might harm Molly
(What does this mean for me?)

↓

RULE/ASSUMPTION
I must make sure I don't harm Molly or I will be a terrible mother
(What does this mean for me?)

↓

RULE/ASSUMPTION
I must do everything perfectly and then I won't be a bad mother
(What does this mean for me?)

↓

RULE/ASSUMPTION
If I make one mistake I will be a bad mother
(If that was true what would be difficult?)

↓

CORE BELIEF
I am bad

Figure 15.3   Anne: downward arrow

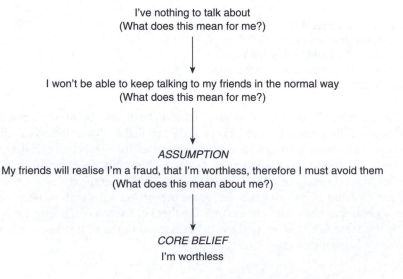

I've nothing to talk about
(What does this mean for me?)

↓

I won't be able to keep talking to my friends in the normal way
(What does this mean for me?)

↓

ASSUMPTION
My friends will realise I'm a fraud, that I'm worthless, therefore I must avoid them
(What does this mean about me?)

↓

CORE BELIEF
I'm worthless

Identifying beliefs using imagery

Sometimes people find it difficult to verbalise their negative thoughts, as discussed in Chapter 13. For these people, it is important to help them make some sense of the images they are experiencing. Images can occur at the thought level or the deeper belief level. Sanders and Wills (2005: 141) suggest that the following questions can be used to gather more information about the deeper level of beliefs:

> What is bad about the events in the image?
> What does that mean about you, others and the world?
> What is the worst that could happen?
> How do you feel now, and in the image? (Identify body sensations and emotions.)
> What is going through your mind in the image?
> Does the image remind you of something earlier on in life?
> If so, when? How old were you? What was happening? What does it say about you now?

Essentially, the same kinds of questions can be used to identify underlying images as well as underlying verbal beliefs.

The above three techniques are the main ways of identifying beliefs and assumptions/ rules. For some people, it may be enough to identify beliefs. The identification process can sometimes provide sufficient insight to enable a person to move forward with their lives. However, in other situations and for other people, it is important to move on to the next step of actually changing core beliefs and assumptions.

Changing core beliefs and assumptions can be a much more challenging process than changing negative thoughts. This is because the beliefs have developed over time and information has been filtered according to the person's beliefs (as in the child's toy example), giving the beliefs the opportunity to grow stronger over time. Thus, changing each belief may take place over a number of months.

Challenging assumptions

Behavioural experiments are one of the main ways of challenging a person's rules or assumptions. Once a rule has been identified, the therapist can work with the client to prepare a suitable experiment to test out the rule. Behavioural experiments were described in detail in Chapter 11. The main rule is that an experiment cannot fail – that is, whatever happens, there is a chance for learning. Sometimes, therapists can do the experiment instead of the client. If, for example, a client was very afraid what might happen if they collapsed in public, the therapist could be the one to do the collapsing and the client could watch what happened from a safe distance. Hopefully, the end result would be less scary than what they had been imagining. (This takes a lot of nerve and is not recommended for the faint-hearted therapist – most try something a little less 'full-on' but we have heard of this example being used!) A client who thinks they would fail completely if they made a small mistake could try out making a mistake to see how it feels and what happens. Obviously, experiments have to be devised in collaboration with the client so they feel comfortable and supported enough to take risks. It may also be important to rehearse the experiment in session before actually carrying it through. This gives the client the opportunity to practise and also to pre-empt any difficulties and to give a better chance for a positive result.

Rules and assumptions have usually been with the client for a long time and have had the opportunity to grow, become ingrained and strengthened. Thus, behavioural experiments may need to be repeated on an ongoing basis in order to have an effect. This may depend on the experiment – it may not be the best idea for a client to try making a lot of mistakes at work.

Another way of challenging assumptions is to have a dialogue with the client, asking them questions about the rules/assumptions they hold and how these rules affect them. The following questions may be helpful:

> What effect has this rule had on you?
> How does it affect your interactions with other people?
> What are the advantages and disadvantages of having this rule?
> Was the rule helpful in the past? How is it helpful/unhelpful now?
> How could this rule be changed in order to make it more helpful?

The client can be asked to think about answers to these kinds of questions for their between-sessions-tasks, as well as having discussions about this within the session.

Changing core beliefs

There are several ways of changing core beliefs and these are described below.

1. *General discussions with the client over time*
   This is a more informal way of challenging a person's core beliefs and works by asking a client curious questions about their beliefs and what they feel other people might believe in their situation. For example, a person who believes they are bad could be questioned about what a good person would be like and also what makes a person bad. They may come up with a list of qualities that they apply to being good and bad and this could lead to a series of discussions using examples of people they know. For some people, this is enough to get them thinking about the beliefs they hold. Other people may need to do a lot more work over time.

2. *List evidence that supports and does not support the core belief*
   This process involves writing each negative core belief down and then writing evidence that supports the belief and evidence that does not support the belief. It is important to write down evidence that supports the belief as the client can feel invalidated if this process does not happen before trying to find evidence that does not support the belief. Clients usually find it much easier to find evidence that supports their negative beliefs.
   When writing down evidence that does not support the belief, it is important to really search for evidence of the fact that the belief is not 100 per cent true. This can be

challenging for clients and *may take a number of months*. It can help to enable the client to look back over their lives for this information, however insignificant it might seem to be. The information can include: achievements, compliments, comments from other people and also qualities the clients may recognise for themselves. Clients can be quick to discount positive information (e.g. 'She only said that to make me feel better') and this may need to be addressed at the same time. Most clients may be aware, from the work they did on challenging negative thoughts, that they discount positive information.

The client can fill out sheets of paper with each negative belief written at the top and collect information on a daily basis that does not support the belief. It does not matter if the client does not initially believe the information. The important part is that they are writing the information down. This helps to gradually change the 'shape of the filters' that are letting information in. It can be helpful to work on one belief at a time and then move on to other beliefs later. Again, these kinds of tasks can be done between sessions which strengthens the client's beliefs that they are the ones making the changes.

3. *Identifying new core beliefs*
   Once someone is used to writing down evidence that does not support their negative core belief, it can be helpful to move to the next stage, which involves developing a new core belief. This needs to be realistic, rather than simply the opposite of the negative core belief. One way of developing a new core belief is to review the information gathered over time that does not support the negative core belief. Therefore, someone with the negative belief 'Everyone thinks I'm stupid' might work towards the belief 'Most people think I'm reasonably intelligent.' The way of doing this can be to write down information in support of the new belief. This, again, can be difficult for clients at first and they may need to be supported through the process and given help so they do not discount positive information. At first, it may be hard for people to have confidence in the new core belief and it may help to get a percentage belief rating over time.

There are other ways of challenging core beliefs but these are beyond the scope of this book. See the Further Reading list for useful books on core beliefs.

Summary

- Working with assumptions and core beliefs usually occurs later in the therapy after the more straightforward interventions have been implemented.
- Core beliefs are the deepest level of cognition and they are global and absolute beliefs, rather than being conditional on certain terms.
- The first step in working with core beliefs and assumptions is to start spotting them: using themes identified in thought diaries; using the downward arrow technique; or using imagery.
- The main way of challenging assumptions is through behavioural experiments.
- Beliefs can be challenged in a number of ways: general discussions over time; listing evidence that supports and does not support the belief; and identifying new core beliefs.

Further reading

Burns, D. (1980) *Feeling Good*. New American Library. New York: Barnes and Noble.
Greenberger, D. & Padesky, C.A. (1995) *Mind over Mood*. New York: Guilford Press.
Sanders, D. & Wills, F. (2005) *Cognitive Therapy: An Introduction*. London: SAGE.
Young, J., Klosko, J. & Weishaar, M.E. (2003) *Schema Therapy: A Practitioner's Guide*.
  New York: Guilford Press.

PART THREE

AND THE REST …

16

Problem Solving

Often clients experience real traumas and life events during the course of therapy. Obviously, it is not appropriate to tackle these kinds of issues with thought challenging and behavioural techniques, and use of these strategies in some situations would be very invalidating for the client and the difficulties they are facing. Problem solving is therefore a technique which helps clients identify the problems they are facing and then create potential solutions. Possible solutions are then studied in more detail and tailored to suit the individual situation, if appropriate. Problem solving is one of the core competencies in CBT (Roth and Pilling 2007) and it can be used as a strategy among other interventions, or as an individual therapeutic technique as described by Mynors-Wallis et al. 2000).

Problem solving can be used in a variety of situations. It is even applicable at a time of crisis although it is usually most helpful when the crisis has reduced or in the prevention of crisis. It can be a strategy that clients weave into their everyday lives to help reduce stress and tension. Hawton and Kirk (1989: 407) suggest the following range of problems as being particularly helped by a problem-solving approach:

- threatened loss (e.g. relationship or job)
- actual loss
- conflicts in which a person is faced with a major choice
- marital or other relationship problems
- work difficulties
- study problems
- coping with boredom
- difficulties concerning child care
- dealing with handicaps resulting from physical or mental illness

Prior to assessment, it is important to consider issues that will determine the effectiveness of a problem-solving approach with any given client/problem. Hawton and Kirk (1989: 413) outline several factors that should be considered:

1 **The client's difficulties need to be specific and definable.** This is not always possible and it may be that client and therapist need to do some initial work together before this point is reached. If, after spending time on this issue, it is still not possible to define specific issues, then problem solving might not be the most useful approach.

2 **The client's goals need to be realistic.** Sometimes clients have goals that are clearly not possible to attain. It is the therapist's job to help the client work towards achievable goals, and to help break goals down into small steps so the client can succeed and move on to more difficult goals.

3 **Absence of severe acute psychiatric illness.** Problem solving is a collaborative approach and therefore the therapist needs to think about whether the person is so severely disabled by psychiatric disorder that he/she cannot be expected to take responsibility to make change, even with support.

4 **There needs to be a clear contract regarding the nature, aims and extent of problem solving.** The client can be taught the approach as a means of dealing with problems that present in the future as well as the ones the therapist is helping the client to solve in the present.

Assessment procedure

Assessment is important and it can be helpful to carry out the following steps:

Identifying the client's problems

The aim here should be to *jointly* draw up a written problem list, with each problem clearly specified.

Attempt to make the list and then get a description of each problem. It's not enough to write 'relationship problems' – the therapist's task is to ask: 'What is it about the relationship?' 'Could you explain more about the problems you're having?'

Sometimes people get symptoms such as anxiety and they're not sure why. It can be helpful to get them to rate anxiety on a 0–10 scale throughout the day, and gradually notice patterns between the anxiety and issues that occur, thus helping them to identify the issues that are causing difficulties.

Explore how the client would like things to be different. A solution-focused approach is quite useful here, that is, getting the client to give a 0–10 rating for their current mood and then getting them to think about what would need to happen to raise their mood up to the next number up on the scale.

Identifying the client's resources

Problem solving generally takes a solution-focused approach in that it helps the client to identify the resources and coping strategies they already use and build on these, as well as potentially developing new coping resources. Clients can find it difficult to identify these resources at times of stress so it can take some skill on the part of the therapist to draw these out. The following list of questions can help to get this information:

- How have you coped with past difficulties?
- Can you think of any possible solutions?
- What could you do to get over this problem?
- Do you sometimes use coping strategies that help in the short term but cause problems in the long term – such as drinking excess alcohol? Are there any coping strategies that might be more helpful?
- Do you have any close friends with whom you can discuss this problem?
- Do you have any professional involvement which may be helpful, for example, health visitor, GP?
- Can changes be made to your environment – housing/employment etc.?

Procedure

When the assessment has been completed, the problem solving can actually be conducted. The following steps can be useful:

- Agree an agenda at the beginning of each session.
- The next step is to choose a problem to be focused on, preferably one that can be easy to solve in the first instance so that the client gets a sense of achievement from the exercise. It is also useful to focus on one problem at a time, although this is not always possible for every client.
- Identify resources that will help the client to solve the problem.
- Start to identify goals together that will help to solve the problem. This can be a 'brainstorming' exercise and it is helpful to look back on the resources identified earlier.
- These goals can then be split into smaller steps which need to be realistic and, where feasible, described in behavioural terms (meaning the actual behaviours the client would need to conduct in order to achieve the goal).
    - 'Brainstorming' can be a good way of identifying these steps.
    - Use 'list of pros and cons', especially to help client with making decisions.
    - Get the client to think about the consequences of each task and any possible difficulties.
- Choose the first target to be tackled – it can be helpful to practise first:
    - Cognitive rehearsal can be beneficial – that is, getting people to imagine what needs to be done and what might happen.
    - Use role play to practise aspects that the client is concerned about. (Always best to call role play something else! Perhaps simply say 'practice', as in 'Let's have a go at practising that.')

- Challenging unhelpful thoughts and beliefs can be useful for addressing issues that are blocking the client from tackling certain tasks.
- Clients may find it worthwhile to plan a reward for themselves after they have addressed a particularly difficult task.
- The therapist can provide information and advice when required or point the client in the right direction in order to access advice/guidance.
- Write the tasks down and get the client to keep a diary so they can see what they've achieved.

Review progress

Progress can be reviewed on an ongoing basis

Examples of problem solving processes

> **Megan**
>
> *Problem list*
>
> - time management in the mornings
> - getting out of the house with Molly
> - sorting out finances
> - dealing with mother's critical comments
>
> *Problem chosen*
>
> - Time management in the mornings: in specific terms, getting up on time, breakfast for self, Molly and Paul and getting out to activities rather than staying in, which can get depressing. (NB: this is towards the end of therapy when Megan has managed to tackle her fears of being alone with Molly.)
>
> *Resources identified*
>
> - Megan's determination: she has tackled many other challenging tasks with regards her mental health
> - good organisational skills
> - support from Paul
>
> *Goal identification*
>
> - going to bed earlier, so less tired in morning
> - preparing breakfast the night before
> - rota with Paul so he occasionally takes the lead in the mornings

- rota for an occasional weekend lie-in with Paul taking the lead
- choosing Molly's outfit the night before
- giving Molly a bath in the evening rather than the morning
- going to local library or asking health visitor about local groups and activities for mums and babies, etc.

The above goals can then be discussed in detail and decisions made about which goals to put in place first. A pros and cons list can be drawn up for each goal if required, but sometimes informal discussion is enough. As the goals are fairly basic, they may not need to be broken down into smaller targets, although sometimes this does need to be done.

Anne

Problem list

- isolation from friends
- whether or not to tell Jack about the affair
- sorting out housework
- communication problems with Jack

Problem chosen

- Isolation from friends: in specific terms, hardly seeing friends, ignoring their phonecalls and finding it difficult/impossible to suggest meeting up with them. When actually meeting up with friends, having very little to say.

Resources identified

- already tackled many goals regarding activity levels
- have a good set of friends with whom have always got on well
- pre-morbidly a good conversationalist
- still able to chat with her children

Goal identification

- getting caller ID so can start graded exposure to picking up the phone
- getting used to picking up the phone to good friends
- gradual exposure to picking up the phone more frequently
- practising phoning good friends
- thinking back to what used to be talked about

(Continued)

(Continued)

- writing down some topics to talk about
- experimenting going for coffee with a good friend, etc.

As before, the above goals can then be discussed in detail and decisions made about which goals to put in place first.

Andy

Problem list

- not seeing friends as much
- cash flow/problems with the flat
- very unfit

Problem chosen

- Cash flow/problems with the flat: in specific terms, finances are stretched especially with being off work and some work needs to be done on the flat – a new window is needed and a damp patch in the kitchen needs to be addressed.

Resources identified

- good organisational skills
- have been good with finances in the past
- have a number of contacts for builders
- logical brain

Goal identification

- work out current financial outgoings and what can cut back on
- work out a savings plan – as the work on the flat does not need to be done urgently, this can be a long-term plan
- explore whether have anything to sell
- think about selling car and buying less expensive one that is cheaper to run
- think about getting a temporary 'stress-free' job to tide self over
- start to get quotes from builders – these can vary a lot and it can be useful to spend time on the quote stage, especially if have time on hands, etc.

As before, the above goals can then be discussed in detail and decisions made about which goals to put in place first.

Summary

- Problem solving can be helpful when clients are facing problems that cannot be tackled with thought-challenging.
- The first step is to draw up a list of problems.
- The client's resources can then be identified.
- Choose an individual problem to tackle first and identify goals and then smaller targets to start working towards solving the problem.
- Review progress on an ongoing basis.

Further reading

Hawton, K. & Kirk, J. (1989) 'Problem solving', In K. Hawton, P.M. Salkovskis, J. Kirk & D.M. Clark (eds), *Cognitive Behaviour Therapy for Psychiatric Problems: A Practical Guide.* Oxford: Oxford University Press.

Mynors-Wallis, L.M., Gath, D.H., Day, A. & Baker, F. (2000) 'Randomised controlled trial of problem solving treatment, antidepressant medication and combined treatment for major depression in primary care', *British Medical Journal,* 320: 26–30.

17

Working with Emotions

In this chapter we will outline some techniques for preparatory work on emotions and make some suggestions regarding when and with whom you might want to use them. We intend this to be a brief introduction rather than a comprehensive guide to working with emotions and therefore make suggestions for further reading. Firstly we will recap on where emotions fit into the CBT model of psychological distress.

Figure 17.1   The cognitive-behavioural model

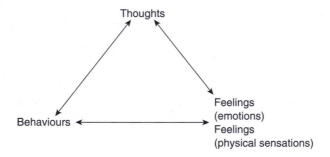

As discussed in previous chapters, CBT interventions target thoughts, feelings and physical sensations to produce positive changes in the client's emotional state. In 'traditional' CBT, emotions are not addressed directly through the interventions, but indirectly through cognitive and behavioural techniques. In our practice we have, however, found it helpful to do some direct work on emotions with some clients before starting cognitive and behavioural strategies to address the presenting problem(s). This is because cognitive-behavioural interventions are more likely to be successful if the client understands the role of emotions in maintaining his or her difficulties.

We would specifically recommend preparatory work on emotions if either of the following applies:

1   Your client is unable to identify or distinguish between certain emotions.
2   Your client copes with difficult emotions in harmful ways (e.g. avoidance, cutting-off, drug or alcohol use or self-harm).

Either of these conditions can interfere with therapy and make it less effective. If your client is unable to identify emotional states, then they will not be able to see the link between specific thoughts and the emotional responses to them – that is, where emotions fit into the 'maintenance cycle'. Cognitive interventions involve keeping records of emotional responses, which will be impossible for the client if they do not have an awareness of their emotional state.

CBT interventions are all about doing and thinking about things differently. This involves change, which can be associated with the experience of new or more intense emotions. It is important that the client is made aware of this possibility before the process of change begins so they are not frightened or confused when they experience changes in emotions. This is often an issue when working with people with anxiety problems, as behavioural work will usually involve exposure to feared situations which have been avoided because of the unpleasant experience of anxiety associated with them. This is sometimes called 'fear of the fear'. The important thing is that the client does not see the emotional experience as something to be concerned about, but as a normal (if unpleasant) response to a given situation. If the emotion is well understood and consequently less feared, then the client will, it is hoped, have more confidence to experience and tolerate the emotion.

Given that CBT interventions have the potential to lead to an increase in either the frequency or intensity of the experience of certain emotions in the short term, it is important that the client has skills to tolerate uncomfortable emotions. Ask your client how they cope with feeling sad, anxious, guilty and low. If the client reports potentially harmful coping strategies such as alcohol or drug use or self-harm, then work on coping with emotions will be important. The client might not voluntarily offer this information, particularly if they find their coping strategies shameful or embarrassing. If you suspect from your assessment that there may be problems around emotional coping, then more direct questions about possible harmful coping behaviours is a good idea. Areas to cover include:

*   self-harm
*   over- or under-eating
*   drug and alcohol use, misuse of prescribed medications
*   overworking
*   obsessional behaviour or cognitions, such as cleaning or counting

We will now outline some techniques for working on emotions, and direct you to further reading for a fuller discussion.

Psycho-education about emotions

The purpose and function of emotions

Learning about the roles of emotions can be useful for individuals who fear the experience of certain emotions. Emotions are a 'normal' part of human experience and have evolved in human beings to fulfil certain functions. They are not, therefore, harmful in themselves, but may be experienced as unpleasant. Have a discussion with your client about the functions of emotions, including the following points:

- Emotions help us to communicate how we are feeling to others, in order to influence their behaviour towards us.
- Emotions are like signals to ourselves – they provide information about what is going on around us.
- Emotions can motivate us to behave in a certain way.
- Our emotional responses will depend on how we *interpret* what is going on around us. (Cognitive interventions work on these interpretations.)

How we learn about emotions and what they mean

Children learn about emotions through experiencing them and having them labelled and responded to by their caregivers. They build an understanding of their own emotions, what triggers them and how to cope with them through this process. If a child's emotions are not responded to appropriately or are dismissed as 'wrong', then the child can develop deficits in the ability to label and cope with his or her own emotional state. If emotions and the experiences associated with them are not validated by caregivers, beliefs that emotions are 'bad' and should be 'hidden away' may develop. This then leads to problems as emotions are a normal and necessary part of human existence, as discussed above. Invalidation of emotions can be overt, such as a denial of abuse or neglect by caregivers, but can also be more subtle. Responses such as 'stop that crying', 'there's no need for that!' or 'never mind' would all be examples of responses that are dismissive of the child's emotional state, yet very common and not intentionally harmful.

Identifying different emotional states in the self and others

For clients who have difficulty in recognising and/or distinguishing between different emotional states in themselves and/or other people, some psycho-education around different emotions will be beneficial. Some key points to include in this work are given below:

- Discuss emotional language; list words used to describe the same, or similar emotions.
- Discuss bodily signs that the emotion is being experienced.
- Discuss common behaviours associated with emotions.
- Discuss situations that are likely to trigger the emotion.
- Discuss the function of the emotion.

Exposure to feared or 'hidden' emotional states

Cognitive and behavioural interventions will result in the client experiencing changes in his or her emotional state. If the client is very fearful of experiencing certain emotions, it is worthwhile working on this in session prior to the introduction of CBT interventions.

The therapist and client can either role-play or imagine situations which induce certain emotions. This can help the client feel an emotion before experiencing it in a 'real' situation. The aim is not for the emotion to be removed, reduced or changed, but rather to illustrate that the emotion can come and go without disastrous consequences. The client will then feel more confident about his or her capacity to tolerate the emotion in real life.

Beliefs about emotions

Some people hold negative beliefs about the experience or meaning of certain emotions. If this is the case, emotional changes produced by cognitive or behavioural interventions may be experienced as very aversive. The client may understandably be less likely to complete homework tasks and might even discontinue the therapy. The problem of negative beliefs about emotions can be addressed by discussing the functions of beliefs as outlined above, and by using cognitive techniques to challenge unhelpful negative beliefs about emotions (see Chapter 14). Negative beliefs about so-called 'negative' emotions such as anger, sadness, guilt and shame are common. Negative beliefs about the 'positive' emotions are also sometimes present, but perhaps less easily identified. They are worth looking out for as, if they are present, they are likely to represent a threat to positive changes in therapy. Typical examples include 'If I feel happy, I am selfish', 'If I experience joy, I am out of control', 'If I get excited, I will only be let down.' For a good practical exercise around challenging common beliefs about emotions see Linehan (1993: 86–7 and 136).

Behavioural responses to emotions

Some clients find the experience of certain strong emotions unbearable, so behaviours which help the client to either avoid or deal with emotional pain naturally develop. These are likely to be effective in the short term, but some coping strategies can have harmful side effects and/or reinforce the fear of the emotion. Examples of behaviours which can help people to cope with emotional pain include drug and alcohol use and self-harm. Avoidance of situations which are linked with the experience of difficult emotions is another common coping mechanism, but this can lead to bigger problems in the long term. Problematic responses to difficult emotional states can be identified in the 'behaviours' element of the CBT model and then behavioural interventions can be used to introduce different ways of responding to emotional experience.

Coping strategies

Sometimes life circumstances mean that difficult emotions are experienced for prolonged periods. Examples can include loss and bereavement, trauma and other changes in life circumstances. If this is the case, your client might benefit from learning some strategies to help him or her take 'time out' from being swamped by the emotion. We would refer you to Chapter 10 on coping strategies if you feel it would be appropriate for your client to learn some strategies before implementing cognitive and behavioural techniques. Remember that it is important that coping strategies are not used as a way of avoiding certain emotions, as this is likely to increase fear of the emotion. It is therefore important to assess fully your client's experience of emotions and associated behaviours before suggesting this work. If you are interested in further work of this kind see Linehan's (1993) chapters on distress tolerance and emotion regulation.

Using imagery and symbolism

Some clients have difficulty in verbally expressing how they feel emotionally. For some people it is easier to use a different medium to discuss emotional states. We have found that using imagery or symbolism are both useful ways of exploring emotions. You can ask the client if they have a name for the emotion, or, if the emotion were an 'object' or a 'thing', what it would look like. A bonus of this approach for clients who are overwhelmed by their emotions is that it can give some separation between the person and the emotion they are experiencing. For clients who are very cut off from their emotions it can be a useful way of exploring their relationship with their emotions. This is a technique 'borrowed' from narrative therapy. If you are interested in reading more narrative techniques White and Epston's book (1990) is a good introduction. Clients are sometimes confused when this is suggested for the first time. It can be helpful to give examples – e.g. anger being experienced as a raging fire, or feeling low being like having a huge weight placed on the body. A further way of exploring emotions is by drawing instead of using words. The client can use a colour or image to represent how they are feeling about their emotions. Some clients can feel uncomfortable with this. It is important to explain to the client that is not about producing a piece of art work (just like talking to the therapist about feelings is not like reciting poetry). It is about representing feelings in a different way. A very good practical workbook is *Draw on Your Emotions* by Margot Sunderland and P. Engleheart (1997). This is a collection of exercises designed to help the client explore their emotions and their relationship to them.

Summary

- Preparatory work on emotions can be helpful for clients who find it difficult to identify emotional states in themselves or others, and clients who cope with emotions in damaging ways.
- Psycho-education around emotions, exposure to feared emotions, challenging negative beliefs about emotions, coping strategies and imagery work can be considered for these clients.

Further reading

Linehan, M.M. (1993) *Skills Training Manual for Treating Borderline Personality Disorder*. New York: Guilford Press.

Sunderland, M. and Engleheart, P. (1997) *Draw on Your Emotions*. Bicester: Speechmark Publishing Ltd.

White, M. and Epston, D. (1990) *Narrative Means to Therapeutic Ends*. New York: Norton.

18

Motivation for Change

This chapter will look at the role of motivation in CBT. We will outline a model of motivation, discuss how to assess motivation for change and address how to deal with poor motivation or ambivalence about change. Motivational work can constitute a therapy in itself. We therefore do not aim to cover the topic in depth but will outline the main issues, suggest some motivational techniques that can be easily incorporated into CBT and suggest further reading.

Motivation is an important factor in the success of CBT, or indeed of any psychological therapy. We shall consider two aspects of client motivation – firstly, motivation to *engage* with therapy, and secondly, the motivation to *change*. The presence of one of these motivations does not necessarily indicate the other. A person may be very motivated to meet with a therapist on a regular basis, but may not have motivation to make changes. Alternatively (and perhaps less commonly) a person may be very motivated to make changes, but lack the motivation to meet with a therapist in order to do this.

It is important first to explore what we mean by motivation. We mean the incentive or drive to do whatever is necessary to achieve the required goals. Motivation is often complicated. A client may believe that they want to achieve a particular goal, but there may be things standing in the way of working towards that goal. The client is often not consciously aware of the things that might be preventing them from achieving change. It can therefore be helpful to examine some of the issues standing in the way of progress before attempting cognitive and behavioural strategies. For some clients, a reduction in symptoms, although very much desired, may result in a new set of problems, which the client may (subconsciously) be avoiding. In other cases, perhaps because of the client's hopeless beliefs about the future or the world in general, there is a lack of incentive to work towards a goal because it seems 'irrelevant' or 'pointless'. Poor motivation is a symptom of depression, and so particular attention should be given to motivational problems in clients presenting with low mood or a diagnosis of depression.

Poor motivation can also result from systemic factors. The client may be very keen to change, and for life to be different, but is prevented from doing so by the system around him or her. Perhaps change would have an undesirable consequence for family members, or the environment that the client lives in makes change difficult. Conversely, the client may be attending therapy sessions not through self-motivation but because somebody else in their life is very keen on the idea of change. Change might be more desirable for a family member, colleague, partner or friend than it is for the client, who might feel they cannot let the other person down, so attend therapy sessions, but without the motivation to engage with therapy or put changes into place.

An important consideration when working with motivation is that clients with poor motivation might not even be consciously aware of the things that are holding them back. The therapist can also be unaware of motivational problems at the start of therapy and may feel frustrated, angry or hopeless at the lack of progress or rapport with the client. It can therefore be beneficial to both client and therapist to explore motivation before embarking on CBT. Obvious motivational problems will be picked up during assessment, and a therapy based on motivational techniques can be considered at this point (see Miller and Rollnick 2002). Motivational problems are, however, often complex and subtle, and have a habit of emerging once therapy is underway. For these reasons we feel that a basic knowledge of motivational theory and techniques is invaluable to the CBT therapist.

The stages of change model (Prochaska and DiClemente 1983) provides a useful framework for understanding client motivation. This model suggests that the process of making a change involves movement through several motivational stages, which tend to occur in sequence (but do not always do so). The important part is that the model suggests that the client's needs, in terms of support in making change, will differ according to the motivational stage at which they are. This model is very relevant for the CBT therapist because it proposes that change-related therapy is unlikely to be successful unless the client is at the appropriate motivational stage. If the client is not, it suggests that preparatory work will be necessary before the active part of therapy can be successful.

Precontemplation

In this stage the person is either unaware that they have a problem behaviour, or is aware but unwilling to change it. Any suggestion of change from others is likely to be met with complete denial or even anger. The client is unmotivated to make changes as they do not believe that they have a problem. Change, unless forced, is unattainable at this stage. If it is forced it is unlikely to be sustained in the long term, unless, as a result of the change, the client gains insight and moves through the motivational cycle. People in this stage are unlikely to present for psychological therapy unless it has been initiated by another person and the client feels obliged to attend, for example, to 'prove' that they are fine.

Contemplation

In this stage the client is 'contemplating' making a change. They are likely to be thinking about the issue more. They might be wondering about their ability to make the change, what the outcomes of the change might be and how it will affect their life. In this stage the person has not actually made the decision to attempt change, but is aware of the issue.

Preparation

The person has made the decision to make the changes and is putting into place all the necessary preparations. This can include talking to friends and family, imagining themselves in the new situation and making necessary practical arrangements and purchases. The length of time needed in this stage will depend on the change to be made, but it is important that the client spends enough time to prepare properly for the change.

Action

This is the stage when the client actually puts the change into action – for example, stops smoking, changes diet, starts taking exercise, becomes more assertive at work.

Maintenance

Maintaining the change can require a lot of energy, especially to start with. The person might feel more comfortable with their old way of being. It involves sticking to a different way of life, when the old patterns can feel more comfortable. Maintenance can be more challenging if important others have failed to make the change, or are unsupportive of the change that the client has made.

(Relapse)

This is in brackets as it does not necessarily occur. The client fails to maintain the change and the old issue re-emerges. The client might start again at the beginning of the cycle following a relapse, or it is possible that they will skip to a later stage directly from relapse.

Motivational strategies

As your client is presenting to you for therapy, they are probably at the 'contemplation' stage or beyond. We will therefore discuss techniques appropriate for these motivational stages. We will focus on motivation for change, rather than motivation to engage in therapy, as engagement skills have been covered in earlier chapters. Sometimes clients in earlier motivational stages do present for therapy, but we find that citing other people as the sole reason for help-seeking is an indication that the client may not be at an appropriate stage of motivation – for example: 'My wife thinks I should see someone', or 'My mum says I can't stay at home unless I come to see you', or 'Work have said that I need to see someone about it.' External motivators like these can still provide reason for the person to change – the client may be fearful perhaps of a relationship suffering. From our clinical experience, however, we do find that clients are usually better able to engage with therapy if they are internally motivated. We do not recommend starting CBT with individuals who are in the 'denial' or 'precontemplative' stages of the motivational cycle, as they are likely to need much more in-depth preparation for therapy.

The motivational strategies discussed below all aim to explore what making the change will mean to the client's life. It is important that the therapist takes a neutral and non-judgemental stance in relation to this. The client needs to be able to consider the meaning of change, particularly some difficulties of making a change, without feeling a pressure from the therapist to view things in a certain way. It is about clients coming to their own conclusions and decisions about change. It is the therapist's job to help clients along in the process of considering the meaning of change, rather than to make the decision for them. This can be difficult, especially when it is glaringly obvious to the therapist how much better the client's life would be if they were able to make the change. If this is the case, bite your tongue. In order for the client to feel free to talk about some of their concerns about change it can help to frame the presence of disadvantages as well as advantages to change as the 'norm'. There can be downsides to even the most positive decisions we make in life and if the client is able to acknowledge what some of these might be, then plans can be made to help them cope. If the client is unable to acknowledge or predict some of the difficulties then they will be less prepared to deal with them. If the client feels unable to cope with a new stressor, then naturally he or she might be less inclined to continue with therapy, deciding that, on balance, they are better staying as they are. We therefore feel that it is as important for the therapist to support the client in considering the potential downsides of change as it is for the therapist to help the client consider the benefits.

Exploring the 'ideal'

This is particularly useful for clients who are at the 'contemplative' stage of motivation. In order for therapy to be successful, the client will need to perceive a gap between how things currently are and how they would ideally like them to be. If the client feels uncomfortable with this gap, they are more likely to engage in therapy. Have a conversation with your client about how they would ideally like things to be, and focus on how 'the problem' is preventing them from reaching this ideal. A conversation of this kind is shown below:

Therapist:	So, thinking about your daughter, how would you like your relationship with Molly to develop?
Megan:	I hope that we are close as she gets older, I hope that she can confide in me, and we can enjoy things together.
Therapist:	And do you enjoy things together at the moment?
Megan:	Sometimes, I suppose – maybe not as much as I would like.
Therapist:	So what would have to change for you to enjoy your time with her more often?
Megan:	Well, don't get me wrong, I do enjoy being with her, it's just this anxiety I have, you know, about germs and things.
Therapist:	And how does that change things?
Megan:	Well, I am constantly on the look-out for what I might pass on to her, or what she might touch that might have germs. I can't bear to see her dirty. I change her straight away.
Therapist:	So it sounds like those worries take up quite a lot of time.
Megan:	Yes, now I think about it I suppose they do. They are constant really. I hadn't really thought of it like that, it has just become so normal.
Therapist:	How do you think things would be different between you and Molly if you did not have these constant worries?
Megan:	I would be able to focus on her more, show an interest in what she is actually doing. I just get distracted as things are at the moment [*becomes tearful*]. I want to enjoy being with her, I really do.
Therapist:	And it seems like these worries are getting in the way of that and it has made you feel sad to think of how things could be different. If we can work on your worries, then it looks like there is real possibility that things can be different. Do you think Molly would notice any difference?
Megan:	Well she wouldn't have to keep getting changed and washed for a start! [*Laughs.*] I think this will be even more important as she gets older, and notices things. I want to show her that I am interested and I definitely don't want her watching me and picking up the same habits.
Therapist:	So it sounds like tackling this problem will be really important for your relationship with Molly …

This dialogue between the therapist and client illustrates an important consideration for this technique. The realisation of how different things are from the ideal can be upsetting for clients. Emotions such as guilt, sadness and loss can be triggered by thinking about what is being missed out on, or how things could be different. For this reason it is not always appropriate for clients presenting with depression or low mood.

Figure 18.1   A decisional bias grid for Anne: decision – overcoming depression

	Pros	Cons
Short-term	I will feel happier I will enjoy the things I used to My family will be pleased I will have more energy	There are things I have forgotten how to do People will expect more of me I will have to go through a difficult process to get there
Long-term	I will have better relationships with my family and friends I will not feel like I am wasting my life I will get more enjoyment out of life I will be healthier I will be able to work again and get a sense of achievement	I will feel as though I don't deserve to be happy

The 'decisional bias' grid

This is a useful and simple technique for clients who are at the 'contemplation' stage and beyond. In addition to being a 'motivational' technique it can help clients prepare for issues that they might not have otherwise considered. More often than not, our decisions are most influenced by the perceived short-term benefits of a particular course of action, but it is often the long-term disadvantages of the choices we make that have the biggest effect on our lives. This technique can help to 'balance' decision making, so that all short- and long-term pros and cons are considered. A completed decisional bias sheet for Anne is shown in Figure 18.1 (a blank sheet can be found in Appendix XIV and is available to download from www.sagepub.co.uk/simmons). The grid has four boxes, relating to the short- and long-term pros and cons of change, to be completed. The decision in question for Anne is a general one about overcoming her depression. These grids can also be used for much more specific changes, for example giving up smoking, taking exercise or communicating an issue or problem to another person.

When the grid has been completed, reflect on the issues with the client. It is often the case that the short-term 'cons' of making the change is what is keeping the person 'stuck', even when they are aware of the long-term 'pros'.

Once the client sees the pros and cons set out like this they are often able to make a 'rational' decision to make the change. Sometimes, however, it is not as clear cut, the client may still feel uncomfortable about the decision despite being able to list many pros. There is a useful extra part to this exercise that can help you to explore the decision further with the client. After the client has identified all the short- and long-term pros and cons ask them to assign a score (for example from 1–10) to indicate how important he or she sees the 'pro' or 'con'. If there is a long list of unimportant 'pros' and one very important 'con' this can then explain why the client still feels uncomfortable about the change. Conversely, if there is just one very important pro and a long list of unimportant 'cons', the client might be unexpectedly positive about the change.

After this exercise is complete it is important you go on to address the issues that have arisen from it in therapy. This will depend on what exactly the issues are, but making use of problem-solving and coping strategies can be helpful (see earlier chapters). It might also be that the client has some negative automatic thoughts about the change, their ability to carry it through or the impact it will have on their life. These can be addressed using the cognitive techniques discussed in Chapters 13 and 14. Below is an outline of how the issues arising from Anne's decisional bias grid were addressed in therapy.

'There are things I have forgotten how to do'.

This was explored further with Anne. She was concerned about many of the everyday things that she no longer did, such as cooking meals for the family, getting public transport and dealing with household finances and bills. What came out of this discussion was that Anne felt unable to do some of these things because of a lack of confidence. The therapist talked to Anne about poor self-confidence as a symptom of depression, which should improve with a lifting of her mood. Some things Anne felt she would not be able to do as she had forgotten what was needed. She was particularly concerned about finances and using public transport. Anne's therapist talked about how they could consider addressing some of these problems as part of the CBT. She explained that the goals could be broken down into small, manageable chunks.

'People will expect more of me'.

Anne initially said that she was concerned that her family would expect her to be back to her old self, and that she could not ever imagine being like that again. On discussion, Anne felt that there were some parts of her 'old self' that she would not want back again. One example she gave was being a 'coper' and just getting on with things, letting things bottle up as a result. On further discussion, Anne wondered whether it was really her family's expectations, or her own expectations of herself. Anne recognised that she would need to cope with things differently to avoid being at risk of feeling low again, but wondered how she could deal with difficult emotions without bottling everything up. This led on to the next issue, 'I will have to go through a difficult process to get there.' Anne and her therapist discussed doing some preparatory work on emotions and coping strategies. They also discussed some ways of communicating how she was feeling to her family.

'I will feel as though I don't deserve to be happy'.

This was an important issue to address as it could lead to a (unconscious) sabotage of progress made. Anne still had many guilty thoughts about things that had happened in her past, and in some ways her depression was seen as the punishment that she deserved. Anne's therapist suggested working on these NATs and underlying core beliefs in therapy. Her therapist also discussed guilty thoughts and self-blame as common among people suffering from depression. Anne was also able to see that if she were happier, then her family would also be happier and she certainly did not want them to be 'punished'.

Letters to the 'problem' as a 'friend' and as an 'enemy'

This is a technique often used with people with eating problems. It is very helpful for clients who have a high level of ambivalence about change, and may have only just started to contemplate making the change. It is similar to the decisional bias grid technique, but the symbolism of 'friend' and 'enemy' can create a useful distance between the person and their problem, which can make it easier to reflect on. The client is asked to write a letter to the 'problem' firstly as a friend and then as an enemy. In the letter to the friend, the client writes all the positive things about having the friend around and what will be missed about the friend when it is gone. In the letter to the enemy the client writes all the negative things about the enemy and why it will be great when it is gone.

Life in five years with the problem and without the problem

The client is asked to write or describe what their life would be like in five years time, firstly with the problem and then without the problem. This is a helpful way of getting the client to consider the longer-term issues in making the change, so is particularly helpful if you feel that the short-term 'cons' of change are keeping the client 'stuck'. This is not usually a technique used for very depressed people due to the pervasive hopelessness about the future that is common among severely depressed people.

Summary

- Theories of human motivation suggest that people go through different stages of motivation in relation to making changes.
- Interventions addressing motivation need to be appropriate to the individual's stage of change.
- If a client presenting for therapy is at an early motivational stage, motivational strategies can be considered before starting cognitive and behavioural change strategies.
- Clients who are in the denial precontemplation stages are unlikely to make or sustain changes.

Further reading

Miller, W.R. & Rollnick, S. (2002) *Motivational Interviewing: Preparing People for Change.* New York: Guilford Press.

Prochaska, J.O. & DiClemente, C.C. (1983) 'Stages and processes of self-change of smoking: toward an integrative model of change', *Journal of Consulting and Clinical Psychology*, 51: 390–95.

19

Therapeutic Endings

This chapter is all about the ending of therapy. Thinking about ending therapy can be difficult for many clients as, for some, this may be the first time they have had the opportunity to really discuss their feelings with another person. Other clients may have had issues with trust previously and they may have taken risks that they had not previously had the opportunity to take. However, it is possible to prepare clients for the final stages of therapy and this preparation is best started as near as possible to the beginning of therapy. Roth and Pilling (2007) see the ability to manage therapeutic endings as a core competency for CBT.

This chapter will outline strategies that can be used at each stage of therapy to ensure that the client is fully aware that therapy will end, and is prepared for its ending. It is important to know when therapy should end and Sanders and Wills (2005) note that therapy generally ends when the allocated number of sessions is completed and, preferably, the client has achieved the goals they originally set for themselves. Sometimes therapy is terminated at an earlier point because it has not been possible to engage in therapy at this time. This does not mean that the client cannot return at a later point.

Assessment

During the assessment, it is helpful to give the client a brief overview of what CBT sessions will consist of and how the therapy is structured. Look back to Chapter 5 for a full outline of this and also how to describe this to clients. One of the main points to get across is that the client will be using the sessions to learn strategies to help with current problems, but also to apply these strategies to future difficulties. A discussion of between-session tasks ('homework') is useful here, along with an explanation that many of the changes a client makes will be due to their commitment to trying out different strategies between sessions. This will help them understand that they, rather than the therapist, are in control of their own changes. Already, the client will, it is hoped, see that their own strength is what will help them make changes in their lives.

Regular reviews

It is good practice to review CBT on a regular basis. A good number of sessions to have (after the assessment sessions) before reviewing is six. This gives the client the opportunity to settle in to the sessions and have some idea about whether they have been helpful so far and if further sessions might be useful.

Clients are often reluctant to say anything negative about the sessions. Therefore, it can be a good idea to let clients know how useful it is to hear constructive criticism, and perhaps even suggest things that other clients have found difficult. Below are some examples of review questions to help the client start thinking about how the process of therapy has been for them so far:

Review questions

What has been helpful about the sessions so far?
What has not been helpful about the sessions so far?
What do you find difficult about attending sessions?
What changes do you feel you have made?
Have there been any things that you feel should already have changed but haven't?
What changes would you still like to make?
What are the specific goals you would like to work on in the next six sessions?
Is there anything else you would like to mention?

Discuss setbacks

It is important to discuss setbacks early on. Most people hope that their recovery will be straightforward and immediate. It is therefore important to stress that changes tend not to occur overnight and that progress can be very up and down. Setbacks are important during recovery. They give the client the opportunity to experience what it feels like to recover and work through obstacles on the path to recovery. Appendix XV has a handout on setbacks which can be given to clients at any time during the therapy process. In fact, the earlier, the better. Clients might also like to write themselves what is sometimes known as a 'rainy day letter', which can be written while the client is feeling positive, to read on days when they are feeling less positive or are having a setback. A short example for Anne is shown below:

Dear Anne,

I know you are having a bad day today and feeling as though you have not made any progress, but I am writing this letter on a good day to remind you of all the changes you have made over the last few months. I need to remind you that you have made many changes, as I know that you find it hard to believe this when you are feeling 'down'. My mood today is really good – not quite back to how it used to be but generally I'm feeling much more confident and seeing friends regularly as well. I feel like I can talk to my friends again and have even started to confide in them a bit more …

This kind of letter can be powerful, as well as very comforting for the person who is in the middle of a setback.

Review between-session tasks (homework) on a regular basis

It is important to make it clear to clients early on in treatment that the between-session-tasks are a vital part of recovery. Clients may struggle with these tasks for a number of reasons:

- *The task feels too difficult.*
  The first few tasks in an exposure programme should be manageable without too much stress. It is important for the client to gain a sense of achievement as this will encourage them to move on to more difficult, and possibly more stressful, tasks.
- *The client wants to fill out the diary/record sheet properly/perfectly.*
  This is a very common problem. Most clients worry that they have filled out the diary/record sheets incorrectly or that their writing is not neat enough. It helps to go through an example or two with the client in session first. Filling in the diary/record sheet in a slightly messy way can help the client to feel more at ease. Stress that you do not mind what the diary/record sheet looks like or even if they haven't filled it in at all – the most important thing is to bring the diary record sheet (empty or not) back to the next session.
- *The client has not understood the task.*
  Again, this can be a common problem – it can be hard for some clients to ask for instructions to be explained, as they think that they *should* be able to understand everything immediately. It can be helpful to go through a number of examples and ask the client questions to check that the instructions are clear. It may benefit some clients to have the instructions written down.
- *The client is unsure how doing the task is going to help them.*
  In this case, the client has been upfront in stating that they are not sure about the task and the benefits of conducting the task. As this is a collaborative therapy, it is important that the client is fully 'on board' or the task will not be of benefit. Explore reasons why the client does not feel the task will be beneficial. Consider other options for tasks. As discussed in Chapter 18, motivational strategies may be helpful to move the client forwards into a position of readiness for change.

Consider the formulation when considering endings

Some clients will find it more difficult than others to finish therapy. This can often be predicted during the course of therapy or from the formulation. If the client has previously had concerns about being abandoned or if they tend to depend on others, then the ending of therapy may be more difficult for them or it may bring up thoughts of other endings. Being transparent with the client about this issue can be helpful, and discussing that it can be hard to end therapy is usually very valuable and enables the client to feel they are not alone. It can be useful to discuss how the ending can be managed and what the client will find most helpful. Some clients like to have a final session, others like to have their file open for a number of months so they can contact the therapist for a booster session if required.

It can also be useful to discuss the strong feelings that the client may experience during the ending phase. For some clients, this may be their first experience of really connecting enough to be able to share their thoughts and deepest feelings, and so to feel they are losing that can bring up strong feelings such as anger and sadness. The client can be encouraged to express these feelings and be open about them as part of the process. Alongside this process of identifying and expressing feelings, the therapist can also enable the client to identify the thoughts and beliefs that might be leading to the strong feelings, so they can either challenge or work through them.

Developing an internal therapist

The client, it is hoped, has been able to see their own part in overcoming their difficulties throughout the therapy process. Some clients find this easier than others. Tasks between sessions can help the client feel that they are working on their difficulties themselves. It can be important to regularly remind the client that they are in control of the changes they make, and also that the time spent in sessions with the therapist usually accounts for only an hour a week or an hour fortnightly. Not very much!

Relapse prevention

It can be helpful to work on a relapse plan with the client in the final sessions. They can also work on this plan between sessions as well. An example of a typical relapse management plan can be found in Appendix XVI and can be downloaded from www.sagepub.co.uk/simmons

End-of-therapy letter

It can be really useful to develop an end-of-therapy letter with clients. This does not have to follow a specified format but it can be helpful to include a written summary of the formulation (using description rather than formulation diagram), a summary of the work completed together and pointers/goals for the future. It can be useful to include book lists and reminders of handouts at the end of the letter. Examples of ending letters for the clients we have been following can be found in Appendix XVII. These letters are most usefully developed during conversations with the client, checking what they would like included and what has been discussed over the course of therapy.

Summary

- Ending therapy can be difficult for many clients and it is important to remind them about ending throughout the process of therapy.
- Use the assessment phase to outline the structure of therapy to clients and discuss the fact that therapy is finite.
- Build in regular reviews.
- Discuss setbacks.
- Review between-session tasks ('homework') and discuss difficulties with these tasks.
- Review the formulation when considering endings.
- Help the client to develop an internal therapist.
- Develop relapse plans and ending letters with the client.

Further reading

Sanders, D. & Wills, F. (2005) *Cognitive Therapy: An Introduction*. London: SAGE.

20

Supervision

As we have mentioned elsewhere in the book, supervision is vital when practising CBT. This continues to be the case even for experienced CBT therapists, although the frequency at which supervision is required usually diminishes to some extent the more experienced the clinician becomes. Supervision has a number of different purposes, and Watkins (1997) notes that supervision 'provides supervisees with feedback about their performance; offers them guidance about what to do in times of confusion and need; allows them the opportunity to get alternate views and perspectives about patient dynamics, interventions, and of course treatment; stimulates or enhances curiosity about treatment and the treatment experience; contributes to the process of forming a therapist "identity"; and serves as a "secure base" for supervisees, letting them know that they are not alone in learning about and performing of psychotherapy' (Cooper and Witenberg 1983; Greben 1991; Hart 1982; Hoffman 1994).

When clinicians first start practising CBT, they may be reasonably new to the concept of supervision and it can take time to learn what supervision is about. The aim of this chapter is to discuss models of supervision and provide some pointers for issues to address with the supervisor when setting up supervision in the first place.

Models of supervision

Models of supervision are useful in that they provide a description of the supervision process and can help to guide the process. Some of the main models of supervision to emerge focus on the 'developmental approach'. These models focus on supervisees and their interactions with their supervisors, and propose that supervisors adapt their style and approach to supervisees' needs in relation to their clients and level of experience (Hawkins and Shohet 1989). There are many developmental models, most of which have been reviewed extensively in the literature (e.g. Holloway 1987).

Bernard and Goodyear (1992: 21) observe that 'developmental models have certain assumptions in common but vary in their applications of those assumptions'. They reviewed a number of models, including the 'complexity model' – initially proposed by Stoltenberg (1981), further developed by Stoltenberg and Delworth (1987) and later by Page and Wosket (1994). This model essentially describes a 'beginner' stage, where the supervisee is dependent on the supervisor, whose main role is to provide support and impart knowledge and skills. In the 'probationer' stage the supervisee is starting to develop their own style and integrate theory and practice when working with clients. Some clinicians will be more autonomous at this stage, others remaining dependent. The 'journeyman' stage is where the supervisee is 'good enough', has a more developed professional identity and is receptive to new ideas and therapeutic orientations. Finally, the supervisee will reach the 'master' therapist stage, where they are secure in their abilities and highly autonomous. Here the supervisee/supervisor relationship is as one between peers: the supervisor is seen more as an 'equal' now.

Using supervision models

There are many other models of supervision in the literature but there is not scope within this book to go into more detail. Do note that the above models are not exclusive to a CBT approach, but can be used as a guide to think about your needs in supervision. Clinicians who are just starting out are more likely to need more of a 'teaching style' from the supervisor, for the supervisor to go into detail about how to conduct certain interventions or help come up with lists of questions for clients as well as working on formulations together in supervision prior to meeting with the client. Sometimes more experienced therapists can feel embarrassed about needing this technical kind of supervision at times, feeling that they 'should' have moved on to being more autonomous – it is therefore important to think of the models in a flexible way and realise that your needs as a supervisee may vary depending on each client and individual situation. So the models can be used as a 'guide in the background' to keep the supervision process on track. Some supervisors may choose to pick out a particular model and may use it to review the supervision, perhaps on a six-monthly basis. In the same way that therapy is reviewed, a review of supervision can allow both supervisor and supervisee to discuss how the supervision has been going and whether it is meeting the needs of the supervisee as well as exploring areas of development and future supervision needs.

Issues to discuss when setting up supervision

As clinicians will have different needs when setting up supervision, it can be helpful to explore certain topics at the start. Below is a list of potential topics to aid discussion:

- needs/likes for supervision
- what is not liked about supervision
- experiences of other supervision
- workload balance – too few clients/too many?
- how risk issues are dealt with – see Chapter 7 for further discussion on this
- work–life balance – what if things come up in personal life?
- what might be difficult to discuss in supervision
- 'you don't have to cure clients'
- how quickly to see clients
- learning style and needs
- process issues versus practical issues
- models of therapy and supervision
- the power differential between supervisor and supervisee, particularly trainees who are being assessed
- who holds clinical responsibility
- reflection on anxieties – both supervisor and supervisee
- confidentiality
- giving feedback – how this is best managed
- letters
- what has not been discussed that feels important
- review of supervision

The above list can be reviewed by both supervisor and supervisee and each topic can be discussed briefly or in more depth, depending on individual needs. Some supervisors like to set up a supervision contract detailing when supervision will take place and how often meetings will be organised.

Summary

- Supervision is a vital component for conducting CBT.
- Individual clinicians will have different supervision requirements.
- Supervision models can be used to guide thinking about supervision needs and to review supervision.
- It can be helpful to consider and discuss a range of issues when first setting up supervision.

Further reading

Bernard, J.M. & Goodyear, R.K. (1992) *Fundamentals of Clinical Supervision.* Boston, MA: Allyn & Bacon.
Cooper, A. & Witenberg, E.G. (1983) 'Stimulation of curiosity in the supervisory process of psychoanalysis', *Contemporary Psychoanalysis*, 19: 248–64.

Greben, S.E. (1991) 'Interpersonal aspects of the supervision of individual psychotherapy', *American Journal of Psychotherapy*, 45: 306–16.

Hart, G. (1982) *The Process of Clinical Supervision*. Baltimore: University Park Press.

Hawkins, P. & Shohet, R. (1989) *Supervision in the Helping Professions*. Milton Keynes: Open University Press.

Hoffman, L.W. (1994) 'The training of psychotherapy supervisors: a barren scape', *Psychotherapy in Private Practice*, 13: 23–42.

Holloway, E.L. (1987) 'Developmental models of supervision: is it development?' *Professional Psychology: Research and Practice*, 18 (3): 209–16.

Page, S. and Wosket, V. (1994) *Supervising the Counsellor. A Cyclical Model*. London: Routledge.

Stoltenberg, C.D. (1981) 'Approaching supervision from a developmental perspective: the counsellor complexity model, *Journal of Counselling Psychology*, 28: 59–65.

Stoltenberg, C.D. & Delworth, U. (1987) *Supervising Counsellors and Therapists: A Developmental Approach*. San Francisco: Jossey-Bass.

Watkins, C.E. (1997) *Handbook of Psychotherapy Supervision*. New York: Wiley.

Conclusion

We hope that this has been both a useful text in conjunction with your clinical training and development and also as a reference guide to recap and refresh the principles of CBT when required. There are many different ways of delivering CBT and we recommend further reading, particularly if you are planning to practise CBT, to broaden your perspective and enhance your clinical skills. Do feel free to make use of the material in the Appendices, in your teaching, with clients or in your studies (photocopiable versions are available to download from www.sagepub.co.uk/simmons).

As we have discussed throughout the book, we strongly advise that anyone planning to use the techniques in this book seek the guidance of a supervisor who is experienced in CBT, and access basic level CBT training. Although we have written this book in jargon-free language and presented some of the techniques as being simple to use, we would like to stress the complex nature of most clients' difficulties and the importance of gaining experience under close supervision.

Appendix I

Referral Criteria Handout

The list below gives some pointers to look for during a general assessment to see if referral for a CBT assessment might be relevant. The person doesn't have to fulfil *all* the criteria but it does help if they fulfil most of them. On the next page are some sample questions to ask clients before making a referral for CBT assessment.

Accessibility of automatic thoughts

- The person needs to be able (even if it takes some prompting) to access negative automatic thoughts, e.g., 'I messed that up', 'People will think I'm odd.'
- It is okay to suggest examples of thoughts that other people sometimes have in these situations, especially if the person is finding it hard to access their own thoughts.

Awareness and differentiation of emotions

- The client needs to be able to gain access to emotions and differentiate between emotions, such as guilt, anxiety, sadness, anger, etc. The therapist needs to be aware of differences in language: 'depressed' may just mean low in mood to some people. Be aware of cultural differences.
- This is not quite as important as the ability to access negative thoughts and some people may not be able to do this at first. For these people, there may need to be some preliminary work on accessing emotions before they start CBT.

The client's ability to make use of therapeutic input – very important!

- An important aspect of therapy is how prepared clients are to make changes in their lives so that they can work on the problems they have. A negative indication might be the question: 'Have you got a tablet that will make it all go away?'

An A4, photocopiable version of this appendix is available to download from www.sagepub.co.uk/simmons

- How motivated is the client? Are they able to collaborate? Or have they been told, by social services or their partner, to come? If the client needs to be persuaded to start CBT, it's most likely an indication that it is not for them at this time. They can always be referred in the future.
- Clients' ability to remain focused on the problem in hand. This may be something that clients have to work towards.

Barriers to therapy

- If someone is 'floridly psychotic'. However, a level of psychotic symptoms can be fine, and CBT for psychosis could be considered.
- If someone is in a current manic phase.
- If clients are cognitively impaired, this may make therapy more difficult but not impossible.
- If there are practical issues, or other referrals are being made, the person will need a care co-ordinator as well.
- If the setting is the NHS, the client will also need to be accepted into the relevant team before therapy assessment can commence.

Questions to consider asking to see if therapy would be helpful

It is most useful to ask the client to describe a situation in which they feel anxious/low/scared, etc. The following questions can then be put.

Accessibility of automatic thoughts

When that situation occurred:

- What were you thinking?
- What went through your mind?
- Sometimes people worry that, for example, if they have a panic attack they might faint, or sometimes people might worry that, for example, if they go out, others will stare at them, etc.

Awareness and differentiation of emotions

When the situation occurred:

- How did you feel?
- What was happening in your body at the time?
- Ask about different situations and how the person felt at that time.

*The client's ability to make use of therapeutic
input*

- What changes would you like to make? (Specific goals are best.)
- What are the advantages and disadvantages of making changes:
  - to the client?
  - to the client's family?
  - to any other significant others?
- What might get in the way of making change, attending sessions on a regular basis, etc.?
- Be aware how focused the client is able to remain on the issue being discussed.

Appendix II

Chapter 3 Exercise

Thoughts

I'm not going to be able to do this.
I feel really self-conscious.
I'm always going to feel this way.
Nothing ever goes right.
I feel out of control.
I'm having a heart attack.
I feel hot and sweaty.
She's being inconsiderate.
I feel really depressed.
I'm a loser.

Feelings

depressed
guilty
feeling blue
feeling discouraged
ashamed
panicky
enthusiastic
humiliated
remorseful
feeling worthless

Physical sensations

sweaty palms
heart racing

An A4, photocopiable version of this appendix is available to download from www.sagepub.co.uk/simmons

feeling dizzy
breathlessness
feeling faint
nausea
feeling tired
feeling in pain
exhausted
dry mouth

Behaviours

seeing friends
avoiding going out
discussing my feelings
checking the oven is off
checking my weight each day
restricting my diet
washing my hands over and over
drinking excess alcohol
telling lies
hiding my shaky hands

Appendix III

Formulation sheet and maintenance cycle

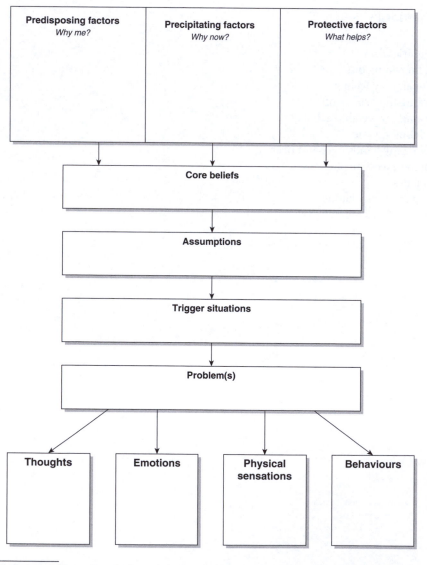

An A4, photocopiable version of this appendix is available to download from www.sagepub.co.uk/simmons

Maintenence Cycle

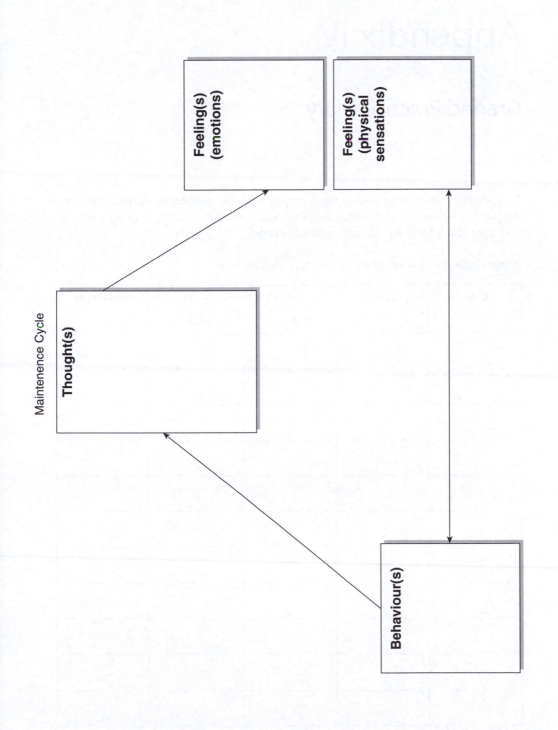

Thought(s)

Feeling(s)
(emotions)

Feeling(s)
(physical
sensations)

Behaviour(s)

Appendix IV

Graded Practice Diary

This is a diary sheet to note down the goals you work on each day/week. Rate the anxiety you feel before and after conducting each goal to see what happens to your anxiety over time and after practising each goal a few times.

Anxiety rating: 1 = low anxiety; 10 = very high anxiety

Date	Goals	Anxiety Rating (1–10)		Comments
		Before	After	

An A4, photocopiable version of this appendix is available to download from www.sagepub.co.uk/simmons

Appendix V

Detailed Activity Record Sheet

Week starting:................................

Time:	Monday	Tuesday	Wednesday	Thursday	Friday	Saturday	Sunday
9–10							
10–11							
11–12							
12–1							
1–2							
2–3							
3–4							
4–5							
6–10							
Mood rating: 0 = low 10 = really good							

Key
P = Pleasure 0–10
A = Achievement 0–10
Write these scores alongside each activity.

An A4, photocopiable version of this appendix is available to download from www.sagepub.co.uk/simmons

Appendix VI

Basic Activity Schedule

Please fill in the following chart for each day of the week. You only need to put in a couple of activities a day to start with. It is useful to try and pick out activities that lift your mood and also note those that seem to lower your mood. Feel free to fill in the comments column and also to rate mood each day on a 0–10 scale (where 10 is very good and 0 is awful).

Week starting:

Day	Activities	Comments
Monday		
Tuesday		
Wednesday		
Thursday		
Friday		
Saturday		
Sunday		

Appendix VII

Thought Record Sheets

Basic Thought Record Sheet

Date	Situation	Emotion(s)	Thoughts and/or images
	Where were you? Who was there? What were you doing? When?	*What did you feel at the time? How strongly did you feel it? (0–10)*	*What did you think? How strongly do you believe the thought? (0–10)*

An A4, photocopiable version of this appendix is available to download from www.sagepub.co.uk/simmons

Detailed Thought Record Sheet

Date	Situation	Emotion(s)	Thought(s) and/or image(s)	Physical sensation(s)	Behaviour(s)
	Where were you? Who was there? What were you doing? When?	What did you feel at the time? How strongly did you feel it? (0–10)	How strongly do you believe the thought? (0–10)	Did you notice any changes in your body at the time?	What did you do after experiencing the thought?

OCD Thought Record Sheet

Date	Situation	Intrusive thought/ image	Appraisal(s)	Emotion(s)	Physical sensations	Behaviours
	Where were you? Who was there? What were you doing? When?	*What was the thought or image that came into your mind?*	*What was your thought about the intrusive thought? How strongly did you believe it? (0–10)*	*What did you feel at the time? How strongly did you feel it? (0–10)*	*Did you notice any changes in your body at the time?*	*What did you do after experiencing the thought?*

Appendix VIII

Questions to Help Identify Negative Automatic Thoughts

- What was going through your mind before you felt guilty/anxious/sad?

- What does this say about you if it is true?

- What were/are you afraid might happen?

- What would be the worst thing that could happen if it is true?

- What does this mean about what the other person thinks about you?

- What does this mean about the other person (or people in general)?

- What images do you have about the situation?

An A4, photocopiable version of this appendix is available to download from www.sagepub.co.uk/simmons

Appendix IX

Thinking Biases

Catastrophising
When the worst possible outcome is predicted and magnified
If I make a mistake I will lose my job.
I can feel my heart beating fast. I am going to die.

Mind-reading
Guessing another person's thoughts
They thought I looked stupid.
She didn't really want to meet up with me.

Fortune-telling
Predicting a bleak future, without evidence for it
There is no point, I will just fail at it.
I am always going to be like this.
No one will ever love me.

All-or-nothing (black-and-white) thinking
Only seeing the extremes, being unable to see the 'grey' area
If I don't get 100 per cent I am a failure.
If he doesn't phone me every day he doesn't love me.

Discounting the positive
When positives are viewed as worthless or meaningless
He was just saying that to be nice.
Anyone could have done that.
NB: Look out for 'yes buts' in response to positive information.

Overgeneralisation
A single negative event is viewed as affecting everything, or as a signal that everything will go wrong
The bus didn't turn up, everything is going wrong.
I burnt the cake, the whole party is a disaster.

Personalisation
Feeling responsible when not at fault
It's my fault no one is enjoying themselves.
They cancelled the trip because they don't want to go with me.

An A4, photocopiable version of this appendix is available to download from www.sagepub.co.uk/simmons

Appendix X

Thinking Biases Exercise

- Photocopy the table of NATs.
- Cut up NATs.
- Discuss each NAT with your client, and 'sort' them into thinking bias categories.
- Discuss how some thoughts represent more than one type of thinking bias.
- Does the client particularly identify with any of the categories?

NATs

It always rains at the weekends.	If a size 12 does not fit me I must be obese.	Unless I get 100% in this exam I have failed.
I never say anything right.	The argument is all my fault.	People are either good or bad.
I will lose control completely.	Politicians always lie.	She was in a funny mood – she doesn't like me.
My heart is beating so fast I could die.	He left the party early because he finds me annoying.	She only said that to make me feel better.
If I make a mistake I will lose my job.	The woman upstairs slammed the door to annoy me.	What, this old thing? I bought it at a jumble sale.
You always forget to do what I ask.	I will always be alone.	We lost the match – it was all my fault.

Possible answers are on the next page (some of them are quite ambiguous and may fit in to more than one category).

An A4, photocopiable version of this appendix is available to download from www.sagepub.co.uk/simmons

Thinking Biases Exercise – Answers

It always rains at the weekends. *Overgeneralisation*	If a size 12 does not fit me I must be obese. *All or nothing*	Unless I get 100% in this exam I have failed. *All or nothing*
I never say anything right. *All or nothing/overgeneralisation*	The argument is all my fault. *Personalisation*	People are either good or bad. *All or nothing*
I will lose control completely. *Catastrophising/fortune-telling*	Politicians always lie. *Overgeneralisation*	She was in a funny mood – she doesn't like me. *Mind-reading*
My heart is beating so fast I could die. *Catastrophising*	He left the party early because he finds me annoying. *Mind-reading*	She only said that to make me feel better. *Discounting the positive*
If I make a mistake I will lose my job. *Catastrophising/fortune-telling*	The woman upstairs slammed the door to annoy me. *Mind-reading*	What, this old thing? I bought it at a jumble sale. *Discounting the positive*
You always forget to do what I ask. *Overgeneralisation*	I will always be alone. *Fortune-telling*	We lost the match – it was all my fault. *Personalisation*

Appendix XI

Thought Evaluation Sheet

Alternative Thoughts

Date	Situation	Emotion(s)	Negative automatic thoughts and/or images (NATs)	Alternative thoughts/images	Outcome
	Where were you? Who was there? What were you doing? When?	*What did you feel at the time? How strongly did you feel it? (0–10)*	*How strongly do you believe the thought? (0–10)*	*What are your new balanced thoughts and/or images? How strongly do you believe them? (0–10)*	1. Re-rate NAT 2. Re-rate emotions (0–10)

An A4, photocopiable version of this appendix is available to download from www.sagepub.co.uk/simmons

Evidence For and Against

Date	Situation	Emotion(s)	Thought(s) and/or image(s)	Evidence for the thought	Evidence against the thought	Alternative (balanced) thought(s)
	Where were you? Who was there? What were you doing? When?	What did you feel at the time? How strongly did you feel it? (0–10)	How strongly do you believe the thought? (0–10)	What direct evidence do you have to support it?	What direct evidence do you have against it?	Rate how strongly you believe this alternative (0–10)

OCD

Date	Situation	Emotion(s)	Intrusive thought(s)/ image(s)	Appraisal of intrusive thought/ image (NAT)	Alternative thoughts about intrusive thought	Outcome
	Where were you? Who was there? What were you doing? When?	*What did you feel at the time? How strongly did you feel it? (0–10)*	*What went through your mind?*	*What did you think about having had the intrusive thought? How strongly did you believe it? (0–10)*	*What are your new balanced thoughts/ images? How strongly do you believe them? (0–10)?*	1. Re-rate NAT 2. Re-rate emotions

Thinking Biases

Date	Situation	Emotion(s)	Negative Automatic Thoughts and/or images	Thinking bias	Alternative thoughts/ images	Outcome
	Where were you? Who was there? What were you doing? When?	What did you feel at the time? How strongly did you feel it? (0–10)	How strongly do you believe the thought? (0–10)	Does the thought seem to fit into any of the thinking bias categories? (see thinking bias sheet)	What are your new balanced thoughts and/or images? How strongly do you believe them? (0–10)	1. Re-rate NAT 2. Re-rate emotions

Appendix XII

Questions to Ask When Evaluating NATs

- Am I only noticing the 'down' side of things?

- Am I expecting myself to be perfect?

- What would I say to one of my friends if they were thinking like this?

- What would one of my closest friends say about this?

- Am I assuming that my way of looking at things is the only way?

- Am I assuming that my way of looking at things is the right way?

- Am I blaming myself for something that is not my fault?

- Am I judging myself more harshly than I would judge others?

- What are the pros and cons of thinking this thought?

- Am I feeling hopeless about the possibility of changing things?

- What is the evidence for the thought?

- Am I making any thinking errors? (Go through thinking errors sheet.)

- Do I often think like this when in a certain state of mind?

- When I am feeling different do I think differently about things?

- Are there certain situations or times when I see things differently?

- Are there any experiences I have had that contradict this thought?

_____

An A4, photocopiable version of this appendix is available to download from www.sagepub.co.uk/simmons

Appendix XIII

Responsibility Chart

Responsibility thought:

....

....

Contributing factors

....

....

....

....

....

....

....

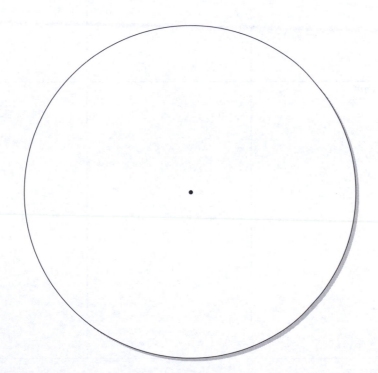

Appendix XIV

Decisional Bias Sheet

The Decision ....

	Pros	Cons
Short-term		
Long-term		

An A4, photocopiable version of this appendix is available to download from www.sagepub.co.uk/simmons

Appendix XV

Handout: Dealing with setbacks during the recovery process

When you are recovering from a mental health problem, it is normal to experience ups and downs and, for most people, recovery is not a smooth process. Setbacks can be frightening especially if you have been feeling much better and beginning to think you can achieve recovery. Prior to starting to recover, when you are in the depths of experiencing mental health problems, one bad day feels much like the next and 'having a bad day' is not that noticeable. However, when you start to recover, you may begin to experience positive feelings again and realise that recovery is possible. It therefore can come as a surprise and a shock when you have a bad day. Bad days can happen for all kinds of different reasons: maybe something specific has happened to trigger it off or maybe you just woke up feeling a bit blue/anxious. Negative thoughts can creep in: 'I'm never going to get better', 'There's no point in even trying to get better.' These negative thoughts can lead you to feel worse.

Setbacks are a completely normal part of recovery. It can be very important to experience at least one setback during the recovery process as it can act as a learning process and teach you that you can climb back out of the setback mode. You can also learn techniques to help you out of the setback and keep a note of these for future use. Once you have experienced recovery from a setback, you will begin to realise that they are not as frightening as you initially thought and you will generally feel more confident that you will be able to make a recovery.

Guidelines for recovering from setbacks

1   Remembering that setbacks are normal

    Once you are actually in the midst of a setback, it can be difficult to remember what might be happening and panic can set in. It can therefore be very helpful to name the process and tell yourself that you are having a setback and that it is a normal stage of recovery. It may also be useful to remind yourself that 'bad days' can feel much worse once you have experienced some 'good/reasonable' days because of the contrast between the two states.

2   Negative thoughts

Once you start to notice you are having a bad day, it can very quickly trigger all kinds of negative thoughts: 'I'm never going to get any better' is probably one of the most common thoughts and it can lead to feelings of hopelessness. You then start to feel worse and have more negative thoughts. These are the kinds of thoughts that could be challenged using a thought diary: think about the sort of advice you might give to a friend who is experiencing a setback.

3   Avoidance

When you have a bad day, you might start to avoid your normal activities. This can make you feel worse, as you will have more time to think about negative things and have less to distract you from your bad day. You may also feel guilty about avoiding things. Try to keep activities going as much as possible. Plan in some pleasant activities that usually help to lift your mood. Make sure you plan some relaxation time. Treat yourself gently and do not blame yourself for the setback. Eat nice healthy foods and get as much sleep as possible.

4   Moving back to first principles

It is easy to feel helpless during a setback and many people can be left wondering how to help themselves out of the hole they feel they have fallen into. It can be helpful to remind yourself of the changes you had made and to reflect on your successes. Do not feel ashamed to go back to the techniques you found helpful at the beginning of your recovery – this does not mean you have failed. Read old handouts you may have been given if you have been in therapy, or old books you used to find helpful.

5   Flashcards and letters

It is hard to remember helpful tips or, indeed, that you have made improvements when you are in the midst of a setback. For this reason, it can be helpful to plan for a setback and make 'flashcards' that can be produced during a setback. These can be pieces of card with short statements written on them, such as:

'I am having a setback which is why I am feeling like this.'
'Setbacks are a normal part of recovery.'
'I will feel better again – I have recovered before.'
'Remember to eat healthy food on a regular basis.'
'Try to get sleep as regularly as possible.'
'Remember to use thought–challenging sheets'.
etc., etc.

Some people write a letter to themselves to read on bad days. This is sometimes known as a 'rainy day letter'. It may read as follows:

Dear Megan,

You are having a bad day today which is why you have chosen to read over this letter. I am writing this letter on a good day to remind you of all the changes you have made. You have made many changes and gained confidence as a mother as well as cutting down on so many of the checks and most of the questions you used to ask. Writing this letter today, I feel so much better and feel I am getting my life back. I know you may be having a bad day today but it won't last …

It is important to write the flashcards and the rainy day letter when you are feeling in a positive mood – it is just too hard to do these tasks when you are feeling low.

6   Specific strategies for dealing with setbacks in depression

- Get active. Start with small goals and keep the goals regular but achievable.
- Be mindful of small pleasures.
- Notice any achievements, no matter how small.
- Try not to compare what you are currently able to do with what you were doing before the setback occurred – this is *such* an important point.
- Try not to criticise yourself. Tackle critical thoughts with thought-challenging techniques.
- Try not to avoid friends, especially those with whom you find it helpful to be in contact.

7   Specific strategies for dealing with setbacks in anxiety

- Remind yourself of coping strategies that help you to feel calmer and more relaxed.
- Go back to practising breathing and relaxation techniques.
- Remind yourself of how to use grounding techniques and practise these.
- Return to easier goals on the hierarchy and practise these very regularly until you feel ready to move on to the next step.
- Tackle anxious thoughts with thought challenging techniques.

8   Specific strategies for dealing with setbacks in OCD

- Re-read the handouts and remind yourself how the OCD cycle is maintained.
- Move back to working on goals you previously found easier.
- Remember how 'thought–action–meaning' fusion works.
- Challenge unhelpful appraisals of intrusive thoughts.

Appendix XVI

Relapse Prevention Sheet

What changes have I made?

What skills have helped me to make these changes?

What have I learned over the last few months (skills and strategies)?

What changes do I want to make in the future?

What will help get me there?

What situations might lead to relapse/setbacks?

What would be early warning signs for me or others to watch out for with regards to relapse/setbacks?

How can I overcome setbacks and move through to the other side?

An A4, photocopiable version of this appendix is available to download from www.sagepub.co.uk/simmons

Appendix XVII

Ending Letters

Dear Anne,

As you know, we have met for a series of sessions of psychological therapy. I am therefore writing in order to summarise the sessions we have had and note down any points for the future.

When we first met, you reported feeling low in mood for about two years but it was difficult to identify what might have triggered the depression. When we discussed this further, it seemed that you had to deal with a number of difficult events at the same time, including the menopause, your children leaving home and difficulties in your relationship with Jack, which precipitated you into having an affair with a work colleague. This last event was particularly difficult for you to cope with as you had immense feelings of guilt and shame and thoughts of worthlessness. It seems that these events may have triggered beliefs developed in your childhood about being worthless. You described your childhood as a lonely time as your father was away a lot with work and your mother was not affectionate. You had a very good relationship with your grandparents but they both died when you were a teenager and you said you felt you may have gone through a period of mild depression then.

When we discussed the symptoms of your depression, you reported that you had been feeling low in mood and tearful and incredibly tired all the time. You described your sleep as being very poor and you found it very difficult to get off to sleep, often waking up several times a night, thinking over your difficulties. You described finding it difficult to interact with your friends in the way that you used to and said you kept thinking that you had nothing to say to them and that they were starting to ignore you. These thoughts left you feeling anxious and low in mood and further perpetuated your difficulties in maintaining conversations with friends in a way that you used to.

You started to challenge yourself to engage in activities you were previously finding it difficult to engage in and also started to notice that certain activities did help to lift your mood. We spent a fair bit of time exploring your thought processes and looking at how you could challenge your thoughts in order to focus on the less negative aspects. We also focused a great deal on how you could change your role with both your family and friends and allow yourself to take risks in terms of letting them get closer to you and offer you support when required. I feel this was a brave step and one which took courage.

You became adept at catching and challenging your negative thoughts and I enclose a sheet of questions you can ask yourself when you need to challenge your thinking. We also spent time talking about the affair you had and you began to process thoughts and feelings around this event. You began to realise that, although you had made a mistake, it did not make you completely worthless and that it was important to move on from this event and put as much into your relationship with Jack as possible. We looked at the pros and cons of telling Jack about the affair and you finally decided against it, as you felt that telling him would only be a means to salving your conscience rather than making things with Jack better.

We have discussed setbacks and that it is normal to have setbacks – they are stages on the way to recovery, not a sign that you will not overcome your difficulties. You have had a number of setbacks during the time we have been meeting and, although these have been very difficult to endure at the time, it is clear that you have learnt a great deal from these episodes. Most importantly, you have learned that you can recover each time. For the future, it will be important to recognise when you are having a setback and to re-read the handouts and relevant books.

Finally, I have enclosed a book list so you can continue to read about and develop your coping strategies into the future …

1. ??

2. ??

3. ??

I feel you have worked hard and shown great commitment and determination during our meetings. It has been a pleasure working with you and seeing the changes that you have made and I wish you all the best for the future. As you know, I will leave your file open until the end of .... and you can contact me at any time if you wish to get in touch. After that time, you will need to go to your GP if you wish to have a re-assessment with our team.

With best wishes

The Therapist

Dear Andy,

As you know, we have met for a series of sessions of psychological therapy. I am therefore writing in order to summarise the sessions we have had and note down any points for the future.

When we first met, it seemed that you had been experiencing feelings of anxiety and panic over the last couple of months, although you had not been feeling like your normal self for about six months. During our initial sessions, you strongly believed that your symptoms were related to your physical health and you found it challenging to think that your thoughts could have such a strong relationship with the symptoms you experienced in your body. During the course of our work together, we tried out a number of behavioural experiments and you learned about your body and how it responds to 'panic and anxiety thoughts'. You were shocked at just how powerfully 'panic thoughts' could affect your body. We spent time discussing how your thoughts, feelings and behaviours form cycles which keep the anxieties going. We talked about how, when you think about going out, you start to worry that you will have a panic attack. These kinds of thoughts lead to you feeling very panicky (which you previously perceived as being unwell/having heart problems). You had started to cope with these difficult feelings by avoiding situations where you might feel panicky/unwell. However, as we have discussed, avoiding anxiety-provoking situations keeps your anxiety going. We explored ways of breaking this cycle and I was impressed with your determination and courage in facing up to some really challenging scenarios. We discussed coping strategies you could use to manage your panic, such as grounding techniques, breathing and relaxation techniques and distraction techniques. You have found the grounding techniques most useful and have been using these on a regular basis.

We made some clear goals together and your first goals were focused on going outside. You found these goals challenging at first but when you realised that your anxiety was reducing each time you tried each goal, you were willing to try facing new situations. You are now going out on a regular basis and have started to see friends again. You have been speaking to your boss about the possibility of going back to work.

We have also spent time discussing self-esteem and confidence and have explored your concerns about the judgements others might make about you. You have started to become less concerned about other people's judgements and are continuing to challenge your thoughts in this area. You have also taken some risks in terms of phoning friends, rather than waiting for them to phone, and you have been surprised by the positive response.

We have discussed setbacks and that it is normal to have setbacks … [see Anne's letter above for the rest]

Dear Megan,

I am writing to you following our sessions together as a summary of the sessions and to note down goals for the future.

When we first started meeting, your main difficulties were the obsessive thoughts you were experiencing about harming Molly and the consequent thought that you must be a bad person to be thinking like this. You were worried that, because you had had the thoughts, you would actually carry them through and harm Molly. You also felt the need to check on her to make sure that she had not become ill. You were feeling extremely panicky if you had to look after Molly on your own, and Paul was having to take time off work. You would also phone the health visitor for reassurance on a daily basis. You gave me some information about your background history and it seems that you had a diffi-cult relationship with your mum while you were growing up. You remember receiving a lot of criticism while you were growing up and your mum was very strict. You also felt she favoured your sister, and that you were the 'pain' in the family, the one who always messed things up. This seems to have carried on through to adulthood and, since you have had Molly, your mum has continued to make critical comments, which has been difficult for you and 'fed into' your beliefs about being a bad person.

Despite the difficulties and low self-esteem you experienced while you were growing up, you managed to cope reasonably well until you gave birth to Molly. It was at this point that you started to have intrusive thoughts about harming Molly and you became extremely frightened about these thoughts and why you might be having them. We dis-cussed the fact that it is normal to have strange thoughts from time to time but that it can cause problems when people start to get worried about the thoughts, or that they might act on the thoughts. Your worries about the thoughts and the possibility that you might act on them then led on to very strong feelings such as anxiety and guilt. You used to cope with these feelings by checking/performing a ritual (e.g. checking on Molly's health), avoiding being alone with her or asking for reassurance from Paul or the health visitor. These behaviours lowered the anxiety in the short term but, by behaving thus, you did not get the opportunity to learn that you would probably be fine without them.

We started to work together to explore these cycles and you started to conduct some small experiments whereby you stopped performing one of the behaviours or stopped avoiding a certain place and learned to cope with the anxiety this caused. This was dif-ficult at first and I was impressed by your courage and determination when tackling these tasks. You gradually learned that you could gain some control over your thoughts, feelings and behaviour and you found that, over time, you were able to face increasingly difficult situations and your confidence grew.

However, despite the changes in the obsessions, you still had very low self-esteem and your thoughts about yourself were very negative and critical. You did not feel that you were a good mother and you lacked confidence in this role. We spent time exploring these thoughts and beliefs. The main themes appeared to be related to your need to be a perfect mother and you were concerned that if you made one mistake it would mean that you were bad. Through the various discussions we had together, you realised that it is normal to worry about new roles, to make mistakes and do things less than perfectly.

You gradually started to have some positive ideas about yourself and have built on these ideas over the last year. There are times when the old beliefs slip back in and it is important to realise when this is happening and challenge the negative thoughts/beliefs if they are getting too strong. I have enclosed a list of questions you can ask yourself to help you with this challenging.

We have discussed setbacks and that it is normal to have setbacks … [see Anne's letter above for the rest …]

References

Beck, A. (1970) *Depression: Causes and Treatment.* Philadelphia: University of Pennsylvania Press.

Beck, A. (1976) *Cognitive Therapy and the Emotional Disorders.* New York: International Universities Press.

Beck, A.T., Epstein, N., Brown, G. & Steer, R.A. (1988) 'An inventory for measuring clinical anxiety: psychometric properties', *Journal of Consulting and Clinical Psychology,* 56: 893–7.

Beck, A.T., Steer, R.A. & Brown, G.K. (1996) *Manual for the Beck Depression Inventory – II.* San Antonio, TX: Psychological Corporation.

Beck, J.S. (1995) *Cognitive Therapy: Basics and Beyond.* New York: Guilford Press.

Beck, J.S. (2007) 'Self-disclosure in cognitive therapy', *Cognitive Therapy Today,* Beck Institute's blog http://cttoday.org/?p=146

Bernard, J.M. & Goodyear, R.K. (1992) *Fundamentals of Clinical Supervision.* Boston, MA: Allyn & Bacon.

Bordin, E.S. (1979) 'The generalisability of the psychoanalytic concept of the working alliance', *Psychotherapy: Theory, Research & Practice,* 16: 252–60.

Burns, D. (1980) *Feeling Good.* New York: New American Library.

Butler, G. (1998) 'Clinical formulation', in A.S. Bellack & M. Herson (eds), *Comprehensive Clinical Psychology.* Oxford: Pergamon.

Cooper, A. & Witenberg, E.G. (1983) 'Stimulation of curiosity in the supervisory process of psychoanalysis'. *Contemporary Psychoanalysis,* 19: 248–64.

Crisp A.H. (ed.) (2004) *Every Family in the Land: Understanding Prejudice and Discrimination against People with Mental Illness.* London: Royal Society of Medicine Press.

Curwen, B., Palmer, S. and Ruddell, P. (2000) *Brief Cognitive Behaviour Therapy.* London: SAGE.

Davis, M., Robbins Eshelman, E. & McKay, M. (1988) *The Relaxation and Stress Reduction Workbook.* Oakland, CA: New Harbinger Publications.

Dols, M.W. (1987) 'Insanity and it's treatment in Islamic society', *Medical History,* 31: 1–14.

Dudley, R. & Kuyken, W. (2006) 'Formulation in cognitive-behavioural therapy', in L. Johnstone, & R. Dallos (eds), *Formulation in Psychology and Psychotherapy: Making Sense of People's Problems.* Hove: Routledge.

Fabrega, H. (1991) 'Psychiatric stigma in non-western societies', *Comparative Psychiatry,* 32: 534–51.

Foa, E.B. & Emmelkamp, P. (eds) (1983) *Failures in Behaviour Therapy.* New York: Wiley.

Greben, S.E. (1991) 'Interpersonal aspects of the supervision of individual psychotherapy', *American Journal of Psychotherapy,* 45: 306–16.

Greenberger, D. & Padesky, C. (1995) *Clinician's Guide to Mind over Mood.* New York and London: Guilford Press.

Hardy, G., Cahill, J. & Barkham, M. (2007) 'Active ingredients of the therapeutic relationship that promote client change', in P. Gilbert & R.L. Leahy, *The Therapeutic Relationship in the Cognitive Behavioural Psychotherapies*. London: Routledge.

Hart, G. (1982) *The Process of Clinical Supervision*. Baltimore: University Park Press.

Hawkins, P. & Shohet, R. (1989) *Supervision in the Helping Professions*. Milton Keynes: Open University Press.

Hawton, K. & Kirk, J. (1989) 'Problem solving', in K. Hawton, P.M. Salkovskis, J. Kirk & D.M. Clark (1989) *Cognitive Behaviour Therapy for Psychiatric Problems: A Practical Guide*. Oxford: Oxford University Press.

Hoffman, L.W. (1994) 'The training of psychotherapy supervisors: a barren scape', *Psychotherapy in Private Practice*, 13: 23–42.

Holloway, E.L. (1987) 'Developmental models of supervision: is it development?' *Professional Psychology: Research and Practice*, 18 (3): 209–16.

Howard, K.I., Kopta, S.M., Krause, M.S. and Orlinsky, D.E. (1986) 'The dose effect relationship in psychotherapy', *American Psychologist*, 41: 159–64.

James, I.A. & Blackburn, I.M. (1995) 'Cognitive therapy with obsessive compulsive disorder', *The British Journal of Psychiatry*, 166: 144–50.

Kennerly, H. (1997) *Overcoming Anxiety*. London: Robinson.

Kuyken, W. (2005) 'Research and evidence base in case formulation', in N. Tarrier (ed.), *Case Formulation in Cognitive Behaviour Therapy: The Treatment of Challenging and Complex Clinical Cases*, Hove: Brunner-Routledge.

Linehan, M.M. (1993) *Skills Training Manual for Treating Borderline Personality Disorder*. New York: Guilford.

Meichenbaum, D.H. (1975) 'A self-instructional approach to stress management: a proposal for stress inoculation training', in C.D. Spielberger & I. Sarason (eds), *Stress and Anxiety* (vol. 2, pp. 237–64). New York: Wiley.

Miller, W.R. & Rollnick, S. (2002) *Motivational Interviewing: Preparing People for Change*. New York: Guilford Press.

Moore, R.G. & Garland, A. (2003) *Cognitive Therapy for Chronic and Persistent Depression*, Series in Clinical Psychology. Chichester: Wiley.

Mynors-Wallis, L.M., Gath, D.H., Day, A. & Baker, F. (2000) 'Randomised controlled trial of problem solving treatment, antidepressant medication and combined treatment for major depression in primary care', *British Medical Journal*, 320: 26–30.

Ng Chee Hong (1997) 'The stigma of mental illness in Asian cultures', *Australian and New Zealand Journal of Psychiatry*, 31: 382–90.

NICE (National Institute for Clinical Excellence) (2004, 2005) *NICE Guidelines* http://guidance.nice.org.uk/CG22/guidance/pdf/English

Niemeyer, R.A. & Feixas, G. (1990) 'The role of homework and skill acquisition in the outcome of group cognitive therapy of depression', *Behaviour Therapy*, 21 (3): 281–92.

Padesky, C.A. (1991) 'Schema as self prejudice', *International Cognitive Therapy Newsletter*, 6: 6–17.

Padesky, C.A. (1993) 'Socratic questioning: changing minds or guiding discovery?' Keynote address delivered at the European Congress of Behavioural and Cognitive Therapies, London, 24 September. www.padesky.com

Page, S. and Wosket, V. (1994) *Supervising the Counsellor. A Cyclical Model*. London: Routledge.

Pavlov, I.P. (1927) *Conditioned Reflexes: An Investigation of the Physiological Activity of the Cerebral Cortex*, translated and edited by G.V. Anrep. London: Oxford University Press.

Pedrick, C. & Hyman, B. (2005) *The OCD Workbook: Your Guide to Breaking Free from Obsessive-Compulsive Disorder*. Oakland, CA: New Harbinger Publications.

Persons, J.B. (1989) *Cognitive Therapy in Practice*. New York and London: Norton.

Persons, J.B., Burns, D.D. & Perioff, J.M. (1988) 'Predictors of dropout and outcome in cognitive therapy for depression in a private practice setting', *Cognitive Therapy and Research*, 12: 557–75.

Prochaska, J.O. & DiClemente, C.C. (1983) 'Stages and processes of self-change of smoking: towards an integrative model of change', *Journal of Consulting and Clinical Psychology*, 51: 390–5.

Roth, A. & Fonagy, P. (1996) *What Works for Whom? A Critical Review of Psychotherapy Research*. New York: Guilford Press.

Roth, A. & Pilling, S. (2007) *The Competencies Required to Deliver Effective Cognitive and Behavioural Therapy for People with Depression and with Anxiety Disorder*. Department of Health Publication.

Safran, J.D. & Segal, Z.M. (1990a) *Interpersonal Process in Cognitive Therapy*. New York: Basic Books, Appendix II.

Safran, J.D. & Segal, Z.M. (1990b) *Interpersonal Process in Cognitive Therapy*. New York: Basic Books, Appendix I.

Sanders, D. & Wills, F. (2005) *Cognitive Therapy: An Introduction*. London: SAGE.

Segal, Z.V., Williams, J.M.G. & Teasdale, J.D. (2002) *Mindfulness-based Cognitive Therapy for Depression: A New Approach to Preventing Relapse*. New York: Guilford Press.

Shapiro, M.B. (1961a) 'A method of measuring psychological changes specific to the individual psychiatric patient', *British Journal of Medical Psychology*, 34: 151–5.

Shapiro, M.B. (1961b) 'The single case in fundamental clinical psychological research', *British Journal of Medical Psychology*, 34: 255–62.

Spitzer, R.L., Williams, J.B. & Kroenke, K. (1999) *Patient Health Questionaire – 9*. Copyright © Pfizer Inc.

Spitzer, R.L., Kroenke, K., Williams, J.B. & Lowe, B. (2006) 'A brief measure for assessing generalised anxiety disorder', *Archives of Internal Medicine*, 166(10): 1092–7.

Stoltenberg, C.D. (1981) 'Approaching supervision from a developmental perspective: the counsellor complexity model', *Journal of Counselling Psychology*, 28: 59–65.

Stoltenberg, C.D. & Delworth, U. (1987) *Supervising Counsellors and Therapists: A Developmental Approach*. San Francisco: Jossey-Bass.

Sunderland, M. and Engleheart, P. (1997) *Draw on Your Emotions*. Bicester: Speechmark Publishing Ltd.

Watkins, C.E. (1997) *Handbook of Psychotherapy Supervision*. New York: Wiley.

Watson, J.B. & Raynor, R. (1920) 'Conditioned emotional responses', *Jounal of Experimental Psychology*, 3: 1–14.

Wells (2006) *Case Formulation in Cognitive Behaviour Therapy: The Treatment of Challenging and Complex Cases*. New York: Routledge.

White, M. and Epston, D. (1990) *Narrative Means to Therapeutic Ends*. New York: Norton.

Young, J., Klosko, J. & Weishaar, M.E. (2003) *Schema Therapy: A Practitioner's Guide*. New York: Guilford Press.

Index

WITHDRAWN